THE NEW COMPLETE
GARDEN MAKEOVER BOOK

Published in 2007 by Murdoch Books Pty Limited
www.murdochbooks.com.au

Murdoch Books UK Limited
Erico House, 6th Floor North
93–99 Upper Richmond Road
Putney, London SW15 2TG
Phone: +44 (0) 20 8785 5995
Fax: +44 (0) 20 8785 5985

Murdoch Books Australia
Pier 8/9, 23 Hickson Road
Millers Point NSW 2000
Phone: +61 (0) 2 8220 2000
Fax: +61 (0) 2 8220 2558

Chief Executive: Juliet Rogers
Publishing Director: Kay Scarlett

Design manager: Vivien Valk
Design concept: Sarah Odgers
Design: Michelle Cutler
Project manager: Sarah Baker
Photo management: Amanda McKittrick
Production: Monika Paratore

A CIP catalogue record for this book is available from the British Library
ISBN 1 921 25925 6
ISBN13 978 1921 25925 8

Printed by Toppan Printing Co. Ltd. in 2007. Printed in China.

THE NEW COMPLETE
GARDEN MAKEOVER BOOK

MURDOCH BOOKS

CONTENTS

DESIGNING YOUR GARDEN

ABOVE A contemporary, low-maintenance garden that has year-round appeal.

OPPOSITE Garden features should be in proportion with the rest of the garden. This arched bridge needs a reasonably large site.

Keen gardeners sometimes decry the notion of design, declaring that a garden is a place for plants. Well, yes it is, but it is much more than a nursery bed for plants. A garden is an extension of the living areas of your home. It's about floors, walls, pools, shade structures, decks, paved terraces and many other elements that we loosely describe as hard landscaping and 'architectural'. Plants too can be architectural, and they are as important an element as the hard landscaping.

We often consciously or subconsciously describe a garden as a place of calm — of peace and rest — yet a garden without design is often the very opposite of these qualities we imagine. A garden without design can be chaotic, unappealing, a maintenance nightmare and a chore.

ABOVE This contemporary water feature incorporates a design trick to make the garden seem deeper: the circular ponds decrease in size as they recede into the distance.

ABOVE RIGHT Part of a restrained formal garden, this rectangular brick pond with stone capping is backed by a feature wall.

OPPOSITE Rows of topiary shrubs make a feature of a front entrance.

A garden is also a place for relaxation and beauty, so we need a space that is 'designed' to meet these needs. How the different elements interact is 'design'. It essentially solves problems in any situation. When you combine the words 'garden' and 'design', what you're really talking about is 'garden problem solving'. Design determines that your outdoor dining space be positioned where it is cool in summer and sheltered in winter. Design tells you where to plant a shade tree so it doesn't obscure the view or invade your house foundations in the future. Design lays out the planting areas so they are beautiful to look at, and it also dictates the best route, width and surface for paths.

Design is also about common sense. After all, it's only practical to place the vegetable garden near the kitchen in an open, sunny position rather than near the front gate, under the deep shade of a tall evergreen tree. It's also practical to make paths leading to service areas such as the clothesline direct and unfettered by foliage: pretty, billowing shrubs spilling romantically over paths are an annoying hindrance when you're carrying a load of wet washing or a set of garden tools. So good design determines where planting techniques like this are appropriate, and where they're not.

And finally, a garden can provide a series of outdoor rooms for cooking and dining, entertaining and children's play. Design elements such as shade structures, decking, paved areas and plant form and colour all play a part in creating an ambience that suits both the architecture of your house and your lifestyle. Getting this combination right can seem a bit challenging at first, but this book will help you with all the aspects of designing your own garden — from landscaping solutions for common garden problems to building features and planting your garden.

LANDSCAPING YOUR GARDEN

Before you start planning and planting your garden, consider the basic elements you have to work with — the climate and aspect, soil type, the gradient of the site — and whether there are any problems requiring attention. Once you've done your site analysis, you can embark on the process of landscaping your garden — installing drainage and improving the soil as well as building hard landscaping features such as retaining walls, raised garden beds, shade structures and steps.

RIGHT The sculpted shape of mop-headed robinias complements the geometric formality of this courtyard garden.

STARTING OUT

A garden is an integral part of the surrounding landscape, and the most successful gardens — and, indeed, the easiest to maintain — come from nurturing the natural environment rather than trying to control it. The prevailing winds, the amount of available sunlight, the soil structure, availability of water and even the nature of the surrounding area should be considered before you even start to turn the soil.

Also, once you consider the built environment — your house, the neighbouring buildings, roads, pools and fences — the landscape becomes a complex interaction between natural and built forms. Take all these into account and your garden will be enjoyed by all.

DEVELOPING A PLAN

The ultimate aim in any garden is to create something that is functional, attractive and easy to maintain. Deciding what to do with your particular parcel of land can be challenging, whether you have land that is flat, sloping, boggy, dry, shady, sunny or a combination of all these. Often the final landscape is formed as a result of solutions to particular problems.

However, before you start work on your garden, spend some time looking at what is already there as well as the natural processes within the landscape. Think about how they affect your day-to-day life and what you can do to improve or enhance the area.

SITE ANALYSIS

Begin by mapping out features, problems, views and existing trees and rocks in relation to your house. The key is to develop a landscape that minimizes hard labour as well as costs and materials. By harnessing natural systems within the landscape, you can keep the garden resource-efficient and save money at the same time.

Here are some key questions to ask in the analysis stage of the project.
* What is the orientation of the site — that is, is it north–south or east–west?
* What slope or gradient does the site have?
* Are there any rocks or natural features?

BELOW A typical example of a site analysis plan (at a scale of 1:100), showing the position of the sun, prevailing winds and any permanent features in the garden.

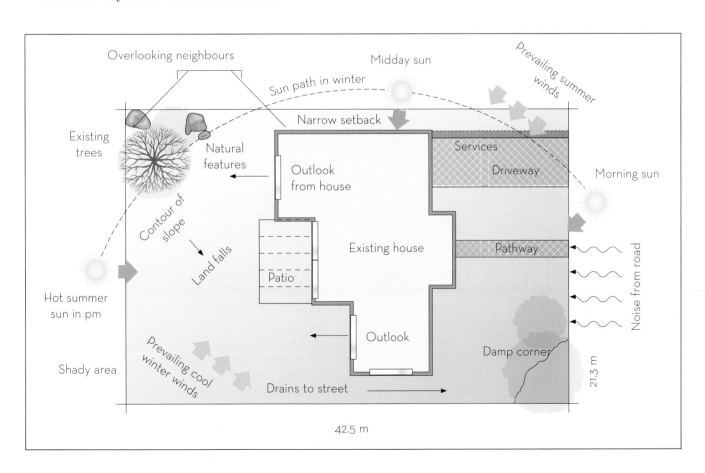

Overlooking neighbours

Midday sun

Prevailing summer winds

Sun path in winter

Narrow setback

Existing trees

Natural features

Services

Driveway

Morning sun

Outlook from house

Contour of slope

Land falls

Existing house

Pathway

Noise from road

Patio

Hot summer sun in pm

Outlook

Damp corner

Shady area

Prevailing cool winter winds

Drains to street

21.3 m

42.5 m

ABOVE If you're starting from scratch, make sure you thoroughly clear the site of any debris such as large stones and old tree roots.

ABOVE RIGHT A well designed garden landscape enhances the built environment and adds value to possibly your biggest investment — your home.

- What type of soil do you have?
- Where does the water drain?
- Where are the services located?
- Are there any problem areas — for example, damp spots, shady areas or areas that are difficult to access?
- Are there any existing trees?
- Are there any views you could incorporate?

If you keep these elements in mind, you'll find planning much easier.

Whether you are designing the garden yourself or employing a landscape designer to do it for you, a landscape plan is essential. It will allow you to focus on one area at a time without losing sight of the overall project. If you decide to employ a professional landscape designer or landscape architect, ask them to specify on the plan as many details as possible on construction methods and techniques. This will help to ensure that any hard landscaping features are structurally sound and built to the relevant building standards.

PROTECTING YOUR INVESTMENT

Changing the landscape around your home will also change the physical and natural processes, such as drainage patterns and volumes, the amount of shade and sun, wind patterns and so on. A house is a major investment, and so it's worth making sure that anything you do in your garden doesn't affect the structure of the house.

Before you embark on a landscaping project, consider these points.

- Make sure you identify and avoid the position and possible depths of any plumbing, telephone or electrical services.
- Make sure that any run-off water from paved areas, roofs or gardens can be successfully directed to the street or existing drainage, unless it is to be collected into a water butt.

- Ensure that any new drains will remain undisturbed by root systems as your garden grows.
- Don't pave, place garden beds or generally raise levels above the damp-proof course around your home. (To locate the position of the damp-proof course, look for the flashing material, which will protrude slightly from the brickwork.)
- Don't backfill against weatherboards or any other cladding material.
- Avoid planting or storing materials close to timber decks, stairs or pergolas as this will encourage decay. It's important to maintain good air circulation around timber.
- Avoid storing materials against the house, as this may encourage damp or algae.
- Never plant trees close to drains.
- Don't plant large trees along side passages or close to footings or slabs.
- Avoid planting large or deciduous trees behind retaining walls.
- Don't plant evergreen trees where they will block out winter sun.

PREPARING THE SITE

Conserving natural resources is important for the environment, and it can often save you time and money when building and planting your garden. As soon as you start preparing the site, consider what can be recycled. The benefits of this will be obvious once you start buying materials.

Also, if you're planning a large-scale project, keep in mind a time schedule so that your landscaping is done in the appropriate seasons. For instance, try to avoid digging when it is very wet as this will damage the soil structure; and do not plant out young plants in harsh summer temperatures.

Clearing and preparing the site will often uncover hidden features and give you a different perspective on the project at hand. Check your master plan and see whether adjustments need to be made. Here are some tips on site preparation that will save you some time and money.

- Clear away any weeds and remove them from the site. If any of these are invasive or hard-to-control species, seek advice from your local garden centre about the best way to remove them. If you have to use a systemic poison, do so well in advance of site works.
- Once you've stockpiled the unwanted vegetation, hire a shredder and create a pile of mulch to use when you've finished planting. Put the stockpiles where they won't inhibit access.
- Sort and stockpile any stones, rocks, bricks, concrete, pieces of tin or timber close to where you might be constructing walls or need fill.
- Keep any well established vegetation on steep banks as this will help keep erosion in check.
- Clear soil and vegetation away from existing structures such as decks or fences so you can assess whether they require any repair.

Once you have prepared the site or area where you plan to do the work, establish what materials you'll require, what you can recycle and where you can stockpile materials during the construction process. This will also help you to assess the suitability of your design for your budget.

ABOVE Don't waste any of your garden clippings and prunings — hire or buy a shredder and use the mulch on your garden beds.

TOP A rotary cultivator makes light work of digging over a large area. Most machines are equipped with a depth adjuster as well as a rear flap that helps to level the soil as you go.

DEVELOPING THE LANDSCAPE

Once the site is cleared and your plan finalised, you can start developing the landscape. The first step is to create suitable areas for outdoor living and relaxing, whether that means terracing a sloping site or adding interest and privacy to a level area.

Providing adequate drainage is an essential part of the landscaping process and should be your next task. Good drainage will ensure that every part of your land is usable and that any structures are protected from damage by groundwater or rainwater. Your soil, too, may require attention if you are to grow healthy plants and lawns.

SLOPING SITES

Sloping sites pose one of the greatest challenges for the landscaper or home gardener, especially if you need to create level areas for outdoor living.

Excavation is one of the most labour-intensive aspects of landscaping, one that requires brute strength if done by hand or a large wallet if done by machine. Meanwhile, the retaining walls usually required after excavation are often the most expensive structures in a garden. It's therefore important to plan your garden so that you minimize the amount of excavation as well as the associated costs.

Terracing is one of the most cost-efficient ways of dealing with a sloping site, and if you design it properly, it can offer rewarding results. A flowing transition of levels is often more appealing to the eye than one abrupt drop, especially when it's combined with wide, gracious steps.

Establish the points of access to and from different parts of the garden on your master plan, and integrate the construction of the steps with that of the retaining walls. The material you use to build the steps should blend harmoniously with other hard landscaping materials, such as that used on the path leading to them.

RIGHT If your sloping site ends in a boggy area, make a feature of it by creating a water garden, planted with appropriate plants such as iris, water lily and gunnera.

OPPOSITE A raised garden bed is one solution to planting on a sloping site.

TOP and ABOVE If your site is below street level, landscaping is essential. Here sandstone retaining walls and steps are cut into a sloping site.

RIGHT Cutting and filling a slope.

CUTTING AND FILLING

Excavating all the way to form a level area will create a large amount of spoil and a large retaining wall. The best method is to excavate halfway and use the spoil to fill an area on the lower side. This way you will have two walls, but they will be smaller and the construction will be easier and less expensive. Also, you can put the spoil to good use rather than remove it at great expense.

* When excavating, start at the top of the site and work the spoil down. This avoids unnecessarily relocating the fill.
* Use a system of pegs and profiles or saddles to mark out the areas you want to excavate (for more information on setting out, see page 340). A string line and level will help you with more precise measurements.
* Use a fixed datum, such as the floor level of your home, to establish the proposed levels.
* Keep retaining walls below 900 mm if you can. Anything over this height should be designed by an engineer and approved by a local Building Control office.
* Once you've cut and filled the site, let the soil stabilize before creating the walls to retain the earth.

BUILDING A DRYSTONE WALL

Stone is one of the most popular materials used for terracing, and you may be able to use existing stone that was stockpiled during the site preparation. As a rule, all walls should be founded on solid substrate such as clay, rock or compacted in situ loam.

1 Using a string line (for straight walls) or a garden hose (for curved walls), mark out the wall, then mark the footing location with lime or spray paint.
2 Dig a trench about 450–600 mm wide down to a solid base. Compact the base with a machine or by hand if necessary.
3 Starting with larger rocks in the centre, gradually build up the wall, at the same time packing and filling with smaller rocks to stabilize the main stones. If you like, use mortar to help stabilize the stones. The

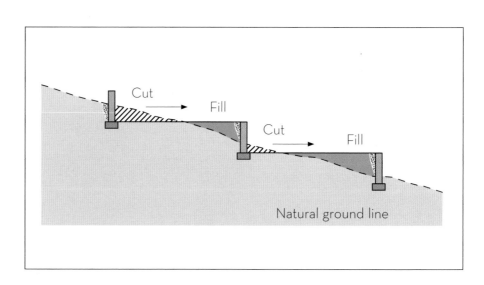

LEFT A drystone retaining wall.

BELOW A cross-section of a stone wall showing the construction method.

closer the stones fit together on the outside face of the wall, the better and neater the wall will look.

4 To provide good drainage, backfill the wall with loose rubble. Any build-up of water behind the wall will put pressure on it; too much pressure and it will eventually fail. You could install an agricultural drain behind the wall to help disperse the water.

5 If there is paving in front of the wall, add a gully.

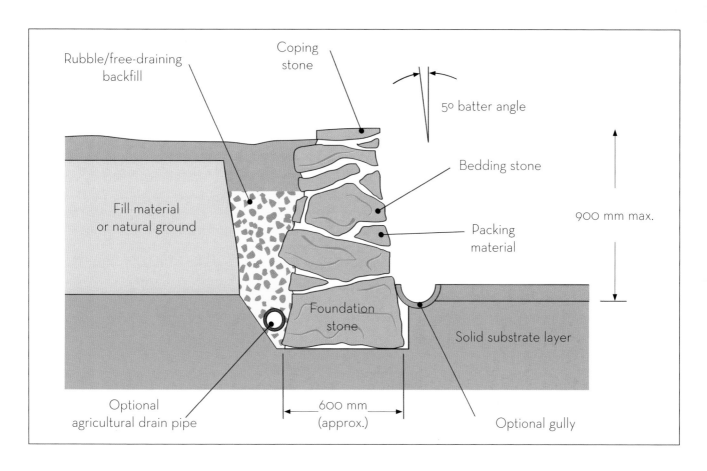

Rubble/free-draining backfill

Coping stone

5° batter angle

Fill material or natural ground

Bedding stone

Packing material

900 mm max.

Foundation stone

Solid substrate layer

Optional agricultural drain pipe

600 mm (approx.)

Optional gully

DRYSTONE RETAINING WALL

TOOLS

- Basic tools (see page 332)
- Long pegs (or 2 m lengths of 12 mm steel rod)
- Water level
- Concrete mixer (if available)
- Brush
- Sponge
- Bucket
- Gloves

MATERIALS

- Selected stones
- Cement
- Sand
- 10 mm coarse aggregate (gravel)
- Agricultural drainpipe
- Gravel for drainage
- Geotextile fabric (optional)

HINT

If a drystone wall is to be met by a grassed area at either the base, the top or both, you will find that mowing is easier if you make a 100 mm wide concrete mower strip at the junction of grass and retaining wall.

Drystone walls are attractive and will last a lifetime if you take the trouble to fit the stones together tightly. The stones in this wall are bedded in concrete for extra strength.

PLANNING

You can construct a small drystone wall without a concrete footing, but you should half-bury the base stones in the ground to prevent movement. In this project, a footing approximately 100 mm deep was excavated to contain a concrete bedding for the base stones.

For greater stability, you can either dry-stack the wall stones or place a shallow bed of concrete beneath each individual stone. The concrete won't be visible from the front and therefore won't affect the appearance of the wall. If you're bedding the stones in concrete, it's best to have two people working on the project — one person positioning the stones while the other mixes the concrete and backfills the wall as it increases in height. Always wear gloves when working with stone.

Remember to check with your local Building Control office, and consult an engineer to ensure that the proposed wall is not too high to withstand the pressures that will be exerted on it.

SELECTING STONES

To create the best-looking and most stable drystone wall, choose the stones carefully. Look for stones that are square and chunky in shape, as these fit together more easily than round or oval shapes. Keep gaps to a minimum so that soil will be retained efficiently and not gradually dribble through the joints.

When choosing the stones for your wall, select three main sizes.

- **Base stones for the foundation** The base stones should be large and heavy (about 300–350 mm long), as they support the rest of the wall. Calculate the length of the wall in metres and multiply it by 3 to give the number of base stones needed. For example, 15 m x 3 = 45 stones.
- **Wall stones for the bulk of construction** These should be medium in size (about 250–300 mm long), with the larger ones laid lower in the wall than the smaller ones. To calculate the number of wall stones you need, multiply the length of the wall (15 m) by the height (0.8 m) and then multiply that by 10 (roughly the number of medium stones in 1 m²): 15 x 0.8 = 12 m² and 12 x 10 = 120 wall stones.
- **Head stones or copestones** These are the smaller, flatter stones (about 200 mm long) that are placed along the top of the wall to give it a level, neat finish. As they can be easily removed or knocked off the wall, head stones are usually seated in a bed of mortar or concrete to hold them firmly in place. In order to calculate the number of head stones

LEFT Naturally weathered rock, purchased from a garden supplier, was fitted together neatly to produce this sturdy drystone wall.

required, multiply the length of the wall in metres by 5. For example:
15 m x 5 = 75 head stones.

PREPARATION

1   Establish the line of the wall, and drive in a long peg or length of steel rod at either end. Position a string line between the two pegs, if possible at the finished height. Use a water level if required to ensure it's level (see page 342).
2   Excavate or cut the bank along the desired line and create a 100 mm deep footing trench.
3   Examine the stones and separate them into the three groups. Grouping stones that seem to work together also saves a lot of time later. Remember that building a drystone wall is like constructing a jigsaw: select and fit one piece at a time. Don't rush this sorting process.

CURVED DRYSTONE WALLS

Drystone walling is the most suitable construction method for curved stone walls. They are easy to build, but you won't be able to use string lines to align the stones. Instead, mark the line of the wall on the ground with a rope or garden hose, or sprinkle a line of flour or lime on the ground.

To create the angled vertical surface, hold a spirit level vertical and measure in from it the required distance to position each stone. Calculate this for each course by measuring in from an end peg at the appropriate height. This is slower than laying to string lines, but a quality finish is possible if you are patient.

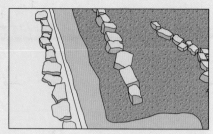

4 Position the base stones in front of the trench, the wall stones behind and the head stones on top of the bank.

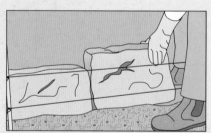

5 Position the pegs at either end of the wall, approximately 400–500 mm from the cut bank.

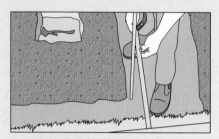

6 With the faces matching the angle of the string lines, butt the stones closely together in the concrete bed.

4 In laying order, position the base stones approximately 500 mm in front of the footing trench. Just beyond the base stones, spread around the medium wall stones. If possible, position the small head stones on top of the bank. This makes them easy to access when you are laying the final course of stone.

5 Position the pegs at either end of the wall, at the front face of the wall, and make sure that they are approximately 400–500 mm away from the cut bank. Angle the pins backwards at about 10 degrees by measuring in from the vertical 100 mm for each 1 m of vertical height. The slant will give the wall greater strength and stability (see the main diagram opposite). Stretch at least two taut string lines between the pins, so that they provide a guide to the correct angle when you're laying the stone.

CONSTRUCTING THE WALL

6 Make a 1:2:4 mix of concrete (see page 335). Starting at one end of the wall, spread a bed of concrete — about 1 m at a time — and position the base stones in it, ensuring that the face of the stones matches the angle of the string lines. Proceed slowly and carefully, making sure that the stones butt closely together. Use stones of different sizes so that you create a mosaic effect, but remember that a square surface on the top edge will make laying the second course easier. Continue laying the base stones until the base course has been completed.

7 Lay agricultural drainpipe behind the base course and cover it with crushed stone or gravel to the top of the base course. Wrap the pipe and gravel in geotextile fabric if you wish (see page 54).

8 Adjust the two string lines upwards for the next course and use the wall stones to construct it. Work in one direction, taking time to carefully select each stone. If a stone doesn't fit well, discard it and try another. Stagger the joints for strength. If you like, bed each wall stone in concrete, making sure the concrete is not visible from the front. To prevent backfill material being washed out through the joints, cover the back of the joints with some concrete as you butt and bed each piece, or position geotextile fabric behind the wall. Backfill with gravel as you work.

9 Use small pieces or wedges of stone to fill any holes and help balance the stones. Tap them into place with a club hammer. Split stone with a club hammer and bolster chisel to create smaller pieces of the required shape or size.

10 Keep repeating steps 8 and 9 to lay as many courses of wall stones as necessary.

FINISHING THE WALL

11 Before laying the smaller head stones, set a string line at the finished height. Check that it's level with a spirit level or water level.

12 To ensure the stability of these smaller pieces of stone, seat them in a shallow bed of concrete. Work from one end of the wall to the other,

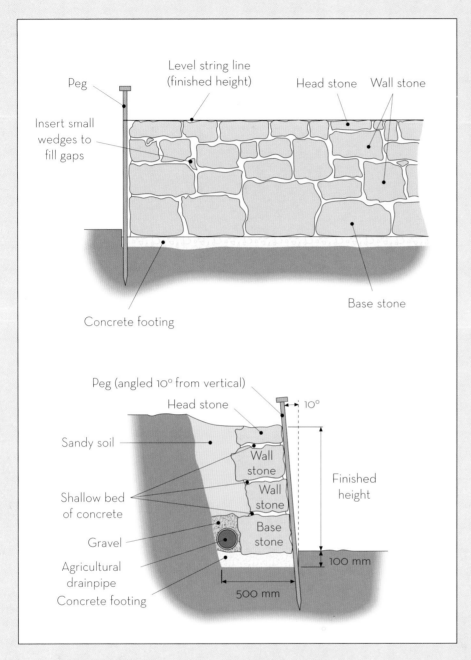

Peg

Level string line (finished height)

Head stone   Wall stone

Insert small wedges to fill gaps

Concrete footing

Base stone

Peg (angled 10° from vertical)

Head stone

Sandy soil

Wall stone

Wall stone

Shallow bed of concrete

Base stone

Gravel

Agricultural drainpipe

Concrete footing

10°

Finished height

100 mm

500 mm

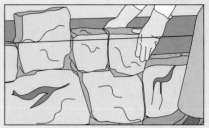

8 Construct the next course, carefully fitting each stone together and staggering the joints.

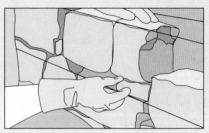

9 Use small pieces or wedges of stone to fill any holes between the larger stones and to help balance them.

LEFT Front and section views.

making sure that the selected pieces finish as close as possible to the final string line.

13 Check the wall and insert small wedges to fill any over-large crevices or to securely balance stones.

14 Wash down the face of the stone to remove any concrete stains. Using sandy loam soil, backfill the wall to the finished height.

RIGHT A simple form of timber edging consists of railway sleepers held in place by timber pegs.

BELOW How to construct a timber wall on a slope.

TIMBER WALLS

The great challenge in landscaping is building a self-retaining garden wall that is quick to install and remains attractive for the life of the garden. Some timber materials, such as CCA-treated timber slabs and hardwood railway sleepers, are especially good for building simple and strong walls. (Sleepers are usually square-edged, while slabs have a rounded edge or face.) The construction method is the same for both.

Sleepers and slabs will usually come in lengths of 1.8–2.4 m and can be worked with a chainsaw and heavy-duty drill. New hardwood sleepers will generally last longer than recycled railway ones. When using treated timber, treat the cut ends with preservative before laying the slabs.

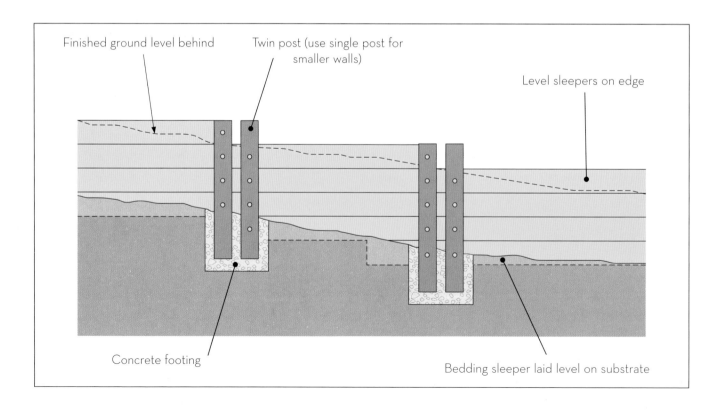

Finished ground level behind

Twin post (use single post for smaller walls)

Level sleepers on edge

Concrete footing

Bedding sleeper laid level on substrate

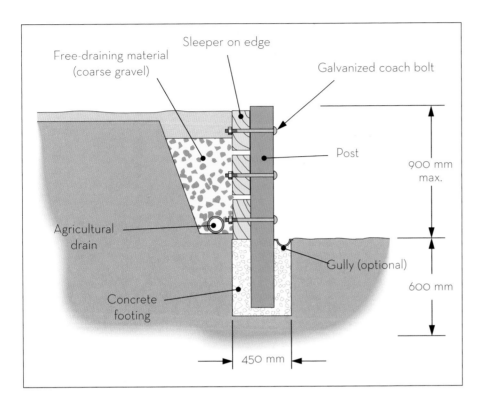

LEFT Side view of a wall constructed with timber sleepers.

PRESSURE-TREATED TIMBER

Pressure-treated softwoods are usually protected by one of three timber preservatives:
* copper chromium arsenic (CCA);
* alkaline copper quart (ACQ); or
* light organic solvent preservative (LOSP).
CCA and ACQ produce a green tone on treated timber while LOSP affects the colour only slightly or not at all. Of the three, LOSP is the least permanent. Timber treated in this way is not suitable for use in the ground.

For more information on levels of timber treatment, see page 28.

CONSTRUCTING A TIMBER WALL

There are several ways to construct timber walls; the post-and-beam method is probably the most reliable. This method uses 150 mm sleepers or slabs with twin posts and is appropriate for a wall up to 900 mm high.

1 Mark out post-hole centres 1800 mm apart. Set out holes for the twin posts each side of the centres, 200 mm long and three times the width of the post. Excavate the holes to a minimum depth of 600 mm, cutting into rock if necessary.
2 Insert the posts, prop them level and fill the hole with high-strength concrete mix. Prod the concrete with a stake or rod to remove air pockets.
3 When the concrete is fully set, clear a solid base behind the post line and prepare a level base for the first sleeper.
4 Set the bottom sleepers dead level, excavating further if required. Start at the lowest point of the wall and work up the slope, leaving a gap at least 10 mm wide between sleepers. If necessary, cut sleepers to half-length. Any half-lengths not supported by a post should be drilled and staked into the sub-base. Make sure that any steps in the wall are the thickness of one sleeper. For extra strength, you can fix the sleepers to the posts with coach bolts.
5 Lay the wall sleepers over the base course, checking levels as required. Use coach bolts to secure them to the posts.
6 When the wall is complete, backfill by hand, first with coarse gravel and then with soil. You can use agricultural drainpipe to improve the drainage. Leave space for a gully at the front of the wall, as water will pass through the gaps in the sleepers (see page 57).
7 Finish by trimming the posts flush with the top sleeper.

TIMBER SLAB RETAINING WALL

TOOLS

- Basic tools (see page 332)
- Water level (optional)
- Circular saw
- Power drill and drill bits
- Gloves

MATERIALS

- Long timber pegs or rods of steel bar
- Railway sleepers, or other logs or timber slabs (see page 28)
- Cement, sand and 10 mm aggregate (gravel)
- 75 x 3.5 mm galvanized lost-head nails
- Coach screws (optional)
- Geotextile fabric
- Agricultural pipe

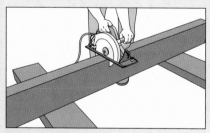

6 To cut a sleeper, lay it at right angles across two others and roll it over as you cut.

This retaining wall consists of horizontal timbers resting on a bed of gravel to preserve them from decay. The timbers, old railway sleepers, are held in place by posts against the outer face.

PREPARATION

1 Establish the position of the wall and prepare the site by cutting away the bank. Position a long peg at each end of the future wall, preferably beyond the ends and aligned with the front of the wall. When driving in the pegs, angle them back at around 10 degrees by measuring in from the vertical 100 mm for every 1 m of vertical height.

2 Mark the finished height of the wall on one peg. Using a string line and spirit level or a water level (see page 342), transfer this mark to the other peg. Stretch a taut string line between the pegs at the finished height. Check that the line is level with a spirit level. Measure down from the string line the height of the wall (allow for complete timbers so that you don't have to cut them), plus 50 mm for a bed of gravel.

3 Ensure the area for the gravel bed is roughly level and approximately 250–300 mm wide.

POSITIONING THE POSTS

4 Calculate the position of the posts on the outside of the wall. They should be centred every 2000–2400 mm, or so that the joints between the horizontal timbers are behind them.

5 Dig holes approximately 400 mm in diameter and 500 mm deep for the posts. Place 100 mm of gravel in the base of each hole and tamp it down.

6 Measure from the string line down to the top of the gravel in the holes to obtain the length for the posts. Using a circular saw, cut the posts to length. If you're using sleepers, lay each at right angles across two other sleepers so you can roll it as you cut.

7 Position a second string line between the two pegs, just above the ground. Locate each post in its hole and angle it back to align with the two string lines. Make sure that the top of the post is exactly level with the top string line so that you won't have to cut it off later.

8 Mix concrete (see page 335). Check each post is at the correct angle with a spirit level and tape, and then fill the hole around it with concrete to 50 mm below the bottom string line. Angle the top of the concrete away from the post. Allow it to set.

LAYING THE SLABS

9 Fill the footing with gravel up to the bottom string line.

10 Set a string line and lay the base course of timbers on edge behind the

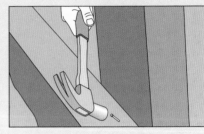

7 Using a vertical spirit level and a tape, set the angle for the post, or align it with the two string lines.

10 Nail each timber in place, nailing at an angle through the top of the timber and into the post.

11 Adjust the string lines up the width of your timber and then lay the remaining courses.

posts, checking the timbers for level with a spirit level as they are positioned. Using 75 x 3.5 mm galvanized lost-head nails, nail each timber in place by nailing at an angle through the top of the timber and into the post. If you're using old railway sleepers, first drill holes with a 4 mm bit so you can nail into the old hardwood. Use butt joints at right-angled corners, reversing the timbers for each layer so that they overlap and trimming the ends so they fit together neatly.

11 Adjust the string lines up 240 mm, or the width of the timber, for each course and lay the remaining courses. Nail each course to the posts; the wall can be made more stable by attaching the top course with coach screws.

TO FINISH

12 Cover the back of the sleeper wall with geotextile fabric, making sure there is sufficient fabric in the bottom of the footing to fully contain the agricultural drainpipe and gravel. The fabric will keep the backfill from direct contact with the timber and prevent premature decay, while allowing water to drain away.

13 Position the agricultural drainpipe behind the base course and inside the geotextile fabric. Cover it completely with gravel, filling as far up the wall as possible. Wrap the fabric around the gravel and pipe to form a bag. Backfill with sandy soil.

ABOVE LEFT Old railway sleepers, cut from hardwood and weathered over many years, make an ideal material for retaining walls, although they are difficult to cut and are heavy to lift. If they are laid on edge, however, you'll need only half as many.

SELECTING TIMBER

Timber used for garden edging is in constant contact with the ground and must be able to withstand damp and attacks by insects. Treated softwoods and durable hardwoods are both suitable for garden edges but the former are easier to work.

Softwoods treated with preservative have been treated with compounds of copper, chromium and arsenic (CCA) (see page 25) and given a 'C' rating, according to their stress-beaming level, usually of C16 or C24. Always wear gloves when handling this timber and a dust mask when sawing it.

For garden edging, select timber with a C24 rating. You'll need to reseal any cut surfaces with preservative.

ABOVE RIGHT Isometric view.

RIGHT Section view.

OPPOSITE A series of retaining walls, each about 1 m high, terrace this steeply sloping site. The rendered masonry walls have been finished with stone coping blocks.

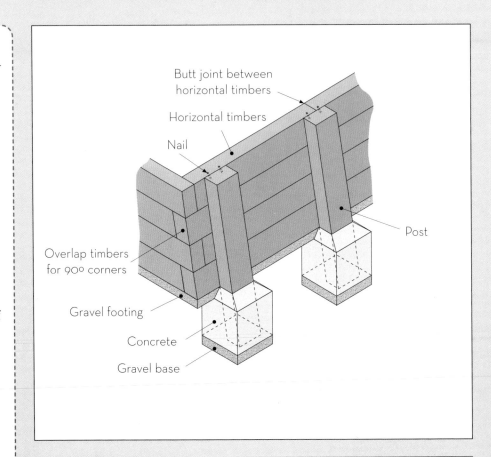

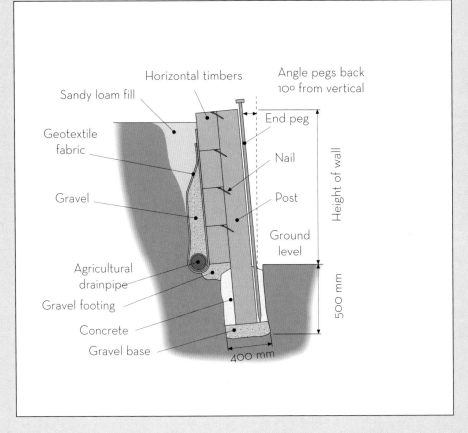

CONCRETE FILL

Old, broken bits of concrete make great fill. It's especially good for filling behind retaining walls as it doesn't compact or break down, and it provides excellent drainage. You can also use very small pieces of concrete gravel as aggregate. Use flat blocks of broken concrete for fill behind a loose retaining wall. However, it's best to discard any concrete that contains steel reinforcing.

RENDERED MASONRY WALLS

Rendered masonry walls look best in formal landscapes and as raised planters in courtyards. They are usually more difficult to build so this is probably not a job for a building novice. With these walls it's essential to install the correct drainage system to avoid capillary water forcing the render off the masonry. Larger walls are best tackled by a tradesperson, but the homeowner can construct smaller ones.

BUILDING A RENDERED MASONRY WALL

Where natural ground or soil is being retained, this wall should not exceed 750 mm in height.

1 Set out the footing line and excavate a trench that is 450 mm wide and 300 mm deep.
2 Consolidate the substrate well. If you find any rock, use this as the footing and apply a levelling layer of concrete or mortar to form the foundation for the brickwork.
3 Place trench mesh at the top and bottom of the trench, then pour the concrete footing so that it finishes with a level surface, stepping the footing with formwork if necessary. Each step should be the height of a brick course.
4 Let the concrete cure and then lay the brickwork, making the first three courses 350 mm wide. Allow for 10 mm wide brick weep holes at 900 mm centres.
5 Continue the brickwork from the fourth course at 230 mm wide, up to a maximum of nine courses.
6 Paint the back of the wall with bituminous compound. Fix a sheet of plastic membrane to the tacky paint and nail it in place. Cut holes in line with the weep holes in the plastic sheet. You should also use some drainage cell, a modular drainage product available from most DIY or hardware stores, to keep the wall dry.
7 Lay agricultural drainpipe at the base of the wall (for step-by-step instructions, see page 54) and then backfill with coarse aggregate (that is, gravel).
8 Apply render, mixed with waterproof additive, to the front and top of the wall and paint it when dry. Alternatively, use oxide additives in the render mix to create coloured walls that won't require painting.

Once the wall has had time to dry and settle, backfill the area behind the wall to the height required. Always backfill with light, sandy loam soils as clay-based soils hold moisture and swell, placing extra pressure on the wall.

OTHER COMMON WALLS

These days there is a wide range of masonry materials in pre-cast form available for the do-it-yourself market. Many of these wall kits are crib walls — that is, their own weight and that of the backfill retain them. The interlocking masonry units come with manufacturer's instructions and are easy for the home handyperson to assemble. Your local DIY store, garden centre, nursery or landscape supplier can source these and other kit-style walling systems for you.

LEFT The combination of a low masonry retaining wall and sandstone blocks suits the informal nature of this sloping garden bed.

BELOW A cross-section of a typical rendered masonry wall.

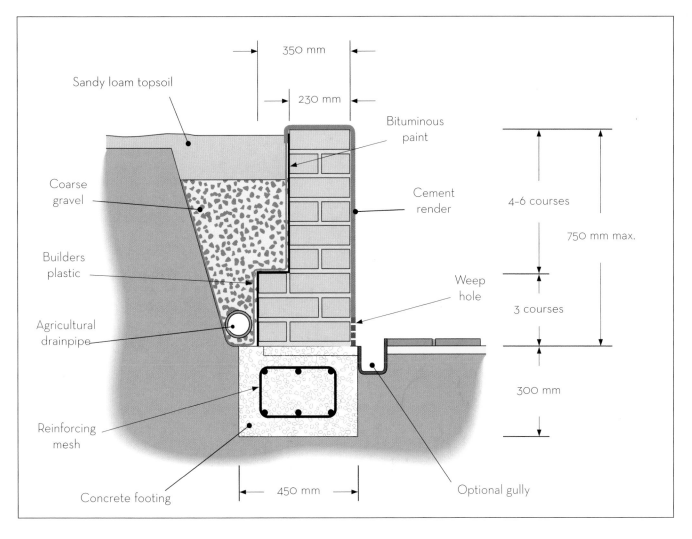

Sandy loam topsoil

Coarse gravel

Builders plastic

Agricultural drainpipe

Reinforcing mesh

Concrete footing

350 mm

230 mm

Bituminous paint

Cement render

Weep hole

Optional gully

4-6 courses

750 mm max.

3 courses

300 mm

450 mm

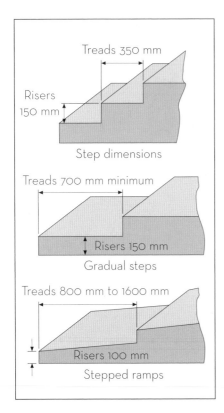

Treads 350 mm

Risers
150 mm

Step dimensions

Treads 700 mm minimum

Risers 150 mm
Gradual steps

Treads 800 mm to 1600 mm

Risers 100 mm
Stepped ramps

ABOVE Different gradients require
different step styles.

ABOVE RIGHT These stone steps have
relatively steep risers that wouldn't be
appropriate for a longer flight.

STEPS

A change in level creates interest and gives character to a garden. Usually
constructed to cope with a sloping site or to terrace a garden, a set of
steps should be made with non-slip paving materials, such as bricks, clay
pavers, wood or sandstone.

PLANNING STEPS

For steps that are both functional and aesthetically pleasing, you need to
consider various things during the planning stage.

* Match the materials used to build the steps with the garden setting and
  the architecture of your home.
* Work out the degree of slope and then decide on the type of steps
  required (see page 148 and the diagram above).
* Step treads should be 250–290 mm deep and, as a rule, the shallower
  the riser, the deeper the tread. For maximum comfort, use the
  following equation to determine the tread:
  $2 \times R$ (riser) $+ T$ (tread) = between 550 and 700 mm
* You can construct steps on a gradient as steep as 1 in 2, but for gentler
  slopes, consider a step-and-ramp combination.
  For more information on designing steps, see page 148.

CONSTRUCTING STEPS

Often you'll need to dig into an earth bank to construct a set of steps. To work out how many steps you need, measure the height of the bank and the length of the slope.

Measuring up

1 Start by placing a peg at the top of the slope, then hammer in a long stake at the bottom of the slope (the stake needs to be at least as high as the slope).
2 Tie a length of string from the bottom of the upper stake to the top of the lower stake, ensuring that the string is level.
3 Measure the distance from the string line to the bottom of the stake. This gives you the height of the slope.

If the slope is too steep for you to measure it in one go, make several similar measurements. To calculate the number of steps, divide the height of the slope by the height of the riser you have chosen. If the gradient is relatively even, this will give you a sound estimate of the number of steps.

Marking out

Once you know how many steps you need, mark out the area.

1 Start by preparing a concrete footing (see pages 340–6) at the bottom of the slope. This should be 15 cm thick and wider than the riser to be used.
2 Peg out the width of each tread and run a string between the pegs where they meet the riser end of the step.
3 Dig out the shape of the steps and then compact the soil. Prepare the entire length of the stairway before starting to mortar or backfill the steps. Start from the base and work up.

Constructing the steps

Use mortar or hard fill as the base for the tread. Mortar the risers into place and backfill the tread with hardcore rubble such as road base, then level the surface ready for laying the treads. Repeat these procedures until all the steps are completed.

To make good concrete steps, either lay concrete over a rough brick framework or use preformed stressed concrete panels available from builders' yards and larger DIY and hardware stores.

MATERIALS

Formal steps are usually constructed from materials such as bricks, pavers, slate, tiles, sawn stone or timber, while informal steps are generally constructed from materials such as old railway sleepers, wood rounds, rock, logs, split stone or various types of loose material. Combination steps involve the use of both groups of materials, such as sleeper risers backed by brick treads.

Constructing steps with informal materials is far less time-consuming as well as easier for a non-professional person to handle. If you prefer to construct formal steps, using tile or brick, you may be better off seeking professional assistance.

ABOVE These timber decking steps could double up as seating — just add some comfortable cushions.

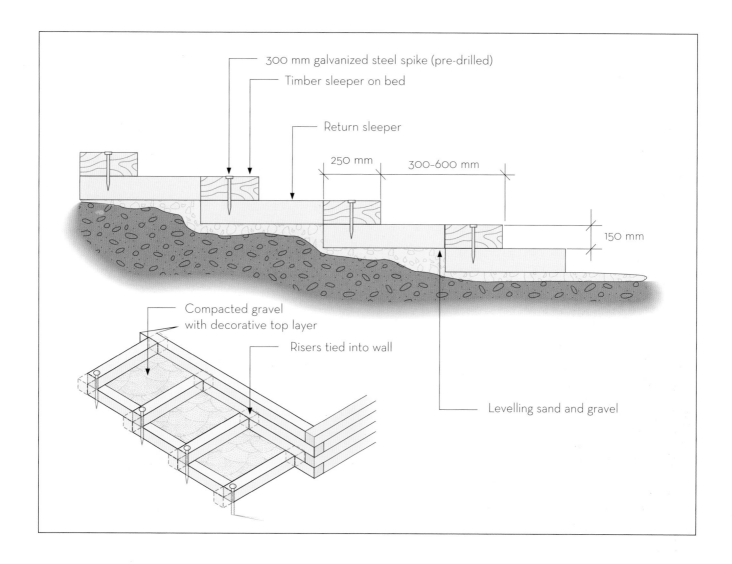

300 mm galvanized steel spike (pre-drilled)

Timber sleeper on bed

Return sleeper

250 mm

300–600 mm

150 mm

Compacted gravel
with decorative top layer

Risers tied into wall

Levelling sand and gravel

SLEEPER AND GRAVEL STEPS

Steps made from timber sleepers and gravel infill are quick and simple to build. They work equally well in formal or casual gardens. You can lay the sleepers flat or on edge to form steeper steps, and hold them in place with 300 mm galvanized spikes.

1 Excavate to the desired width and depth of the step, making the rise one or two sleepers high, with the tread a minimum 300 mm deep.
2 Cut a level base for the bottom sleeper and use road base or sand as a foundation. Compact it well so that it finishes 50 mm below ground level.
3 Mark out and cut the sleepers. Drill holes 100 mm in from each end, large enough for the spikes.
4 Lay the first sleeper level on the foundation and secure it with spikes. If appropriate, tie the sleeper into adjoining retaining walls.
5 Lay sleepers at right angles to each end of the first sleeper to form the sides of the landing and retain the gravel.
6 Place the next riser across the end of the two sleepers and secure it to them with spikes. Repeat the process for each landing.
7 Backfill the landings with spoil, compact it and then finish with gravel.

ABOVE Cross-section of typical sleeper steps with an isometric construction detail.

OPPOSITE Sleeper and gravel steps are sturdy and safe.

The tread depth and shallow risers on both these sets of steps make them comfortable and safe to use.

STONE STEPS

Use these step-by-step instructions as a guide to your situation.

1. Calculate the number of steps you need by measuring the height between the two landing areas and dividing by the riser height. Risers should be a minimum of 150 mm and a maximum of 190 mm for comfortable climbing. (Allow for the depth of mortar as well as the depth of the particular material you're using.) All the risers should be the same height or climbers will stumble.
2. Establish the tread depth (see page 32).
3. To establish the overall length of the flight of steps, multiply the number of risers by the tread.
4. Starting from the top of the flight, excavate a rough flight of steps from the earth, allowing for the thickness of the material to be used.
5. Provide a mortar or concrete bed for the bottom riser. Use the smaller pieces of stone for the risers, saving the larger pieces for the treads,

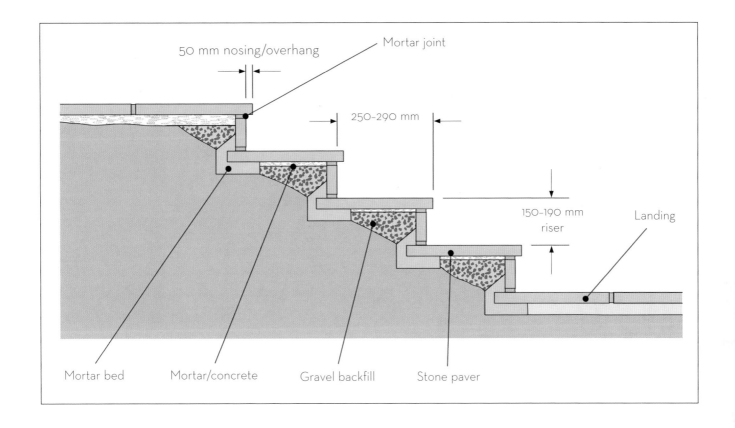

50 mm nosing/overhang

Mortar joint

250–290 mm

150–190 mm
riser

Landing

Mortar bed

Mortar/concrete

Gravel backfill

Stone paver

ABOVE Cross-section of a typical stone stair construction.

although the material for the riser should be thick enough to provide a good solid bearing. The height of each riser stone should be adjusted so that the tread stones finish at the calculated riser height. Make sure the bottom riser is tied into the bank or wall to give it strength. Backfill the riser with crushed aggregate (gravel) to provide good drainage and a good foundation for the tread.

6   Cut the stone for the tread, allowing for an overhang on the riser below and a bearing for the riser above.

7   Apply mortar to the top of the riser and use mortar or concrete to provide a level base for the tread. For the mortar, use good bricklaying sand or loam and a ratio of 4 parts sand to 1 part cement, adding a conditioner, such as detergent or a proprietary product, to keep the mortar workable longer. Use white cement with light-coloured stone and wet stone before applying the mortar so that the stone doesn't soak up the moisture of the mortar and weaken the bond. Keep an old sponge and water handy to smooth off the joints, and also to wipe up any excess mortar.

8   Lay the stones for the tread with the square edge facing outwards and work from the outside. The gaps between the stones should be uniform (about 10–20 mm).

9   Place mortar on the back of the tread to provide a bond for the next riser, and continue the process to the top of the flight.

10 Use a mortar mix to point up the gaps between the stones on the treads and risers. A neat finish on the joints will improve the look of the steps.

ABOVE A timber boardwalk protects
the natural environment.

TIMBER DECKING

A great way to create either a level area for entertaining or a walkway for
protecting sensitive plants and landscapes is to build a timber platform or
boardwalk. This eliminates the need for heavy earthworks and retaining
walls, and allows free drainage of the site.

These projects are often best tackled by a reliable tradesperson, but
if you're keen and have the right tools, it's a lot simpler than it looks.
Whether you want to build a boardwalk or a platform, the methods are
much the same. The main issue is to avoid timber spans that will lead to
sagging because of insufficient support. Ask your timber supplier for more
information. For outdoor projects, always use treated timber or hardwood
and galvanized fixings. Treated pine is easier to work with and is insect
resistant if the cuts have been sealed properly.

1   Using a straight line, measure and set the outer limit of the platform,
    then mark off the footing centres, remembering to keep the set-out
    square in the process. (For instructions on setting out a 90-degree
    corner, see page 342.) Generally, the centres of the footings should be
    no more than 1800 mm apart, and, for a neat, cantilevered effect, set
    them back 450 mm within the outer limit.

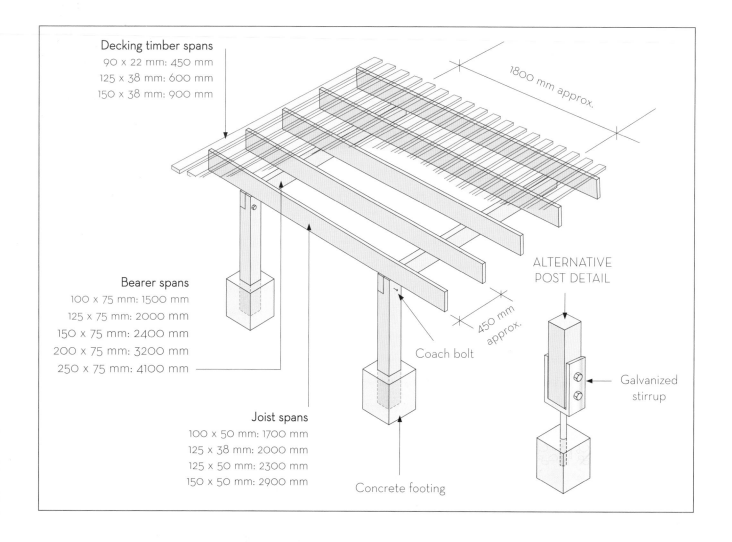

Decking timber spans
90 x 22 mm: 450 mm
125 x 38 mm: 600 mm
150 x 38 mm: 900 mm

1800 mm approx.

Bearer spans
100 x 75 mm: 1500 mm
125 x 75 mm: 2000 mm
150 x 75 mm: 2400 mm
200 x 75 mm: 3200 mm
250 x 75 mm: 4100 mm

Coach bolt

450 mm approx.

ALTERNATIVE
POST DETAIL

Galvanized
stirrup

Joist spans
100 x 50 mm: 1700 mm
125 x 38 mm: 2000 mm
125 x 50 mm: 2300 mm
150 x 50 mm: 2900 mm

Concrete footing

2 Excavate the footing hole to approximately 300 mm deep and make it 450 x 450 mm. Reset the string lines once you've completed the holes.

3 Set posts in the holes and brace them in position with timber offcuts, using a spirit level to check that each one is vertical. Alternatively, set galvanized stirrups in the concrete footings and attach the posts to them. For larger platforms you can build brick piers and use metal caps to expose insect activity.

4 Pour in pre-mixed concrete and again check that the posts are vertical with the spirit level. Cut off the posts at the same level.

5 Cut the bearers to length, allowing 300 mm overhang at each end. At the top of each post, mark and cut a housing for the bearer. Use coach bolts to fix the bearers to the posts.

6 Cut the joists to length, allowing 300 mm overhang at each end, and lay them out perpendicular to the bearers. Skew-nail through them into the bearers.

7 Lay out the decking timbers perpendicular to the joists and nail them in place, fixing at each joist centre. Use a piece of dowel or timber offcut to space the decking timbers about 5 mm apart. The gaps allow for timber expansion, as well as air movement and water drainage to help avoid rot. Paint, oil or stain the timber to suit.

ABOVE LEFT and RIGHT You can adapt the method for building boardwalks and decking to make walkways over water courses and damp areas.

OPPOSITE BOTTOM Typical deck/boardwalk construction. *Note:* The spans shown, using C24 treated softwood, are approximate.

BOARDWALK ACROSS WATER

TOOLS

- Groundwork tools
- Woodwork tools
- Maul
- Spirit level
- Aluminium ladder
- Scaffold plank
- String line
- Paint and paintbrush
- Polythene sheet

MATERIALS

- Sleeper beams: 150 x 75 mm
- Ballast or sharp sand
- Posts: 50 x 50 mm
- Deck slats: 125 x 37 mm
- Galvanized nails: 150 mm and 63 mm
- Wood stain
- Chicken wire
- Staples

In wet or boggy areas, a boardwalk is a useful substitute for a more conventional path. There are several methods worth considering.

Smaller bodies of water can be spanned using large natural flagstones, perhaps sandstone or slate, depending on the site. Railway sleepers also work well, since they are solid and long lasting, and don't require any complicated construction techniques. Two side by side are much safer than one. If the water is wide enough, stepping stones would be fun. You could make these from paving slabs bedded onto concrete blocks or use natural boulders bedded into the base of the pool. For a wider span, consider either a galvanized steel walkway in a high-tech design.

The boardwalk for this project was painted with a blue stain and finished with a layer of chicken wire to provide a non-slip surface.

LAYING AND FIXING THE BEAMS

1 The simplest base construction for a single span boardwalk is to lay half a sleeper beam bearer at each end. First decide on the finished height of the boardwalk above the water: not so high that it needs to be supported above ground level on the banks at either side but, if you are bridging a natural watercourse, high enough to cope with any changes in the water level. The underside of the proposed boardwalk beams will give you the finished height of the supporting bearers. Cut a sleeper in half to give you the bearer for each end of the boardwalk, then dig out a trench, allowing for the depth of the sleeper and a bed of ballast or sharp sand. Lay the first bearer and thump it down with a maul to the finished level. Check with a spirit level that it runs level across its length.

2 Excavate and lay the second bearer on the opposite bank. Then lay one of the beams across the water from one bearer to the other, and use a spirit level to check that the two bearers are level. Knock the second bearer down with a maul until both are level. If it's not easy to gain access to the opposite bank to complete this stage, then you could lay an aluminium ladder and scaffold plank from one side of the water to the other to act as a temporary bridge.

3 Using a long galvanized nail, fix the first beam in position by nailing through its side into the bearer. Check that it crosses the bearer at 90 degrees and fix the other end with a nail in the same manner. The beams need to be fairly substantial, so use 150 x 75 mm timbers. Position the second beam parallel to the first by measuring and checking that the space between the two beams is the same at each end. The width across from the outside of one beam to the outside of the other should allow for deck slats to overhang at each side by about 75 mm.

4 Firmly anchor the beams by driving in long 50 x 50 mm posts. Drive them in with a heavy hammer hard against the point inside the beams

2 Use a spirit level to check that the bearer is level.

4 To firmly anchor each beam, drive a post into each of the corners where the beam meets the bearers.

LEFT If you have a large enough body of water in your garden, a boardwalk makes an interesting feature.

5 Begin to nail the boards into position. One edge of each board should align with the taut string line you've set up.

6 Continue laying the boards across the water. Nail the board in front of you as you go.

where the beams meet with the bearers, as far into the bank as they will go. Nail each post to both the beam and the bearer, and then cut off the post to just below the top of the beam.

5   Cut each of the deck slats to the same length. Nail one slat of decking board into position at each end of the boardwalk, then pull a string line taut between them along one edge. Check for square (see page 342). Now start to lay the rest of the deck slats, nailing them into position with one edge just touching the string line. Use a nail as a spacer to leave a small gap between each board. This gap will accommodate the natural expansion of the timber and allow surface water to drain away. At this stage, only knock in one nail at each end of the board and leave them proud in case you need to remove and realign any of the boards.

ADDING THE SLATS

6   Work your way across the water, nailing in boards in front of you as you go. When you have completed approximately half the boarding, it's a good idea to lay out the remaining slats without nailing them down. This will indicate whether you need to increase or decrease the gap slightly between each board in order to fit all the boards neatly, without having to cut any of them down to a thin strip. If no adjustments are needed, fix nails at the end of each board. Once you've fixed all the boards, check along the opposite edge to the line to make sure that the ends there are all even too. If any are not even, trim them with a panel saw and sand them to make them smooth.

TO FINISH

7   You will now need to check the entire boardwalk to see if you need to touch up any of the boards with stain, since cutting the boards may have resulted in some accidental removal of the stain. If re-staining is required, be sure to lay a sheet of polythene over the water to protect it from splashes, which can contaminate it.

8   Finally, tack chicken wire to the surface with staples. To do this, stretch the wire taut over the slats and curl it around the edges before fixing it down. This wire will help to provide a good grip on the surface, especially in damp and slippery areas.

7 If you need to touch up the boardwalk with stain, lay a polythene sheet under the board.

8 To protect your boardwalk and to provide a good grip on the surface, fix chicken wire to the boards.

LEFT Building up new garden beds is a simple solution to poor clay soils.

OPPOSITE TOP A small level courtyard has been simply treated with raised beds, a water feature (far left) and a gravel floor.

OPPOSITE BOTTOM Mounds create visual interest on a large level site.

LEVEL SITES

A level site is both easy to maintain and ideal for entertaining or children's play. However, it can be difficult to create visual interest in a large flat area, and you're likely to encounter problems, such as poor drainage.

Changing the contours by mounding can improve drainage by diverting surface water runoff. Be careful to direct the flow towards a natural drainage path or existing drain; and try to avoid creating areas that collect water. Added contours can also provide visual interest.

You can also transform an uninteresting garden, especially a small space such as a courtyard, with raised planters. Use them to display favourite plant species and help define a particular space.

BUILDING A MOUND

The soil structure is made of different layers of topsoil, subsoils and the substratum; each has different levels of drainage and nutrients. When excavation is carried out on a site, the soil structure is often destroyed and the different types of soil mixed haphazardly, upsetting the drainage patterns. So when you add soil to a site, it's important to provide as natural a grading of soil types as possible or the results may be disappointing.

1 Where possible, remove the useful topsoil and vegetation from the designated area, then dig or hoe the remaining soil to allow good drainage through the subsoil layers.
2 Create a mound on the proposed area, either by using free-draining subsoil from the site or importing weed-free and free-draining fill. Make sure the material can drain freely once it's been compacted.
3 Compact the fill by hand or machine to a point where it's stable and drains well. To help the compaction process, water in the fill.
4 To create the planting medium and ensure the mound grades smoothly into the surrounding levels, spread imported or reused topsoil over the mound to a depth of 300 mm. On large or steep mounds, use erosion control mats to help retain the topsoil.
5 Plant out with soil-binding groundcover species. Finish with mulch.

ABOVE A timber edge makes a simple raised bed, ideal for vegetables or any plants that need a free-draining soil.

BELOW If you prefer a curved but formal wall for your raised beds, brick is one of the best materials to use.

RAISED BEDS

Raised beds are a simple way to improve the soil and change the growing conditions for plants that might need a little help in terms of drainage, deeper, richer soil or other requirements that might not be local to your area. For instance, use raised beds to grow vegetables so you can add more organic matter for fast growth, or if you have heavy clay soil and want to grow plants that prefer sandy surface soil. Succulents and alpines require a fast-draining medium and different growing conditions to those in the rest of the garden; a raised bed can provide the right conditions.

Another advantage of a raised bed is that watering and fertilization are more economical. The soil of a raised bed warms up faster and excess soil moisture drains away, reducing damage from overwatering. Because of the warmer soil, a raised bed also allows earlier planting, particularly in cold winter areas, and is usually ready to plant several weeks before a regular garden bed. Root crops grown in a raised bed are stronger and yield more produce in less space.

Raised beds are also a stylish addition to the urban garden and can double as seating when entertaining. Anyone with limited space will find that a raised bed improves access and increases the available arable ground, so whether you live in a small modern townhouse, retirement villa or penthouse with a rooftop garden, use raised beds as a design element that also solves practical space problems. This type of garden is particularly practical for gardeners who are wheelchair-bound.

BUILDING A RAISED BED

You can adapt this method to suit your situation and design.

1 Using a string line and lime powder, set out the area for the bed. (For instructions on setting out, see page 340).
2 Excavate a trench around 450 mm wide by 300 mm deep for the foundations. Compact the base of the trench, using a spirit level and straight edge to ensure that the base is level. Where the ground slopes down or up, create a step in the base of about 200 mm at a time.
3 Set up a string line within the trench to mark the top of the brick footing, about 180 mm from the base of the trench.
4 Build a concrete footing (see pages 340–6), or a footing from bricks. (Use the oldest and roughest bricks laid on edge in a mortar bed.) Check that the top of the footing is level.
5 Lay brickwork on the footing to a maximum height of about 600 mm. Leave gaps in the bottom courses for weep holes so that any water can escape, otherwise it will be retained and cause damage.
6 For decorative effect or to make a seat, add a capping course of bricks laid header style, sandstone slabs or pre-cast concrete blocks.
7 If you plan to render the brickwork, add a waterproof membrane to the inside of the walls.
8 Backfill with rubble up to the height of the weep holes. If you wish, lay geotextile fabric or drainage cell over the aggregate and up the walls.
9 Install free-draining planter box soil mix (with a high sand and/or ash content). Plant out the raised bed and add mulch to a depth of 75 mm.

BELOW A cut-away section of a raised brick planter.

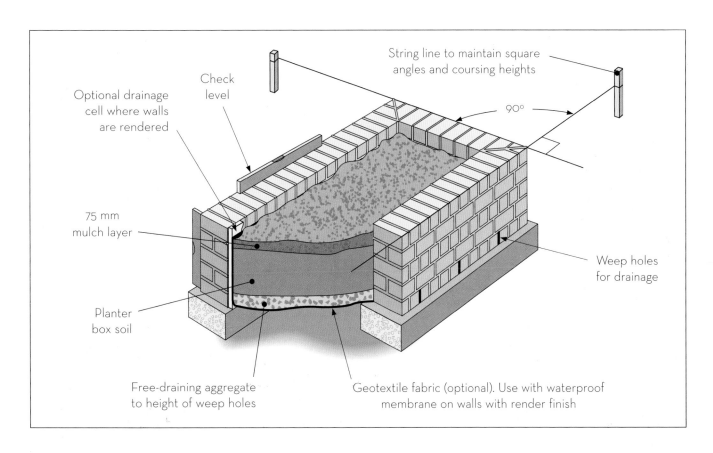

String line to maintain square angles and coursing heights

Check level

Optional drainage cell where walls are rendered

90°

75 mm mulch layer

Weep holes for drainage

Planter box soil

Free-draining aggregate to height of weep holes

Geotextile fabric (optional). Use with waterproof membrane on walls with render finish

CONCRETE RAISED BED

TOOLS

- Basic tools (see page 332)
- Circular saw or handsaw
- Chisel
- Electric drill
- 18 mm hole saw or spade bit
- Steel mesh cutters or angle grinder
- Edging tool
- Paintbrush

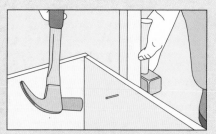

6 Ensure the sides are level before fixing them to each peg with one nail near the top of the side.

Concrete is an ideal material for a raised bed. Make sure you provide adequate drainage so that the soil inside doesn't become waterlogged. The formwork should be constructed accurately and be strong enough to contain the wet concrete.

CONSTRUCTING THE FORMWORK

1 Mark out the 1800 x 1200 mm sheet of exterior ply, dividing it lengthways into four strips 300 mm wide. Likewise, mark out the 1200 x 1200 mm sheet into four strips 300 mm wide. Cut the strips using a circular saw, with a straight edge as a guide, or a handsaw.

2 On two 1800 mm pieces, measure along 1484 mm and mark the length, and on two 1200 mm pieces, measure and mark the length at 884 mm. Nail the two pairs together and cut the lengths square.

3 Construct the outside box using two 1800 mm and two 1200 mm lengths (see the main diagram on page 51). Nail the butt joints together using 65 x 3 mm plywood nails, but nail only to the first head. This will allow you to remove the nails easily when dismantling the formwork. Use three equally spaced nails per joint.

4 The inside box cannot be nailed together like the outside one because, once the concrete is poured, it's impossible to remove the nails. Therefore, nail 300 mm long timber cleats flush to both ends of the long sides, using three 40 x 3 mm bullet-head nails. Position the short ends of the box and nail through the plywood into the timber cleat with two nails.

5 Prepare the 1836 x 1200 mm site, removing grass or unwanted vegetative matter. Roughly level the ground to make it easier to position the boxes.

6 Position the outside box on the ground and measure both diagonals to ensure it is square. Adjust and temporarily brace across the corners if necessary. Position three outer pegs equally spaced along each long side against the formwork, driving them in with a sledge hammer or club hammer until they are firm. Add a peg in the middle of each short side. Use a spirit level to ensure the sides are level. If necessary, prop up the sides to the correct height before fixing them to the pegs with 40 x 3 mm lost-head nails. Nail only once near the top of the sides to make dismantling easier.

7 Position the inside box, ensuring there is an even 140 mm space between the inside and outside boxes. Position an inner peg against each inner face of the inside box, in the centre of each side and, once again, drive it into the ground until it is firm. Lay a spirit level or straight edge across both boxes, and lift and match the finished height of the outside box. Fix it by nailing through the top of the plywood into the pegs, using one 40 x 3 mm lost-head nail per peg.

LEFT Concrete makes a sturdy raised garden bed. The concrete can be coloured or given a textured finish so that it blends more easily into the landscape; this bed was given a coat of textured paint.

CONCRETE FOOTINGS

The size of the footing for a masonry raised bed is determined by what you'll plant in the bed. Large trees can lift and crack small footings. To contain them, a footing 300 mm wide and deep, reinforced with a three-bar steel cage, is appropriate. For smaller trees, shrubs or palms, a footing 300 mm wide and 100 mm deep with a single layer of three-bar is sufficient. For annuals and small plants, a brick footing below ground level is adequate.

MATERIALS*

- 1800 x 1200 mm sheet of 18 mm exterior plywood
- 1200 x 1200 mm sheet of 18 mm exterior plywood
- Timber pegs
- 4 x 300 mm long 75 x 50 mm softwood cleats
- 1400 mm long piece of 50 x 25 mm timber for spreader
- 6 x 500 mm long pieces of 50 x 25 mm timber for buttresses
- 10 x 140 mm long 50 x 25 mm timber spacer blocks
- 40 x 3 mm lost-head nails
- 65 x 3 mm lost-head plywood nails
- 18 mm flexible plastic conduit pipe
- 6 m of three-bar steel reinforcement tie wire and bar chairs
- Vegetable cooking oil or light motor oil
- Portland cement
- Sand
- Coarse aggregate (gravel)

* To construct a garden bed 1800 x 1164 mm and 300 mm high.

8 Place the spreader across the centre of the long sides, nailing it to the tops of the centre pegs.

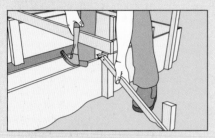

9 Fix buttress supports to the outer pegs, angle them down and fix them to the extra pegs at ground level.

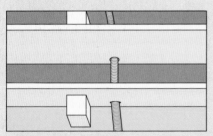

10 Drill holes through both boxes and place plastic conduit pipe through the holes as a channel for the water.

FINISHING THE FORMWORK

8 As concrete is particularly heavy when wet, strengthen the box so that it doesn't lose shape or move sideways during the pour. Place the spreader across the centre of the long sides. Check that the sides of the box are parallel and equally spaced before fixing the spreader to the tops of the centre pegs with 40 x 3 mm lost-head nails.

9 To prevent the formwork flexing sideways, hammer in extra pegs about 250 mm outside the box. Nail buttresses to the outer pegs at the level of the top of the sides and then angle them down and fix them to the extra pegs at ground level.

10 To provide drainage holes through the concrete, drill 18 mm holes through both boxes. Position the holes 50 mm above ground level and every 600 mm along the outside box (line up the holes in the inside box with these). Place 18 mm of plastic conduit pipe through the pairs of holes to provide a channel for the water (the ends will be trimmed off later).

11 Using steel mesh cutters or an angle grinder, cut two 1700 mm and two 1100 mm lengths of three-bar steel reinforcement. Position the lengths between the sides about 50 mm above ground level on bar chairs and tie the corners together with tie wire.

12 Cut ten 140 mm long timber spacer blocks, and space them equally within the formwork to help keep the sides parallel. As the concrete is poured, gradually lift the spacer blocks higher until the concreting is completed, then remove them.

13 Use a paintbrush to coat the inside of the formwork with oil. This will make it easier to remove the formwork and prevent the concrete surface from honeycombing.

ADDING THE CONCRETE

14 Mix the concrete (see page 335) and pour it into the formwork. This can be a difficult job, so consider carefully whether you should mix it yourself or have it delivered. Ensure there is access to the site, and construct a wheelbarrow ramp if necessary.

15 Once the concrete is in place, level the surface with a float. Tap the formwork sides with a hammer to help settle the concrete, remove air pockets and prevent honeycombing on the surface. Run an edging tool along both sides of the top surface to push the aggregate down.

16 Allow the concrete to set for 1–2 hours. Once the top of the concrete feels firm when pressed, finish the top surface with an edger.

17 Remove the nails from the outside formwork only and begin to pull it away. If the concrete does not wobble or move, it's safe to continue. Weather conditions can affect the drying time of concrete, so if there is any movement, wait for another hour.

18 Use a wooden float on the vertical face, working horizontally to prevent damage to the top edge. The wooden float will give the surfaces a textured look. Fill any holes in the surfaces with a mix of 1 part sand and 1 part cement. To prevent damage to the edges, it's best to float from the corners to the centre.

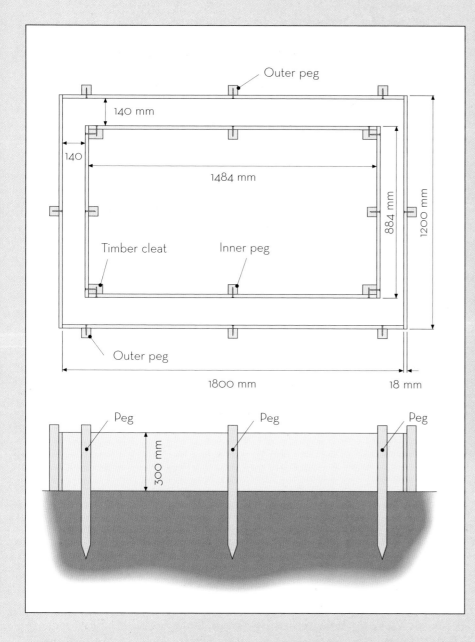

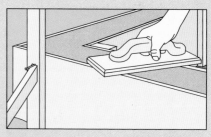

15 Level the top surface with a float wide enough to bear on both the inner and outer boxes.

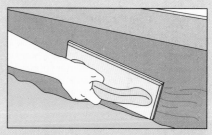

18 Use a wooden float on the vertical face, working horizontally to prevent damage to the top edge.

LEFT Top and side views of formwork.

TO FINISH

19 Allow the concrete to set fully. Split the cleats away with a hammer and chisel, and pull away and lift out the inside formwork.

20 Cut off the drainage pipes so that they are flush with the surface of the concrete. Fill the base of the garden bed with a layer of broken bricks, tiles or gravel for drainage before adding soil and compost.

ABOVE and ABOVE RIGHT On a sloping site it's critical to install the correct drainage system. Agricultural drains have been used on this site.

DRAINING THE SITE

Water can be both friend and foe in a garden, and managing that water efficiently can reduce the amount of maintenance required, improve plant growth and protect your investment. Draining the site correctly is an important part of the natural system that makes up a garden landscape.

The best location for any type of drain or sump is the lowest part of the particular paved or lawn area; this point will be obvious if the pavers are mossy or if the lawn is soggy and unhealthy. Getting rid of the unwanted water is a simple process: use drains and pipes that connect to either the street gutter or water easement, as long as the connecting point is lower than the area you want to drain. Otherwise use a dispersion trench.

CHOOSING THE RIGHT SYSTEM

If you are starting a project from scratch, the time to start installing drainage is after you have constructed retaining walls and established finished levels. Once you are left with clear, level areas you can assess the amount of drainage you need.

There are different types of drains for different situations and most are simple to construct. The table opposite will help you select the right system for your particular situation.

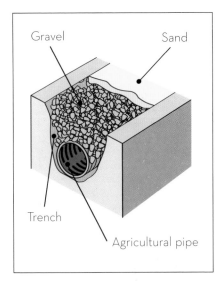

TYPES OF DRAIN

DRAIN	WHERE TO USE IT
Agricultural drain	Gardens, lawns
Channel drain	Driveways, paths, pool surrounds and paved areas
Siltation pit	Driveways, large areas of paving or lawn
Gully	Paths and paved areas
Open pebble drain	Gardens
Dispersion trench	Poorly drained sites

AGRICULTURAL DRAIN

One way of dealing with a boggy area is to create a system of agricultural drains. They are designed so that they fill from the bottom of the trench and disperse the water as it rises in the pipe.

1 Set out the drain perpendicular to (that is, at right angles to) the contour of the site and so that the downhill end leads into a larger soak pit or, preferably, a drainage system provided by a plumber. For large areas, lay a network of drains in a herringbone pattern.

2 Next, dig trenches about 150 mm into the subsoil and to an overall depth of at least 300 mm. Grade the trenches so that they have a minimum 1 in 100 fall.

3 Lay enough geotextile membrane in the bottom of the trench to fold back over the top of the trench.

4 Add a layer of gravel, or coarse aggregate.

5 Lay agricultural drainage pipe on the bottom of the trench and connect it to the drainage system or other pipes in the network. Test the fall of the drain to ensure that water won't pond.

6 Backfill the trench with gravel, then fold the membrane back over the trench. Add a final layer of sandy loam topsoil.

ABOVE Isometric view of an agricultural drain.

LEFT Without adequate drainage, the bottom of a sloping site such as this one will become damp and boggy.

LAYING AGRICULTURAL DRAIN

Installing an agricultural drain is a simple process, although you'll need to do a lot of digging.

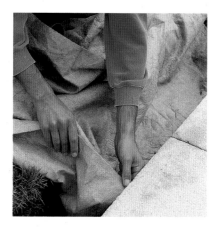

1 After you've excavated a trench, lay geotextile membrane to prevent any soil from being washed into the pipe. Allow for plenty of excess as you'll need to fold it over the trench later.

2 Next, add a layer of gravel before laying the pipe, then backfill with some more gravel over the top of the pipe.

3 Fold the geotextile membrane back over the top of the filled trench. Cover with topsoil and turf, if appropriate.

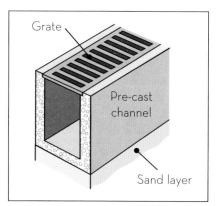

Grate

Pre-cast channel

Sand layer

PRE-CAST CHANNEL DRAIN

There are several different types of pre-cast channel drains, varying in size, depth and material. If you are installing one under a driveway, you will need a more robust unit; otherwise a standard unit will be sufficient.

1 Lift the pavers along the line where you want the drain to be installed, leaving at least one row against the wall or edge of the paved area.

2 Excavate a trench with a minimum fall of 1 in 100. It should terminate at a water pipe junction or at a point where you can install PVC pipe to connect to the junction. Make the trench deep enough for the channel to finish flush with the pavers when on a sand/cement base that is at least 50 mm deep. Check the fall with a spirit level and straight edge.

3 To provide the footing for the channel, place a dry mix of coarse sand and cement in the trench.

4 Set up a string line and level to show the fall and to set a straight edge for the channel. It will be easiest if you start at the junction (dispersal) point and work back. Align the channel with the string line, setting it into the mortar mix where necessary. Connect it to any water lines and seal with a recommended bonding agent. Pack a wet mix of mortar around the sides of the channel.

5 Cut pavers to finish flush against the channel, laying them so that they fall towards the drain, thus maximizing the drainage catchment.

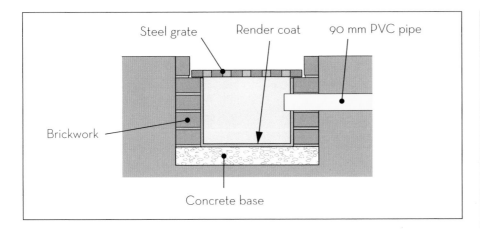

Steel grate Render coat 90 mm PVC pipe

Brickwork

Concrete base

ABOVE A statue or other garden ornament can be used to disguise a siltation pit.

ABOVE LEFT Cross-section of a brick siltation pit.

OPPOSITE TOP Isometric view of a pre-cast channel drain.

OPPOSITE BOTTOM A pre-cast channel drain in a paved area.

BRICK SILTATION PIT

If you have a large area to drain but a channel drain is unsuitable, the alternative is to construct a siltation pit or sump. A siltation pit can handle runoff from a large area and have the added benefit of allowing dirty runoff to settle, thus reducing the risk of a blocked drain.

The size of the pit will depend on the size of the area you want to drain. As a guide, a 470 x 470 mm pit should effectively drain around 50–80 square metres of paved area or about 100 square metres of lawn. Larger pits will suit larger areas or where accumulated runoff from neighbouring land increases the amount of water collecting on the area you want to drain.

1 Assess the connection point and install any lines required to take away water that will collect in the pit.
2 For a 470 x 470 m pit, dig an 800 m square hole 700 mm deep. Compact the base of the hole.
3 Add a layer of sand about 50 mm deep and line the inside of the hole with a sheet of builders plastic.
4 Pour a level concrete slab about 500 x 500 mm and 75 mm thick in the base of the pit. Leave it to cure for a few days. (For information on laying concrete, see pages 332–51.)
5 On the concrete slab, set out and then lay the brickwork walls, checking they are square and will accommodate the grate you have purchased (check that the nibs of the grate can be inserted in the brickwork). About two courses from the top of the pit, leave a gap in the brickwork for a 90 mm diameter pipe.
6 Install a section of the pipe and seal around it with cement mix. Attach a sleeve to the pipe for connection to the main line.
7 Line the inside brickwork with a render mixed with waterproofing agent. A heavy-bagged finish will suffice.
8 Install the grate. Repair the turf or pavers around the pit so that the pit finishes about 10 mm below the surface.
9 Disguise the pit with a garden ornament, such as a piece of statuary, and spread decorative pebbles around the base. The water will drain freely through the pebbles and you can use the ornament as a focal point in the garden.

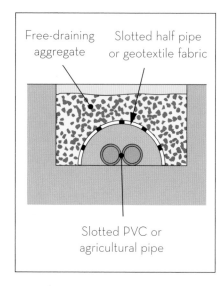

Free-draining aggregate

Slotted half pipe or geotextile fabric

Slotted PVC or agricultural pipe

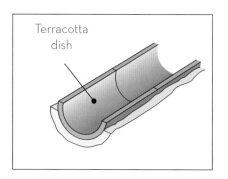

Terracotta dish

TOP Dispersion trench.

CENTRE and ABOVE A gully is usually made of terracotta.

ABOVE RIGHT A trench disguised as a natural stream.

DISPERSION TRENCH

If you want to drain an area that has no way of connecting to either an easement or a street gutter, such as when your land slopes away from the street, a simple dispersion trench may be the solution. Dispersal systems are usually only recommended where there is either no alternative or where there are large areas of lawn or garden to cope with overflows. The soil profile must also be deep enough to cope; dispersion trenches are unsuitable for sites with exposed bedrock.

Selecting the right location for a dispersion trench is critical if water is to be dispersed effectively without affecting neighbouring structures. It should be large enough to disperse large quantities of water, be as long as possible and run parallel to the contours of the site. Small systems that relieve only small areas of drainage catchment are available. They are based on the same principle as the systems referred to here.

1 Excavate the trench to a minimum of 1 m long and 300 mm wide.
2 Take a large-gauge agricultural pipe, or similar slotted or perforated pipe such as the type used in septic systems, and lay it along the trench as shown in the diagram (see top left). Connect it to incoming drainage lines. Cover the agricultural pipe with a slotted half pipe or a geotextile fabric.
3 Backfill the trench with rubble to cover the pipe and then continue to backfill to a depth of about 300 mm with smaller aggregates, finishing with 20 mm recycled aggregate. Backfill the remaining trench with sand and compact evenly. Finish with topsoil and turf.

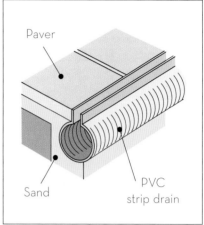

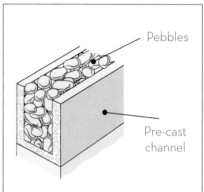

OTHER DRAINAGE METHODS

There are several other types of drain to consider. The size of your garden and the particular problem will help determine which drainage system is appropriate for your situation.

- **Gully** Consisting of a terracotta dish, this shallow open drain is used to divert water into a larger collection pit. It can be set into paving or lawn and garden areas.
- **Swathe or culvert** A larger version of the gully, it's used to divert water from large areas.
- **Strip drain** This proprietary system is usually made from PVC and it has an opening approximately 25 mm wide along the top. The water drains into this. It is generally used across the fall of pedestrian areas and wherever it's desirable to minimize the visual impact of grated drains.
- **Open pebble or decorative gravel drain** This open trench can be disguised as part of a gravel or pebble bed and is particularly useful beside paths and patios where runoff is heavy and other drains can be unsightly. It's often used in tropical climates and can be adapted.
- **Natural dry stream bed** This solution is often used on large sites or where there is heavy runoff in wet climates. Runoff areas are graded towards a large, open trench, which is then landscaped to replicate a natural stream bed. Large rocks, logs and plantings are used to break the water flow. The trench often terminates in a pool or water storage area.

TOP PVC strip drain.

ABOVE Pebble or gravel drain.

ABOVE LEFT A stream bed is an attractive solution to the problem of heavy runoff.

ABOVE When you install irrigation pipe, make sure there are no kinks or twists, otherwise the pipe will creep as it fills with water.

TOP To check the water flow per hour on a seephose system, place a container, such as this small jar, into the soil below the pipe so that the rim is level with the soil surface.

IRRIGATION

Irrigating a site is an important part of landscape management. Simple systems can help in the establishment of plants and provide additional water in dry times. However, water is a valuable resource to be used sparingly so, before you install an irrigation system, ensure the water needs of your garden are minimized. Select plant species tolerant of local conditions, mulch garden beds to prevent evaporation of soil water and design a garden layout that conserves water.

Where possible, rainwater should be collected for use on the garden. You can install simple reservoirs by connecting roof water disposal systems to water butts or even by constructing a pond to collect rainwater.

IRRIGATION SYSTEMS

A simple micro-irrigation system will help you to develop and manage your garden beds and lawns. First, check whether your local water company has regulations concerning installation licensing, tap connection and back-flow devices. If you live in a drought-stricken area, such as the south-east of England you may not be able to use an irrigation system at all, so again, check with your local water authority.

Most DIY stores and garden centres have a large range of irrigation products and can provide advice for the home landscaper. Look closely at the flow rate of each spray or drip fitting: overburdening the system will result in weak flows and poor coverage.

You'll need to plan the layout to suit your water pressure. To identify the flow rate or pressure of your water supply, turn the tap on full and time how long it takes to fill a 10-litre bucket. This will allow you to calculate your flow rate as a ratio of litres per second. Most proprietary irrigation systems include instructions to help you calculate the coverage of the system and its spray heads.

The higher your water pressure, the greater the diameter of pipe you can use, but it's better to use a thinner line with drip or directional fittings. This will help conserve water.

POP-UP LAWN IRRIGATION

This system is ideal for large areas of lawn. The spray nozzles sit flush with the surface of the soil and pop up when the water is turned on.

1 Before you select the spray fitting, calculate the area of lawn you want to irrigate and check the compatibility of your flow rate with the product. The packaging or the fitting itself usually identifies the spray pattern. When designing the irrigation pattern for each area of lawn, use a selection of half, three-quarter and full-circle spray patterns (see page 60). Roughly mark out the radius of each spray fitting, allowing for small overlaps. Use half circles to run parallel to garden beds or paving and three-quarter circles for corners. The fewer the fittings, the better the flow pressure will be, so minimize the branches off the main line.

LEFT Many areas are now subject to drought and water restrictions in the summer, so this type of irrigation system is more likely to be found in parks.

2 Use a spade to excavate for the plastic line, being careful to save turf strips for replanting. Set the line into the trench so that the pop-up fittings sit flush with the top of the soil. This will ensure that they won't be cut up by the lawn mower.
3 Using connector fittings and clamps, connect the lines in the trenches. Try to minimize right-angled corners.
4 Connect the pop-up fittings to the lines and the main line to the hose cock, using a back-flow device and/or filter unit where required.
5 Test run the system and adjust it as necessary.
6 Backfill the trenches and test the system again.

GARDEN IRRIGATION

Garden polypipe systems tend to be more efficient than lawn systems as the spray distances don't need to be as long. By running a main line along the centre or front of a garden bed, you can usually service most plants effectively, perhaps with the additional use of feeder lines or 'spaghetti tubing'. The position of the main line will depend on accessibility and the position of plants within the bed. In those gardens with borders — that is, smaller foreground plantings and larger background plants — run the line at the front, while in those with a more even layout of similar sized shrubs, run it along the centre. To run a line along walkways, position the polypipe at the front of the bed or beside the path so that the spray heads can be directed towards the garden.

As a general rule, use drip fittings for larger trees and shrubs, and spray systems for smaller shrubs, ferns and groundcovers. Fine spray heads will create humid conditions for delicate ferns or tropical

HOLIDAY CARE

If you're going on holidays, prepare your garden for a dry spell.

• Place an organic mulch such as peat moss or grass clippings around plants to conserve moisture. Keep mulch clear of trunks or it may cause rot.
• Thoroughly water the garden before you leave. First, make a small depression around trees and shrubs, then water. When water soaks into the soil, refill 2–3 times as the water soaks away.
• Install a trickle irrigation system on a timer: at the programmed time, a small volume of water will automatically drip onto soil at the base of plants.
• Water pot plants well, then bury them up to the rims and cover them with peat moss, dead leaves, grass clippings, pebbles or bark.

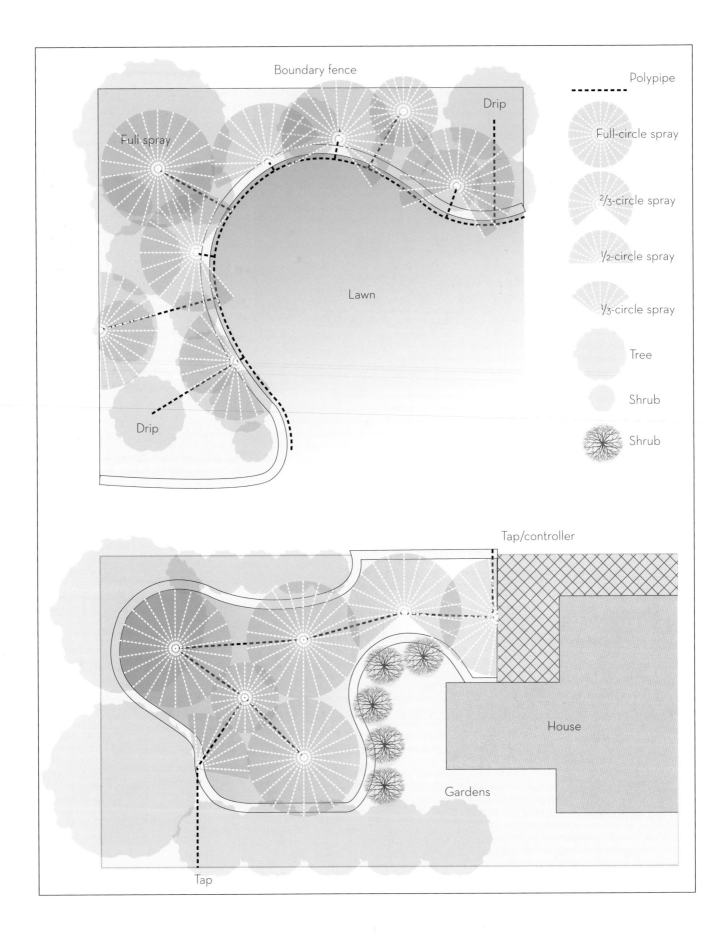

Boundary fence

Polypipe

Drip

Full spray

Full-circle spray

²/₃-circle spray

¹/₂-circle spray

¹/₃-circle spray

Lawn

Tree

Shrub

Drip

Shrub

Tap/controller

House

Gardens

Tap

landscapes. Use drip fittings at the base of plants to avoid 'water burns' on sensitive flowers.

1 Run the selected polypipe along the garden bed. Select and connect each fitting to achieve the greatest coverage without being wasteful.
2 Bury the polypipe under a heavy layer of mulch or just beneath the soil in order to keep any spray risers in an upright position.
3 Connect and run the system. Adjust the fittings to provide the most efficient coverage.
4 Clean and test the spray heads regularly to ensure plants are receiving the maximum amount of water for optimum growth.

PROGRAMMING AND MANAGEMENT

You can use computer control devices to manage your watering times. They are simple to programme and connect, and many run on 9-volt batteries. For a larger, more complex system, you'll need to get a professional irrigation installer to set up a master controller. Whatever the programming system, it's important to use a programme that conserves water and maximizes growth. Generally, watering systems should be designed to enhance the natural weather cycle so as to provide more suitable conditions for all plants, and to help youngsters in the early stages of growth.

Here are a few simple guidelines for irrigation management.

* Restrict watering times to early morning or evening to avoid evaporation and 'leaf burn', which is caused by the magnification of the sun in water droplets on the leaf.
* If the planting is young, set the system to provide it with water at least 3–5 times a week until the plants are established. Scale back the watering after about a month.

ABOVE and ABOVE LEFT These spray risers are part of a garden polypipe system.

OPPOSITE Some sample irrigation designs for small gardens.

CLOCKWISE FROM ABOVE There are five main types of soil: loam, chalk, silt, peat and clay.

BELOW Dig in manure and other organic matter, such as straw, to improve the texture and add nitrogen to the soil.

WORKING WITH THE SOIL

Soil provides plants with the nutrients they need to sustain growth as well as anchorage so that they can grow to their mature heights. In addition, soil provides moisture for the root system, and often contains a delicate balance of micro-organisms that assist a plant's nutrient intake.

For good plant growth, it's important to provide and maintain a balanced soil medium. It's usually quite obvious when the soil system isn't operating properly; plants will yellow and wither or become infested with insects if their nutrient intake is insufficient to keep them healthy.

It isn't a huge job to develop a suitable soil profile for plant growth. By understanding the key components of a good growing medium, you can improve most soils almost immediately and develop their fertility and workability over time. You may also need to consider how to minimize any erosion as well as take into account drainage and watering requirements.

First, you need to establish what soil type you have; depending on the size of your garden, you may have more than one.

CLAY SOILS

Although clays are very high in nutrients, heavy clays can result in poor plant growth. Usually, the problem is that the soil's compact structure won't allow root penetration, hindering air, water and nutrient intake. There are a number of ways to deal with clay soils, and each will encourage healthier growth.

Clay soils are usually identified by a hard or lumpy soil structure and poor plant growth. They have very fine particles that tend to compact or clump easily. They also swell when wet and contract when dry, causing paving to crack. In most cases, it's sufficient to dig plenty of humus-rich material, such as garden compost, into the soil, but if the clay is heavy and sticky, you may need to do add grit and sand to improve drainage.

IMPROVING A CLAY BED

Where soil is very clayey, you can use this method for planting individual plants or improving an entire garden bed.

1 Break up the clay with a mattock or bar, and apply garden lime according to the directions on the package.
2 Add about 200 mm of sandy loam to the soil and finish with a similar depth of loam and compost mix, such as John Innes No. 2 or 3.
3 Gently cultivate these layers. They'll produce better conditions, allowing better drainage and aeration, and thus better plant growth.
4 Dig a well in the loam and place the plant in it, spreading the roots from the base. Be careful not to dig the well into the clay, as water will sit in it, drowning the roots and killing the plant. Also, don't pile the soil around the stem or on top of the root system, but use it to create a ridge around the plant.
5 Water in well.
6 Add mulch.

PLANTS FOR CLAY SOILS

- *Abelia*
- *Ajuga reptans*
- *Aster* cv.
- *Aucuba japonica*
- *Berberia*
- *Choisya ternata*
- *Cotinus coggygria*
- *Helenium* cv.
- *Hydrangea* sp. and cv.
- *Monarda didyma*
- Roses (many).
- *Thalictrum*

BELOW You can improve a clay bed by building on it with compost and loam.

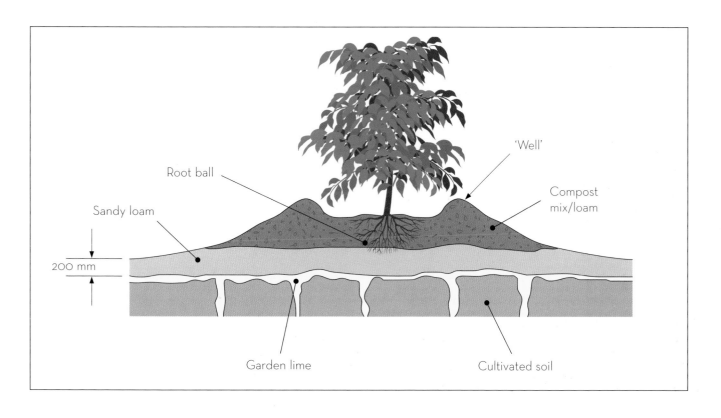

'Well'

Root ball

Compost mix/loam

Sandy loam

200 mm

Garden lime

Cultivated soil

ABOVE The vibrant flowers of the gazania, which copes with sandy soils.

PLANTS FOR SANDY SOILS

- *Allium*
- *Brachyglottis* 'Sunshine'
- *Caryopteris x clandonensis*
- *Convolvulus sabatius*
- *Dianthus* sp. and cv.
- *Erodium* sp.
- *Grevillea* sp.
- *Helichrysum* sp. and cv.
- *Muscari*
- *Phlomis fruticosa*
- *Scilla*
- *Sedum* sp. and cv.
- *Silene* sp.
- *Tulipa* sp.

REPLACING LAWN ON A CLAY SOIL

If poor lawn growth is due to a compacted clay soil, it's best to remove the turf and work in some grit before laying new turf.

1 Either remove the existing turf with a turf cutter, or kill it with a systemic herbicide.
2 If the lawn area is compacted, break up the clay and apply grit and lime (see 'Improving a clay bed' on page 63). You can use a rotivator, but if you have heavy clay, be careful that the machine doesn't further compact the soil.
3 Apply sandy loam and dig it into the clay, stopping about 50 mm clear of the subsoil.
4 Lay a suitable turf, depending on the use your lawn gets.

SANDY SOILS

Sandy soils are not usually a problem as they drain well and promote root growth. Many plants can cope with sandy conditions, but if you want to grow moisture-lovers, you may need to enhance the soil condition. The key is to retain the moisture so the plants can utilize it. Organic mulch and compost usually improve a sandy soil quickly and effectively. Heavy mulching, which reduces evaporation and retains the moisture content, is also essential.

It's worth noting that sandy soils can be impervious, or the nutrients can be leached out, resulting in poor plant growth.

COMPACTED SOILS

In dry weather, clay soil can become so hard on the surface that water cannot penetrate it. The water simply pools on the top of the soil and doesn't drain through at all. If you want to plant as soon as possible, use the advice given on page 63, 'Improving a clay bed'. However, the best long-term way to improve the situation is to dig plenty of organic matter to open up the soil structure, and to add a thick organic mulch on the soil surface. If you are preparing the area for planting, dig in the organic matter before you plant and water the soil very well after planting, then add the mulch (see page 76). Don't add a mulch on top of dry soil. If the problem occurs in an existing flowerbed, work the compost carefully into the soil around the plants and water very well before adding the mulch on top.

This type of treatment should be repeated at least once a year, preferably twice — in spring and autumn — and over a few years the soil will become much more workable.

LEACHED SOILS

If plants are stunted and growing poorly, it's likely that the nutrients are being leached out as the water drains through.

1 Work some good quality organic compost into the soil.
2 Mulch the bed with leaf litter or well-rotted bark, which will continue to break down into the soil over time.

SHALLOW SOILS

Shallow soils present several problems. Because there is not much depth for plants to get their roots into, they may not be able to obtain the water and nutrients they need and, in the case of larger plants, they may also be unable to grow deep enough roots to stabilise themselves, which means they are vulnerable to falling over in strong winds. Conversely shallow soils often have underlying rock, which can make drainage poor.

One way of dealing with the problem is to select plants adapted to the conditions, such as the native species of the area. Approaching the problem in a holistic manner will often give the best results. Look around gardens in your local area to see what is thriving, and choose the plants you like the look of for your own garden. Plants such as *Alchemilla mollis* (lady's mantle), *Aquilegia vulgaris* (grannies bonnets), *Digitalis purpurea* (foxglove) and *Buddleja davidii* are among many that can put up with challenging conditions. Alternatively, construct raised beds and use planters to overcome the lack of soil depth.

COPING WITH A SLOPING SITE

If you have a sloping site with shallow soil and little or no plant growth, there are several things you can do to create planting pockets.

1 To reduce the possibility of erosion and prevent any topsoil being washed away, create buffers with rocks, logs or culverts. Biodegradable erosion control matting will provide good protection on extreme slopes, especially when it's combined with rock or log buffers.
2 Using similar materials, create planting pockets on the slope. Each pocket should be deep enough to hold a 100 mm pot.
3 Plant the pockets with groundcover plants and shrubs.
4 Finish with a composting mulch. You can also plant taller species that will eventually shelter the soil and further enrich it with leaf litter.

ABOVE You can cope with a sloping site by creating planting pockets, or even by positioning large pot plants like this one.

BELOW Here are two solutions for sloping sites — either using rocks, logs and plants or planting into erosion control matting.

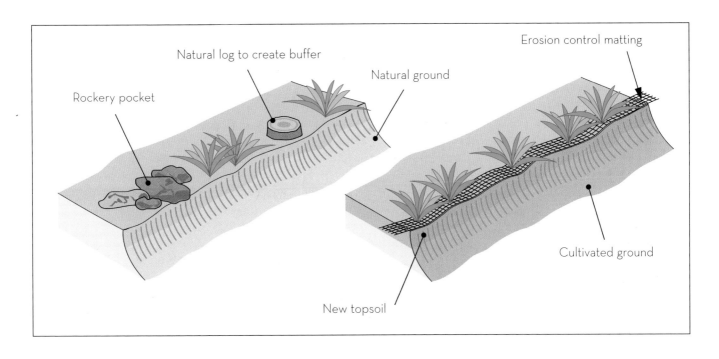

Rockery pocket

Natural log to create buffer

Natural ground

Erosion control matting

Cultivated ground

New topsoil

ABOVE A newly planted rock garden demonstrates the importance of positioning the rocks effectively.

ROCK GARDENS

One way of dealing with a sloping site, or a site with little topsoil, is to build a rock garden. Typically composed of artfully arranged stones, which provide the right habitat for plants that grow naturally among rocks in the wild, a rock garden also makes an attractive feature. In Victorian times, when the craze for collecting succulents, alpines and small herbaceous perennials was at its peak, rock gardens were a popular way to display plant collections. With succulents now among the most fashionable of contemporary plants, the rock garden is enjoying a revival.

SUITABLE SITES

Sloping sites are ideal for rock gardens. Erosion can be a serious problem on a slope, especially when it has been cleared of vegetation. Partially submerged rocks both prevent soil washaway and retain soil and moisture. They provide protected pockets for plants and cool, moist growing conditions for roots.

If you have a flat site, a rock garden can improve your landscaping potential. For instance, use it to add variation or direct traffic — a mounded rock garden provides a 'natural' obstacle for a path to wind around and, if it is correctly sited, prevents unwanted passage through your garden.

If you have enough space and the budget to build on a large scale, your rock garden could resemble a natural rock formation, and could even include ponds and cascades that take advantage of the fall of the land. But plan carefully: the costs of materials — especially pumps, pool liners and rock — can be expensive. You should also consider the drainage effects on the remainder of the garden and the likely effect of shade and tree cover in future years.

ABOVE A dry stream bed that has been transformed into a rock garden.

PLANTS FOR A ROCK GARDEN

In a larger garden, a rock garden is a haven for small, delicate-looking plants that need to grow without interference from the roots and shade of trees and large shrubs. Rock gardens can also provide a microclimate, trapping heat in a cool site and providing a cool root run in a warm one.

Alpines benefit from the reflected warmth absorbed by the stones, and the roots of succulents enjoy an even temperature while surface temperatures may rise and fall wildly. Southern African plants that grow naturally on rocky slopes are also good candidates, as are other specialist collections of desert or dry-adapted plants, such as succulents and some cacti (these may need to be planted in pots and brought indoors over winter). Rock gardens also improve the drainage for any plants that need fast-draining soil.

The type of plants you intend to grow should determine the location of your rock garden. A sunny south-facing position, unshaded by large trees, is the best position for an alpine or succulent planting. On the other hand, a shaded rock garden with a northerly aspect can be used for growing ferns and other plants whose natural habitat is wooded slopes. Also, keep in mind that a rock garden is an informal garden feature so it should be compatible with the rest of the garden.

PLANTS FOR ROCK GARDENS

- Alpine plants such as *Phlox subulata* and *Lewisia* sp.
- *Arenaria*
- *Sempervivum* sp.
- *Arabis* sp.
- *Sedum* sp.
- *Gentiana* sp.

SOIL FOR A ROCK GARDEN

You can use good garden loam for a rock garden but as most rockery plants need sharp or excellent drainage, a special growing medium will usually yield better results. Equal parts of coarse sand or fine gravel, leaf mould or peat and good garden loam should do the job. To make a freer-draining mix, increase the amounts of sand or gravel; however, if the loam is particularly sandy or has coarse particles, this should not be necessary.

CONSTRUCTING A ROCK GARDEN

The secret of a well designed rock garden is in the placement and scaling of the rocks and boulders. In its basic form, a rock garden is a mound of rocks filled with free-draining soil. The stone is added in layers: the larger rocks at the base anchor the whole construction and make it stable, while successive layers comprise rocks of decreasing size. This gradation of scale helps the rock garden to look natural.

PLANT AND ROCK SHAPES

Successful rockery planting depends on finding the right plants to complement the stones. When choosing plants, take into account height, shape and spread as well as colour. Use trailing plants to soften edges and partly cover deep rocks; mounding and cushion plants that follow the horizontal lines of some rocks; and erect plants to echo and complement vertical rock shapes.

For ideas on how to use stones effectively in your rock garden, look carefully at rock formations in nature — on local hills or heathland. You can lay stones either flat or upright, but it's best to keep most of them stratified in a single plane, but on different levels, of course. Put the most attractive rocks in the most prominent positions. Look for attractive markings and natural form as you select rocks for their shape, colour and texture. Avoid using damaged or obviously artificially cut rocks for the visible parts of your rock garden.

For large rock gardens, use large boulders and larger plants, and for smaller gardens use smaller ones. Where dominant shapes, forms or colours are evident in the surrounding landscape, replicate that form or colour in your garden. When rock gardens first became popular, it was quite common to construct them from rock that had been quarried from moorland, uplands, or other environmentally sensitive areas. Besides being expensive, this is no longer ecologically acceptable, and it is best to try to obtain local rocks, from building sites or similar sources.

If you're starting on a level or near flat surface, excavate an area, add a layer of rock rubble for drainage and cover it with garden soil to create a slightly mounded base. Start from ground level and work up, laying each stone at the same angle. In nature, rocks follow a single plane and usually two-thirds of each rock is buried. Remember this when setting rocks in place. Backfill with soil and set back the next layer of stones to create a slight slope. Repeat this process for each outcrop. For variety, allow some stones to protrude at odd angles.

For a sloping site, follow these steps.

1   When choosing the location for your rock garden, position it where it will seem to be a continuation of the natural landscape. Mark out a free-form area, incorporating any slope or bank.

RIGHT Choose appropriate plants to grow in the small pockets of soil in your rock garden.

2 Working up the bank, position the larger boulders to retain the bulk of the soil. Where necessary, excavate the bank so that you can set the boulder into it. This will not only result in a more natural effect, it will also secure the boulder on the slope.

3 Using the same method, group smaller rocks around the larger ones, but be careful to position any parallel sides together to enhance the natural look. Using smaller stones as packers, secure the boulders and, at the same time, bring in soil to backfill any pockets you create.

4 Accent feature rocks with groundcover plants and spillover plants. Use shrubs to bind the soil and rocks together.

5 Place logs or branches to enhance the natural look, and finish the area with leaf mulch or gravel.

ABOVE Handsome stone retaining walls solve two problems at once — a sloping site and dry, shallow soil.

WET OR SODDEN SOILS

Wet soils are often the result of either shallow bedrock or shallow clay subsoil. They can both be remedied in much the same way.

1 Divert the runoff by exposing the impervious layer at or near the source of the runoff, such as at the top of a slope or beneath a natural spring.

2 Excavate a trench into the rock or clay to a maximum depth of 300 mm, so that it diverts the water towards a natural drainage point. Repeat this procedure at intervals as required. Water will collect in the trench and be diverted away from the impervious layer. (See pages 52–7 for more information on drainage.)

3 Backfill the trench with pebbles or coarse sand.

4 Create mounds for planting or add soil to lawn areas. Raising the beds will give plants more space for root growth and avoid 'wet feet'.

RIGHT Agapanthus, shown here in bud, cope with wind and salt spray.

PLANTS FOR SALTY ENVIRONMENTS

- *Crambe maritima*
- *Hebe* sp.
- *Hibiscus* sp.
- *Lavandula* sp.
- *Leptospermum* sp.
- *Rosmarinus officinalis*
- *Tamarix* sp.

SOLVING PROBLEMS

Most gardens have a problem area. Sometimes this is a result of the natural environment — such as salt spray in coastal areas — and sometimes the problem develops over time — for example, as trees grow, they cast areas of the garden into deep shade.

When you're planning your garden, identify existing problem areas and try to foresee where problems may develop in the future. You'll then be able to construct your garden in the most effective way, as there are solutions for all landscaping problems.

SALTY ENVIRONMENTS

Planting in a salty seaside environment can be challenging but rewarding. You'll have to cope with sandy soils and salt-laden winds, which can have a detrimental effect on a large range of plants. For example, it is likely that you won't be able to grow an herbaceous border full of lush perennials.

Creating a landscape that is comfortable for both you and the plants requires a range of techniques.

- Improve the soil with compost and organic matter.
- Provide heavy mulch to retain water in the soil.
- Install a watering system.
- Form some protected microclimates by creating windbreaks with hedges and screens.
- Where appropriate, place birdbaths, ponds and water trays around the more sensitive plants to keep the humidity level up.

Once you have provided protection for the plants, you can select from a range of species to enhance the landscape. Choose only plants that tolerate salt environments and dry, light conditions. Look at neighbouring gardens for ideas.

POOL AREAS

The areas around swimming pools can suffer the same problems as coastal environments, so if you want to avoid salinity problems, select your plants and landscape materials accordingly.

Choose only galvanized or stainless steel fixings (nails, screws and bolts) and use non-corrosive or easily maintained surfaces, such as glass, timber or powder-coated steel fences and furniture. If you plan to lay pavers, check with the manufacturer to make sure they resist salt corrosion and don't become slippery when wet.

The landscaping around a swimming pool should include plants that can cope with chlorine.

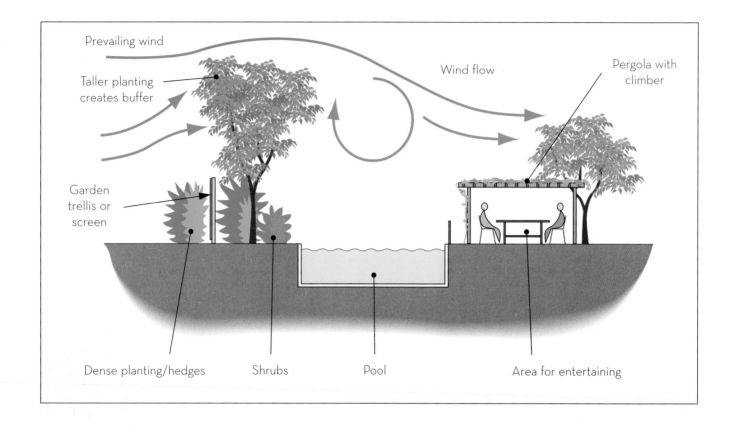

Prevailing wind

Taller planting
creates buffer

Wind flow

Pergola with
climber

Garden
trellis or
screen

Dense planting/hedges   Shrubs   Pool   Area for entertaining

ABOVE Some simple ideas for
windbreaks and shelters.

OPPOSITE TOP *Oleander* (*Nerium
oleander*) is a popular windbreak in
warm climates.

OPPOSITE BOTTOM Constructing
a windbreak or screen.

WINDY AREAS

Strong winds not only make outdoor entertaining difficult, they also help
dry out the garden, as they increase the evaporation rate and so leave you
struggling to keep up with watering. One solution is to try to modify the
wind pattern around your home, creating a microclimate that can support
a broader range of plant species and make outdoor life more comfortable.

If you're planning an outdoor entertaining area, pool or lawn area, try
to position it behind the house, a large tree or other structure that can act
as a buffer from the prevailing winds. If this isn't possible, consider using
plants or a screen to create your own windbreaks.

WINDBREAK PLANNING

Trees naturally absorb energy. Not only do they convert the sun's energy
to oxygen, but also their branches absorb the sometimes damaging
strength and energy of the wind. Thus, the more trees you have in your
garden or neighbourhood, the more protected the environment will be
around you.

For an effective windbreak, use fast-growing tree species native to
your area and position them to help alleviate wind eddies.

WINDBREAK TRELLIS

Open streets and passages between houses can often create wind tunnels.
One way to block the wind and create a more comfortable garden is to
build a simple trellis, which makes a good windbreak as well as an
attractive backdrop.

The trellis below consists of standard 1.8 x 1.8 m lattice panels that are secured to posts. For a more unusual look, you could use 50 x 50 mm timber battens instead of lattice. Secure the battens to the top and bottom rails at equal spacings.

1 Calculate the centre position for each post, allowing for the width of the panel and the depth of the rebated frame.

2 Set out post holes in the desired position and dig them to a depth of 450–600 mm. (For more information on setting out and digging post holes, see page 353.)

3 In each hole make a solid foundation by using gravel or breaking up an old brick. Consolidate and roughly level the foundation.

4 Position the posts and prop them up with offcut lengths of timber. Use a spirit level to ensure they are vertical both ways.

5 Pour ready-mixed concrete around the posts and water it in.

6 Check again for vertical and reposition the props as necessary.

7 While you're waiting for the concrete to set, measure the opening and prepare the lattice panels. Using a mitre saw or handsaw and mitre box, cut the mitred corners of the rebated frame, being careful with the measurements.

8 Fit the lattice into the frame and nail it together.

9 Using hexagonal-head self-drilling screws and making sure the panels are level, fix the panels to the posts. Cut off the tops of the posts 100 mm above the top of the frame.

10 Finish off the posts with newel knobs.

11 Plant selected climbers or decorative specimens against the trellis.

TREES AND SHRUBS SUITABLE FOR WINDBREAKS

- *Crataegus* sp.
- *Escallonia* sp. and cv.
- *Euonymus japonicus* cv.
- *Ilex aquifolium* cv.
- *Olearia* sp.
- *Picea* sp.
- *Sorbus* sp.
- *Taxus baccata*

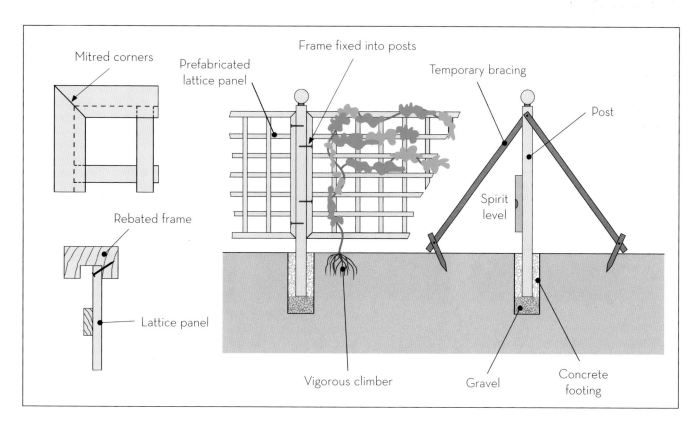

Mitred corners

Prefabricated lattice panel

Frame fixed into posts

Temporary bracing

Post

Rebated frame

Spirit level

Lattice panel

Vigorous climber

Gravel

Concrete footing

RIGHT Plants suitable for wet or boggy areas thrive around this garden pond.

PLANTS FOR BOGGY AREAS

- *Arum* sp.
- *Aruncus aethusifolius*
- *Astilbe* sp. and cv.
- *Caltha palustris*
- *Cornus alba* cv.
- *Gunnera manicata*
- *Iris pseudacorus*
- *Lysichiton americanus*
- *Osmunda regalis*
- *Rodgersia* sp.

MAKING A GRAVEL GARDEN

Gravel gardens can be made where soil is very damp or as an attractive feature in their own right. You can use different grades of pebble and gravel, but grey or blue slate chippings will provide a foil for green foliage.

1 Start by clearing and levelling the area. Place a sheet of thick black landscaping material over the bed and bury the edges at least 15 cm deep. Firmly close the groove in the soil with your heel.

2 Cut a cross in the fabric where each plant is to be placed and dig out a planting hole. Place the plant through the fabric into the hole. Firm gently into place. Fold the flaps back into position.

3 Tip piles of slate chips or gravel onto the plastic around the base of the plants and over the whole area, spreading it out evenly and making sure all the fabric is completely hidden.

WET AREAS

Damp areas in the garden can be caused by many factors, including natural springs, shallow soils, bad drainage, septic overflows and subsoil depressions. The soils in these areas are sometimes anaerobic — that is, devoid of any oxygen that supports soil organisms — which can be easily identified by pungent sulphuric smells.

Sometimes you can fix damp areas by improving the drainage (see pages 52–7), but if there is a natural depression, a spring or shallow soils, you may need to look at other solutions, such as: creating a bog or gravel garden; aerating the soil and adding humus-rich compost to break up the clay subsoil; creating a raised garden bed; building a wooden walkway where access is required; and planting moisture-absorbing trees or shrubs.

BUILDING A BOG GARDEN

Creating a bog garden is a very simple, attractive solution to planting a wet area. Some bog plants, such as gunnera, have large leaves that will help evaporate excess water, and if you carefully prepare the area and add a pebble surface, you should be able to keep maintenance to a minimum.

1   Make the most sodden area the centre of the bog garden and roughly mark out a free-form shape to encompass the damp area.
2   Remove existing weeds and groundcovers, as well as any anaerobic, boggy soil. If you wish, cover the depression with plastic sheeting.
3   To provide a free-draining medium, add a layer of stones or gravel.
4   Lay fresh topsoil, mixed with coarse sand, over the area and position some large rocks to make the area look more interesting and natural.
5   Plant out with the species you've selected.
6   Finish the bed with pebbles in various sizes, loosely grouping the different sizes together to replicate a dry stream bed. Continue the dry bed beyond the bog garden if you wish.
7   Water the plants in well and finish the edges of the area with groundcovers, irises and other water-loving plants.

BOGGY LAWN

Boggy lawns can result from any of the situations discussed at left and should be dealt with in the same way as any damp area. If runoff and poor drainage are the cause, one way to deal with the problem is to create a system of agricultural drains to disperse the runoff (see page 54).

BELOW A cross-section of a typical bog garden.

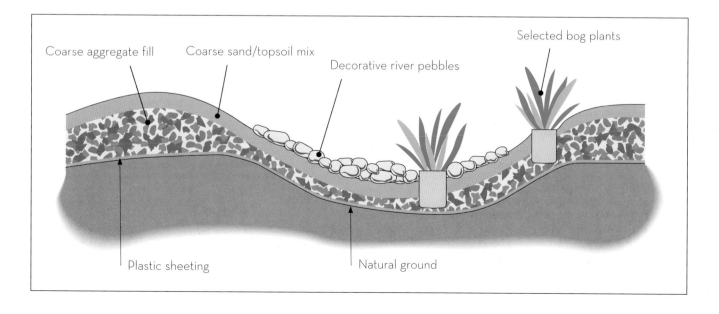

Coarse aggregate fill   Coarse sand/topsoil mix   Decorative river pebbles   Selected bog plants   Plastic sheeting   Natural ground

MULCHING

When mulching your garden beds, you can use inorganic substances, such as gravel, or organic substances, which add nutrients, such as home-made compost, bark chippings or straw.

DRY AREAS

Sometimes gardens contain spots that are always dry, no matter how much water you give them. Once again the soil structure is often the root cause of the problem, with rocky or sandy subsoils draining too rapidly to sustain most plants. Other causes include: too much direct sun; excessive wind, causing evaporation; proximity of garden or house walls; and large, thirsty trees and hedges.

To sustain a healthy garden, it's often better to work with the land type rather than try to change the natural soil system. However, if you have an established garden with deep soil profiles that has persistently dry beds or lawns, there are some simple things you can try to improve conditions.

MULCHING AND IMPROVING

So long as there is a reasonable depth of soil in the flower beds, adding plenty of organic matter and a thick layer of mulch will go a long way to improving a soil's water-retaining ability. It is almost impossible to add too much organic matter, and the more often you can top it up, the better.

Once you have planted the flower bed, apply a thick mulch over the top. Alternatively, prepare the flower bed, lay a sheet of landscaping

APPLYING A MULCH LAYER

A 75 mm thick layer of leaf, bark or gravel mulch on garden beds will help retain the soil moisture by reducing evaporation. Before laying the mulch, however, it's a good idea to improve the soil with compost, manure or other organic material to help it retain moisture. Always water this material in well before adding the mulch layer.

1 Landscaping materials, such as woven plastic, are effective but look unsightly. Cover them with ornamental gravel, chippings or some other decorative surface.

2 Shredded bark, wood chippings or other types of organic mulch will compost when in contact with the soil. Fungal moulds may grow, but these don't harm plants.

3 To provide good weed control and prevent moisture loss from the soil, organic mulches should be 5–10 cm deep.

material over it, and plant through it (see box, page 74). To increase your chances of success, choose plants that can cope with dry conditions - there are plenty.

INSTALLING A ROOT BARRIER

Some trees tend to soak up all the available moisture at the expense of adjoining plants. One solution is to limit the spread of the thirsty roots by creating a root barrier.

1 Around the problem tree, dig a 500 mm deep trench so that it's about two-thirds the radius of the canopy out from the trunk.
2 Cut any large roots cleanly and paint them with horticultural sealant to prevent disease entering the tree.
3 Install a barrier of builder's plastic or a more robust material to retain the roots.
4 Backfill the trench with fresh, friable soil. The roots of plants outside the barrier will thrive in this tilled soil.
5 To compensate for the root loss, prune the tree back to the same diameter as the trench barrier.
6 To minimize the compaction that occurs under the drip line, lay a wide edging of bricks, pavers or the like, and mulch the base of the tree.

PLANTS FOR DRY GARDENS

- *Armeria maritima*
- *Buddleja* sp. and cv.
- *Cistus* sp. and cv.
- *Delosperma* (*Mesembryanthemum*)
- *Eryngium* sp. and cv.
- *Lavandula* sp. and cv.
- *Leucanthemum vulgare*
- *Perovskia atriplicifolia*
- *Portulaca grandiflora*
- *Potentilla fruticosa* cv.

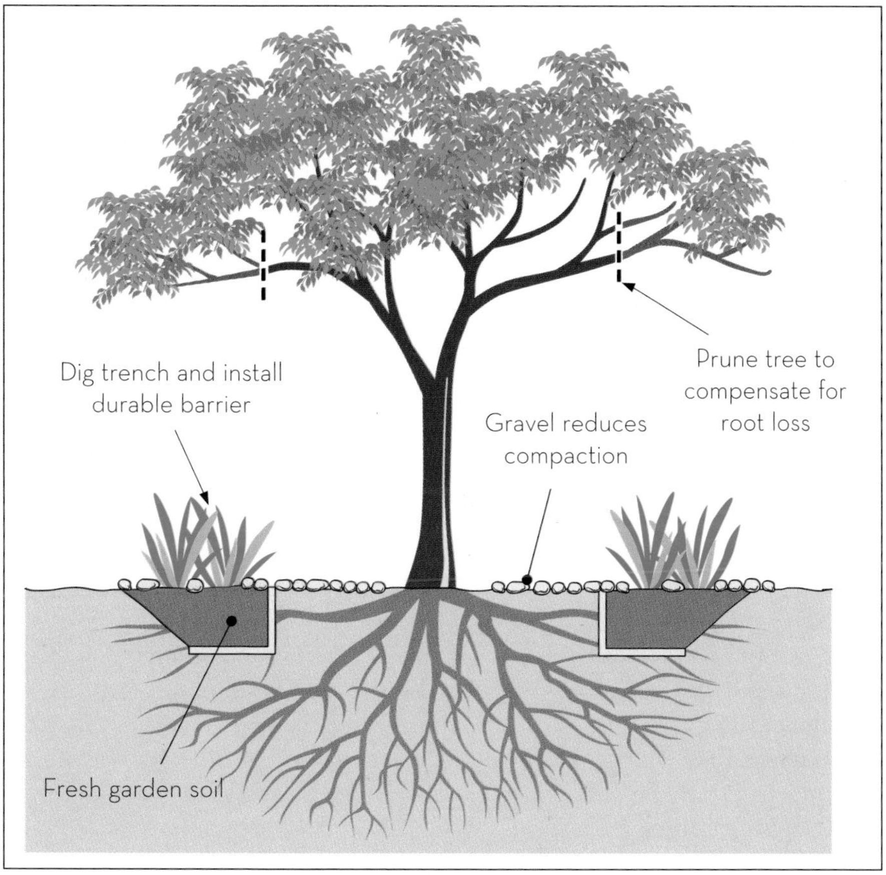

Dig trench and install durable barrier

Prune tree to compensate for root loss

Gravel reduces compaction

Fresh garden soil

LEFT To grow plants beneath a tree's drip lines, you'll need to recondition the soil where it's become compacted, and prune the tree.

RIGHT The brick piers on this freestanding pergola will support a vigorous and long-lived climber such as wisteria.

BUILDING A SHADE STRUCTURE

Sometimes it's best to deal with dry areas by creating shade, either by planting trees with large canopies or by building a structure to reduce the impact of the sun. For example, a large arbour or pergola correctly positioned and covered with climbers will create shade to help protect delicate plants at the hottest part of the day. The structure can also create a focal point in the garden, define a walkway or frame a pleasant view.

Ideally, build a structure such as an arbour or pergola from materials that reflect the architectural elements of the house. For example, if brick columns are used to support the verandah or patio roof, then use brick for the garden structure; similarly, if timber posts support the verandah, use timber to support your garden structure. And make sure you echo any decorative elements, such as timber fretwork.

The instructions below are for a simple pergola with four piers. It's easy enough to add more piers to make a longer structure. Check with your timber merchant to ensure the timber you buy for the beams and rafters is suitable for the spans between the piers.

For more ideas and projects on shade structures, see page 168.

1   Using string lines, set out the positions for the four piers at centres of approximately 2400 mm one way and 3600 mm the other way. If you want to vary these dimensions, check the timber span tables available at your local timber advisory service centre. Check that the set out is square (see page 342).

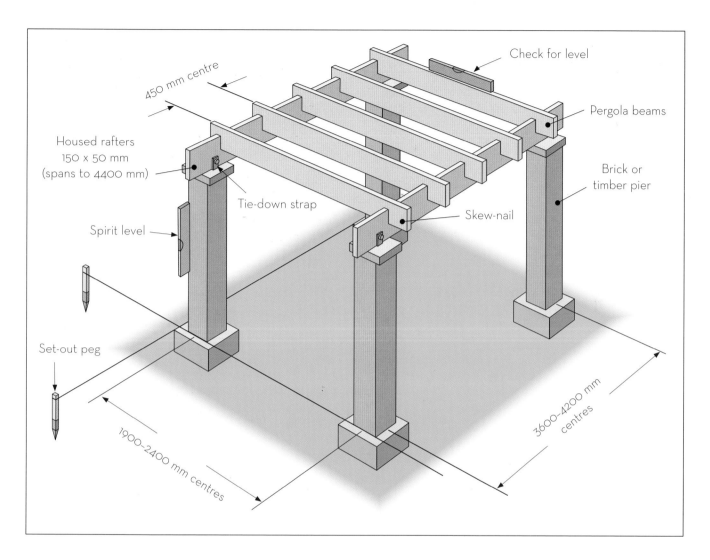

Check for level

Pergola beams

450 mm centre

Housed rafters
150 x 50 mm
(spans to 4400 mm)

Brick or
timber pier

Tie-down strap

Spirit level

Skew-nail

Set-out peg

3600–4200 mm
centres

1900–2400 mm centres

2 Excavate the holes for the concrete footings, which should all be 450 x 450 mm and 450 mm deep. Establish a level for the tops of the footings. Pour in the concrete and, using a water level, check that the tops of the footings are all level.

3 Build the brick piers, using a spirit level and a builders square to ensure each pier is square and plumb. The piers should measure approximately 350 x 350 mm and have a minimum height of 2100 mm. Insert a tie-down strap in the top course.

4 Measure and cut the beams. They will run along the long side of the structure. Secure them to the top of the piers with the strapping, which will also help to brace the structure. If you wish, cut decorative patterns on the ends.

5 Fix the rafters perpendicular to the beams by skew-nailing every 1200 mm into the top of the beams. To minimize timber warping, you could also house them into the beams.

6 To provide shade, fix timber battens across the rafters, or plant climbers. To support the climbers and provide a decorative effect, add garden wire in a criss-cross or grid pattern.

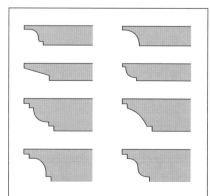

ABOVE Some decorative cuts for beams and rafters.

TOP Constructing a simple pergola. This design can easily be adapted or extended.

NARROW SPACES

The way in which a house is positioned among others can often result in a narrow side passage or small, irregular spaces that more often than not are neglected; they can also become wind tunnels. However, with a little imagination and effort you can make these areas useful parts of the garden. The key is to keep them functional and minimize maintenance by using plenty of mulch or impervious surfaces.

Use hardy plants with a minimal spread to create a visual rhythm when seen from within or outside the passage. They also create attractive contrasts with paved surfaces. For shady canopies in these areas, choose trees with attractive barks and small root systems, and for low-maintenance hedges or screens, plant narrow conifers.

RANDOM STEPPING STONES

To create visual interest in narrow areas, use random stepping stones rather than a straight path. Lay the stones on a solid base of compacted sand and secure with a collar of cement if necessary.

1 Randomly place the stones so that they wind through the passage, but pace out their positions for comfortable steps. As a rule, set them at centres of approximately 450 mm. Try not to place them too erratically; they should look natural.
2 Mark the positions and remove the soil to a depth of about 100 mm. Compact the soil.
3 In each spot spread a sand base and compact it evenly.
4 Lay the stones on the compacted bases and secure them with a mortar collar if necessary.
5 Plant hardy species and groundcovers between the stones.
6 Finish the area with decorative gravel or bark mulch so that it's flush with the top of the stones.
7 Thoroughly water in both plants and stones to settle the landscape.

MATERIALS FOR STEPPING STONES

- Concrete pads/sections
- Hardwood sleepers
- Pre-cast units
- Sandstone flagging or squares
- Secondhand bricks
- Timber rounds

ABOVE A stepping stone path set in a bed of gravel is a sensible solution for a narrow space.

LEFT It's probably best to pave a shady side passage as it will be much easier than gravel to keep clean.

OPPOSITE Another way to create interest in a small level courtyard is to use simple plantings in an elegant way. Here limestone pavers are defined by lilyturf (*Ophiopogon*) in a grid pattern.

PLANTS FOR SHADY AREAS

- *Astrantia major*
- *Dicentra spectablis*
- *Erythronium* sp. and cv.
- Fern sp. and cv.
- *Helleborus* sp. and cv.
- *Hosta* sp. and cv.
- *Leucojum aestivum*
- *Primula vulgaris*
- *Trilium grandiflorum*
- *Vinca* sp.

ABOVE An accumulation of dirt and grime on wooden decking encourages the growth of algae. Scrub decking with a solution of mild detergent about once a year.

ABOVE RIGHT It's often difficult to grow plants in the shade of a large tree, which will suck up all the available moisture in the soil.

SHADY AREAS

Most problems associated with shady areas result from dampness, as ground water takes longer to evaporate in these places. However, some shady areas, such as those under large tree canopies where the water intake is dominated by the tree, can suffer from dryness (for more information, see page 76).

SLIPPERY PAVERS

Brick paving laid in a shady area is likely to be mossy and slippery. Because bricks are porous, the water soaks into them as if they were sponges and remains there until it evaporates, thus providing the perfect medium for moss and other water-loving plant life and moulds.

Kill off the moss using a proprietary moss-killer — readily available from your local garden centre or DIY store. The most effective solution to this problem, however, is more holistic: you need to increase the evaporation process.

1 Prune or thin any overhead branches to increase the light levels and the amount of air circulation.
2 Take up and re-lay the paving bricks over a base of at least 100 mm of compacted coarse sand as a base. Provide plenty of fall drains where possible. Alternatively, remove random pavers and dig out the soil in these pockets as much as you can, replacing it with coarse sand and gravel. These pockets will help the surface to drain and will also provide opportunities to plant hardy groundcovers, such as creeping Jenny.

SOIL COMPACTION AND ACIDITY

Soil can become compacted underneath tree drip lines. As the tree sheds rainwater, the area directly below the outer branches receives heavy water droplets, and this eventually results in hard soils that plant roots have difficulty penetrating.

Here the best solution is to till the soil and add coarse sand at a ratio of 1 part sand to 5 parts soil. A thick layer of mulch will help add organic matter and also protect the soil from compaction.

Some trees that consistently drop bark or needles, such as eucalypts and pines, cause the soil to become quite acidic over a period of time. Add lime to balance the soil pH, but bear in mind that it may harm the tree if you apply it consistently. It's better to plant the area with acid-loving plants than to try to change the natural pH balance of the soil.

OTHER SOLUTIONS FOR SHADY AREAS

Where acidity, compaction, damp and lack of light make plantings or lawn too difficult to manage, think about replacing them with other garden features. Consider the following options.

* Garden seat
* Wide garden edge
* Water feature
* Rockery
* Gravel garden
* Path or paving

TOP *Pieris* sp., a plant that tolerates acid soil.

ABOVE LEFT Keep a stone path swept clean of leaves and other debris, otherwise it will become slippery and dangerous in wet weather.

ADDING FEATURES

In the garden, the details set the mood, establish a theme and give a finished look, creating a place for relaxation and enjoyment. Whether you have a large country plot or a small inner-city courtyard, you can use focal points, seating areas, paths and garden beds as well as features such as arbours and pergolas to create outdoor living rooms, space for contemplation and areas that are designed to surprise and delight.

ABOVE and TOP Sometimes it's the details that make the difference — the symmetry of a pair of topiary shrubs or a 'window' into the landscape beyond your garden.

RIGHT Proportion is an important element in garden design. In a large garden, small trees and low plantings would be out of scale with the landscape as a whole.

THE PRINCIPLES OF DESIGN

Design principles are nothing more than rules of thumb, things that have been tried and found to work. We can use these principles or rules to elicit emotion and manipulate how we perceive a garden, how it looks in different seasons and how we move around it.

You can use the elements of design — levels, focal points, views and materials — by mixing hard elements and living things such as trees, screening and foundation plantings to create texture and colour patterns to suit your lifestlye, your taste and the architecture of your house. The best garden designs use elements such as unity, repetition, transition, balance, mystery and surprise to create a space with soul or ambience.

There are three main types of design principles — the look and feel of the garden, and movement within the garden.

THE LOOK

To achieve a certain look in your garden, you need to work with three basic elements — form, line and texture.

Form covers both the hard landscaping — such as paving, fences and garden structures — and the soft landscaping, the plants. Plant forms vary considerably, from tall upright cypresses to ground-hugging creepers. You can also manipulate form in the way you position plants and by using various planting and pruning techniques. A single plant can be used as a highlight or focal point but, together, plants form part of the garden architecture, helping to create an overall look.

Line gives a garden a three-dimensional quality, and it applies to both plantings and landscape features. Use hard landscaping, such as stone borders to flower beds or paths, to lead your eye to different parts of the

ABOVE In this courtyard, square and rectangular shapes are repeated in the garden beds and paving to create a sense of unity.

ABOVE LEFT A seaside garden needs protection from salt-laden winds.

FORMAL DESIGNS

You can design a formal garden in a contemporary landscape by using some appropriate feature plants. Incorporate paths, terraces and formal planting patterns, and grow exotic species for dramatic effect. Arches, fountains, topiary and espaliers are all possible components. Constant maintenance will be required to maintain the effect: you'll need to clip hedges regularly, constantly mow lawns and keep paths and beds free of weeds.

garden. Trees with strongly horizontal branches direct your eye to the side and suggest restfulness. Upright plants such as *Frachycarpus* that have foliage that splays out at the top, suggesting action and excitement. In a contemporary garden, you can mix these strong upright shapes with zigzag hard landscaping patterns to suggest movement and space.

Texture is similar to both form and line. Plants can have a strong textural quality in a garden composition. Some suggest movement, forcing you to look up and away from the ground, while others can be soft, romantic or sensual. For instance, the soft woolly texture of lamb's ear (*Stachys byzantina*) invites you to touch the leaves. In hard landscaping, texture can be found in the surfaces and patterning of stone, tile or brick. The contrasts provided by these textures are also visually useful.

THE FEEL

Another key design principle governs the overall feel of the garden, which can be broken down into three elements — proportion, transition and unity.

Proportion relates to the size of components in the garden compared to both people and the broader landscape outside the garden. For instance, small groups of low shrubs and groundcovers planted near an imposing house in a large garden will look just as out of proportion as a huge tree planted in a tiny courtyard.

Gradual change enables comfortable changes in proportion and scale. Transition applies to many different elements in the garden, from plant size to hard landscaping and structural elements, such as houses or terraces. The more seamless the transition from one element to another, the more harmonious the garden will seem.

Unity is the element that ties all the little bits together. Without it, a garden lacks harmony, giving an overall impression of confusion. Planting a low hedge around disparate garden beds is just one way of creating a sense of unity.

MOVEMENT

Finally, there are three elements that create movement in a garden — rhythm, repetition and focal points.

This design technique involves repeating elements in a garden to create pattern. For instance, you can create a sense of rhythm or movement by paving a circular terrace in a spiral pattern, or by alternating two different plants along a path.

Repeating a theme — whether you use specific plants, foliage or flower colours or hard landscaping — helps to create a balanced composition. For example, you could repeat a rectangular shape in lawn, paved areas or garden beds to unify the design.

A focal point is a plant or object placed in the landscape in such a way that it draws your attention. It can be used to deflect attention from an unattractive view or lead you along a path to a viewpoint. Both techniques help create movement in the garden. Lines do the same thing, whether they are provided by paths, borders, hedges, screens or fences.

OPPOSITE A formal garden relies on symmetry, proportion and repetition.

ABOVE This beautifully designed path is an example of how you can use colour, texture and proportion to draw the eye to a distant focal point.

OPPOSITE A hedge of camellias (*Camellia sasanqua*) allows a view of the neighbouring or 'borrowed' landscape.

FOCAL POINTS

A focal point is anything that catches your eye and focuses attention on itself. In the garden, it's a great way to distract you from less desirable areas or to draw you into other parts of the garden.

You can distribute focal points around the garden and use art, statuary, plants, urns, lanterns, topiary or a large structure such as a pergola, gazebo, arch, bench or arbour, which may have a dual practical and aesthetic purpose. A focal point could also be something that's not immediately obvious but needs to be sought out and discovered — for example, a small collection of coloured pebbles, a wall plaque in a corner or a pot of sculptural succulents.

A focal point can also be an entire view. In the large classical or country garden where there is plenty of space, there may be a natural focus, such as the vista provided by an avenue of trees, walls or high hedging. In the smaller garden, you need to create focal points yourself.

DRAWING THE EYE

Straight lines are more direct and attract attention faster than curved ones. In a small garden, however, you'll create a greater impact if you draw the viewer's attention slowly — use flowing lines as they have a more measured impact.

Symmetrical style intensifies the effect, while an asymmetrical design softens or even avoids it. You can easily achieve this by placing an attractive focal point on an uncluttered lawn or area of paving so that nothing else competes with it.

Focal points are also used in interiors. In a well-designed room, a painting or a piece of furniture will be placed so that it draws your attention. When you visit a new city or town, the chances are you'll immediately focus on objects in order to fix your bearings. A focal point is part of the process of orientating yourself to strange surroundings, even when you do something as mundane as look for the level and sector number of the car park in your local shopping centre.

Partly hiding focal points creates mystery and tension. When garden designers talk of tension, they really mean the gentle unfolding of surprises that whet your appetite and make exploring a garden an adventure to be savoured. If you see everything in the garden at once, there is no invitation to go in and explore.

THE BORROWED LANDSCAPE

Most gardens are fenced off to provide privacy and mark the boundaries of the property, but bare fences are not attractive and fences also reduce the outlook or view. To get the most out of the surrounding landscape and achieve a feeling of spaciousness, think about blurring these boundaries. Here are some ways to 'borrow' the landscape beyond your boundaries.

- When designing a planting layout, use low shrubs in the foreground and larger shrubs near the fence to 'break up' the boundary line.
- Plant trees and shrubs similar to those in the neighbourhood to help maintain a unified character for the area.
- Frame a view with trees or structures, such as arbours. This will encourage you to focus beyond your boundaries.
- Place trees and shrubs to block views of neighbouring buildings, telegraph poles or sheds. This creates a more natural landscape.
- If natural landscapes are close to your boundaries, continue the theme with similar materials and native plants, and eliminate fences wherever possible.

POSITIONING FOCAL POINTS

There are two techniques to using focal points. The more direct method is to position a focal point along a main axis or at the end of the garden, where it can be seen from the viewing point. For instance, imagine entering the garden from the back door or patio and seeing an object at the far end of the garden.

Alternatively, for supplementary interest, you could place a focal point along a path or passageway. For instance, a small seat in a clearing may draw you towards it or it may simply stop you in your tracks as you admire the surrounding planting.

By slowing you down or directing your attention to something other than the main view, focal points make the garden seem bigger and fuller than at first glance. In effect, you're inviting the viewer to walk around and explore the garden.

VIEWING POINTS

The necessary corollary of a focal point is the viewing point. Focal points vary and change roles as you move around the garden. A distant gazebo, for instance, can be both a focal point from one angle and a viewing point when you reach it.

BELOW A period water feature is an effective focal point at the end of a formal path.

A garden can have many focal points, but too many of them seen from the one viewing point become confusing — busy to the eye and unpleasing to the mind — so keep them to a minimum. The old adage 'keep it simple' is a good one to follow. Aim for one striking piece and the element of surprise. Instead of placing a feature in every corner, aim for simple sweeping lines and perhaps an understated architectural planting or a simple ground surface of gravels to attract your attention as you walk around the garden.

Try to design your garden so that focal points gradually appear as you move around. In most cases, a single focal point is needed in any given spot. You can position focal points along a straight axis but partly hide them with planting or structures, curved paths or walls.

You can also position a focal point so that you can view it from inside the house. Consider parts of the garden you see from doors, windows and from upper level windows. You could site a focal point so it's seen from one of these points of view. Key rooms, the ones where you're most likely to be looking out the window, are the kitchen and dining and living rooms.

You should also consider the views from outdoor spaces, such as patios and balconies. Remember, the view will change as you move, so look at the proposed position for a focal point from as many perspectives as you can. Place an object that is roughly the same size as your proposed focal point so you can judge how well it can be seen.

ABOVE A curved path shaded by covered arches draws the eye.

CHOOSING A STYLE

Displaying focal points requires some sensitivity to style and period. Most pieces benefit from being set in surroundings that suit them, so choose plants and ground surfaces that will complement the design of the piece you use. In some cases, a statue, urn or object needs to stand alone in splendid isolation. In others, partially obscuring the piece with plants enhances its allure. You should also decide whether your chosen piece should be seen at ground level or raised closer to eye level by being placed on a plinth. Some are better seen from above.

Finish off the area around your focal point with a gravel surface, stone pavers or a ground-covering plant. Water makes another fine base for displaying some statues. Your choice depends on the scene you want to create as well as on your budget.

Modern pieces need similar treatments. Choose materials that have a contemporary edge and look in keeping with the style of the piece you wish to display.

TEMPORARY FOCAL POINTS

Focal points needn't be permanent features. A flag banner or swag can serve as a focal point for a celebration or party. For instance, the Balinese like to hang long fabric banners in different colours. For a party at night you could light a path or a terrace with glass candleholders. Consider choosing colours to match the event, such as red and green for Christmas or rainbow shades for summer events.

ABOVE Poppies going to seed in a cottage garden in midsummer.

SEASONS IN THE GARDEN

Whether you live in an area with a mild climate or a cold one with plenty of frosts in winter, you can still enjoy the garden all year long. It's simply a matter of carefully planning the features, architectural elements and, above all, the planting in your garden.

WINTER APPEAL

If it snows or there are heavy frosts in winter where you live, the landscape takes on a cleaner, uncluttered aspect, and a few select deciduous plants with coloured stems will stand out brilliantly against the white background. The best are the dogwoods. *Cornus alba* 'Sibirica' has brilliant red stems, while *Salix alba* 'Vitellina' provides yellow highlights. The white stems of *Rubus cockburnianus* are also effective, especially if they are under-planted with a dark foliage groundcover, such as *Bergenia cordifolia* 'Abendglut' or *B. crassifolia* 'Bressingham Ruby', both of which have large burgundy leaves. The thorns of *Rosa sericea* 'Pteracantha' even glow red when they are backlit by the afternoon sun, which can be very appealing.

Winter also has some interesting scented flowers, such as wintersweet (*Chimonanthus praecox*), several daphnes (*Daphne bholua*, *D. mezereum* and *D. odora*) and *Viburnum* x *bodnantense* 'Dawn', which has candy pink flowers. Use bulbs, such as snowdrop (*Galanthus nivalis*), followed by crocus and muscari to extend the season, and mix them with early-flowering perennials, such as hellebores, for their charming blooms.

SPRING ABUNDANCE

Spring often seems to take care of itself, but it pays dividends to focus on the burgeoning new growth on deciduous plants. Spring growth is not just green. It starts out as pink, bronze or even fluorescent lime green and then slowly changes. The changes may take place in a few days, but often stretch to a week or more, but the impact can be breathtaking. Take the *Toona sinensis* 'Flamingo'. Its new leaves open a startling pink and graduate through cerise to purple and finally green.

RELAXED SUMMER

Summer is a time when we enjoy the heat and the long days, but we also need shade and cooling places. For most gardens, deciduous trees are the ideal choice. They provide a dense cover of shade when it's most needed. Stepping under the canopy of a tree on a hot summer's day is like walking into an air-conditioned room. If you have a largish garden, plant several slow-growing trees together to form a small, shady copse — silver birch is a popular choice. With a small garden select, just one slender delicate-leaved specimen, to provide dappled shade, without being oppressive.

If you can't have a tree, consider an umbrella, or a pergola covered by ornamental grape. Think of tavernas in Greece, or market umbrellas in Tuscany, and try to create a similar ambience in your summer garden.

Many summer-flowering plants have a wonderful fragrance, which will enhance your enjoyment of the garden. Honeysuckle, roses, mock orange (*Philadelphus*) and many hebes have perfumed flowers. For a more tropical ambience, grow jasmine, which is fairly hardy, or frangipani (*Plumeria*) and Angel's trumpet (*Brugmansia*), both of which will need to be overwintered in a greenhouse or conservatory. The flowers of Angel's trumpet are most strongly fragrant in the evening, so position pots near a window or on the patio.

ABOVE Once the frosts begin, most of the soft foliage dies down and the garden takes on a different character, the forms and shapes of trees and shrubs becoming more prominent.

AUTUMN SHADES

Autumn is often considered the most beautiful of seasons, not only because of its startling foliage effects, but also because of the slight nip in the air combined with warm, clear and sunny days and the crescendo of colour and change. The last of the summer perennials seem more vivid in autumn; the late ones are taller, more vigorous and somehow more dramatic. The first leaves fall during this display of flower colour.

Berry-bearing bushes also push the display well into winter. Beauty berry (*Callicarpa* sp.) has brilliant purple fruits that are popular with flower arrangers. Snowberry (*Symphoricarpos* sp.) has beautiful white fruits, while *Skimmia japonica* is an evergreen that boasts persistent red berries on female plants.

GARDEN EDGINGS

Garden or lawn edgings help prevent vigorous turf or groundcover entering garden beds and choking the shrubs and trees. They allow you to cut the grass right to the edge without slicing off some emerging bulb or perennial if runners have invaded the lawn after the hiatus of the summer holidays. Edgings also hold back soil, stop mulch spilling over onto lawns and paths, provide definition between garden beds or paths and contain gravel on a terrace or path. And, of course, they protect plants. Tree guards, a form of edging, prevent bark from being damaged by edge trimmers and lawn mowers.

Edgings are often the most underrated garden details. They give the garden a clear outline, and they also give it a finished and loved appearance. Without edgings, not only does a garden appear half-completed but also maintenance tasks can be more arduous.

EDGING STYLES

It's a good idea to determine the layout of garden edges in the design stage. They can be very simple, so that there is a natural transition from lawn to garden bed, or constructed from materials that make a strong visual statement, so that they become a feature.

Edgings take many forms. They can be ugly concrete strips between garden beds and the lawn, or they can either be crisply or subtly defined areas of your garden. You can use edgings to enhance the design of your garden. Victorian and Edwardian gardens were often edged with decorative wire or glazed edging tiles, decorated with flower or rope patterns. Traditional Japanese gardens used similar glazed tiles, perhaps decorated with a stylized chrysanthemum pattern but always with a subtle brown salt-glazed finish.

Try to keep the chosen edging in character with the style of both the house and the garden. When used well, edgings enhance this effect; however, when used poorly, they detract from it. Edgings can be either formal or informal, traditional or contemporary in style. For a period house, the Victorian and Edwardian edgings suggested above would work well, as would old dark-coloured bricks. However, modern, concrete or pale blond bricks would be completely inappropriate in this setting.

Hedges, too, are a form of soft landscaping edge, and are so important for putting the 'form' in formal gardens. Hedges tend to be trimmed into exact geometric shapes, but a more rounded, looser cut can give an edging a softer, informal feel that retains a strong sense of discipline.

REPETITION

As with other garden elements, repetition is a good design tool for edges. Combining the architectural elements and the soft landscaping of plant forms is an interesting way to not only define the beds but also to differentiate sectors of the garden. Sometimes a garden can be divided into room-like spaces with separate and distinct characters or functions —

Whatever material you use, garden edgings give a neat finish to beds and make it easier to perform maintenance tasks such as mowing.

ABOVE You can soften stone edges with creeping and spreading plants.

LEFT Here a brick edge prevents grass runners from invading a gravel strip.

for instance, you can separate a vegetable garden from the main part of the garden or screen a dining patio from the lawn, especially if it's exposed to the street.

MATERIALS

The materials you choose for edgings should blend in with the rest of the garden, especially the house and paths. Consider materials for their practical uses as well as for the feeling they lend a garden. Bricks have an earthy, warm feel. They look good in a cottage garden or in a traditional garden around a period house, and turning them on their sides produces a neat edging that suits a well-kept perennial border.

If using stone, concrete or terracotta edging, lay it at the same time the path is laid. The reason for this is simple. Generally, the outer edge of a brick or stone path is laid on a footing of concrete with the edge hidden under the surface. An edging such as terracotta or concrete tile needs to abut the path, but this is impossible if the path is already established. (See 'Paths' on page 137.)

EDGING FOR LAWNS

Edging treatments for lawns need to be level with, or slightly below, the level of the lawn itself. These keep grass back and also provide a firm surface for the wheels of the mower. Without them, the blades of the mower can slip, leaving a scalped edge. Once this happens, the grass suffers and weeds can take hold.

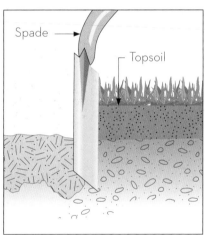

ABOVE Use a sharp spade or half-moon tool to keep the lawn edges neat.

TOP A brick edge contains this bed of vegetables.

Plastic edges designed for lawns should be laid flush with the level of the grass or just below. Such edges rarely enhance the look of your garden in themselves, but they work discretely by keeping the lawn edge well defined and reducing the invasion of grass runners into the flower beds.

A lawn edging can be a mowing strip of concrete, bricks or pavers laid on a footing of concrete. Edges can be of stone, terracotta or timber, but if they are raised above the surface of the lawn, as they almost invariably are, the mower won't be able to provide a clean cut. The solution is to use a strimmer whenever you mow the lawn.

MAKING A GRASS EDGE

For a neat and attractive, plain grass edge, use a half-moon edging tool once a year in spring and, at every mowing trim the edges with shears. This style of edging is labour-intensive but looks good in informal gardens and where borders are large with many curves. It is also effective in a garden where plants are the dominant features and where the beds and lawns are regularly maintained.

1   Use a hose, string line or straight edge to lay out the edging.
2   With a sharp spade or half-moon edging tool, cut the edge of the turf, prise it away and expose a deep edge or trench along the garden border.
3   Remove any grass from the garden bed.

INSTALLING TIMBER EDGING

Timber edging has the same effect as a plain grass edge but provides a solid barrier between the lawn and garden. It therefore requires less maintenance. It's best to keep timber edging discreet, although it will work well in straight lines or in free-form garden layouts.

1   Use a hose, straight edge or string line to mark out the border, then use a sharp spade to cut away the turf along the line.
2   Lay a length of 90 x 22 mm timber. If there are tight curves in the layout, make shallow cuts 2–5 mm deep in the back of the timber and use the pegs as fulcrums for bending the timber.
3   Drive 50 x 50 mm stakes securely and vertically into the ground behind the edging, at centres of around 2400 mm. The tops of the stakes should finish flush with the lawn. Use double stakes where lengths of timber join.
4   Using galvanized nails or self-tapping screws, secure the edging to the stakes so that it finishes flush with the lawn.
5   Backfill the lawn edge as necessary. Check the edge is flush, then raise or drive in the stakes as necessary.

BUILDING WIDE BRICK EDGING

If you want a perfect mowing strip and a very low maintenance border, consider wide brick edging. Although the materials can be expensive and the labour required is intensive, this makes a decorative border for all styles of gardens, especially those with strong geometrical layouts.

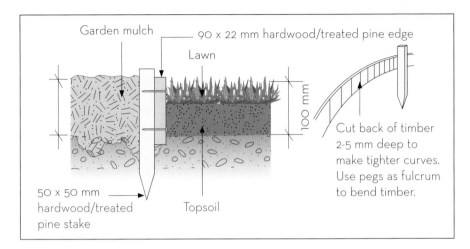

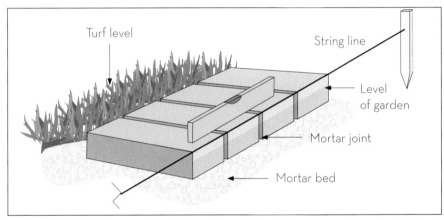

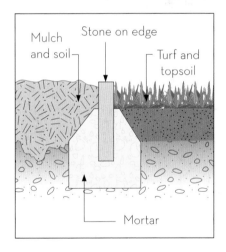

1. Lay out the edge and mark it with lime. Dig a shallow trench about 300 mm wide and 150 mm deep from the top of the existing or proposed lawn level. Compact the base.
2. Using either pre-mixed mortar, or a 5:1 ratio of bricklayers sand and cement, make up a mortar mix. Add plasticizer or 1 part lime to make the mortar more workable.
3. Use a mortar trowel to lay a bed of mortar on the base of the trench.
4. Lay the bricks side by side on the base, trowelling mortar to the side of the brick as you lay. Make a 10–15 mm joint between each brick and keep the top of the edging level by tapping and adjusting with the spirit level. Leave the bricks to set.
5. Fill any gaps with mortar and use a damp sponge to wipe off any excess mortar.

ABOVE Stone edging.

TOP Stone should be laid on its end in a bed of mortar.

TOP LEFT Timber edging.

ABOVE LEFT Brick or paver edging.

STONE EDGING

A similar method can be used to lay stone edging. For a more rustic effect, use flat stone pieces, such as sandstone flagging, worked to a regular shape or dimension. Where the garden is higher than the lawn, the stones can be set upright to retain the bed itself, providing you use a thick mortar or concrete collar to hold them in place.

STONE EDGING

TOOLS AND MATERIALS

- Basic tools (see page 332)
- Natural (that is, not dressed) stone
- Cement
- Sand
- 10 mm aggregate (gravel)

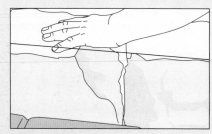

5 Using the string line as a guide, bed each stone firmly in place.

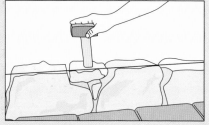

6 Fill gaps by tapping into place small pieces of stone that have been cut to fit.

HINT

If you use irregularly shaped stones next to lawn, construct a mower strip. Fix all stone edges in place by bedding the stones into a 20–50 mm footing of concrete.

Stone makes a natural, hard-wearing edging for the garden. In this project natural stone was set into a bed of mortar to make a raised edge. You can buy stone by the square metre from landscape supply or garden centres. Ask the supplier to work out the amount you need from the length of your edging. Flat-faced, chunky stones are most suitable for close-butted, unmortared joints.

PREPARATION

1 Establish the line by setting a string line. To mark a curved edge, lay out a rope or garden hose, or sprinkle flour or lime.
2 Excavate a trench about 300 mm wide (depending on the width of the stone) and 100 mm below ground level so that you remove all vegetation. If you're adding a mower strip, increase the footing width by 100 mm and make a 100 mm vertical cut at the front of the excavation.

LAYING THE STONE

3 To give you a rough idea of how the edging will look, lay out the stone about 500 mm in front of the excavated edge. Reposition individual pieces of stone, turning them or swapping them with other pieces until you are satisfied with how they will butt together. If you want the top edge of the stones to be level, adjust the depth of the trench to suit each stone (see the diagram opposite). If you want the top of the edging to be irregular, place the stones on a flat bed.
4 Prepare the ground for concrete by wetting it. This will prevent the concrete bed drying and hardening too quickly. Mix your own concrete so that you can lay small sections at a time. A load of commercially delivered concrete will go hard before you can lay all the stone. For instructions on mixing concrete, see page 335.
5 Spread a bed of concrete 50 mm thick and approximately 1 m long. Using the string line as a guide for an even top edge, position each stone in turn. Give each stone two or three twists to bed it firmly in place, making sure it is hard up against the edge and also closely butted against the last stone.
6 Fill any gaps with small pieces of stone. Cut them to fit with a club hammer and bolster chisel and tap them in place. Use concrete at the back of each joint to prevent soil washing out through the joints.

TO FINISH

7 Fill any narrow gaps between the stones and the hard edge with a sand and cement grout, or sand. Allow the concrete to dry before filling in behind the edging with garden soil.

LEFT The natural stone used to edge this garden bed suits the informal character of the garden.

BELOW LEFT Front and side views of the stone edging.

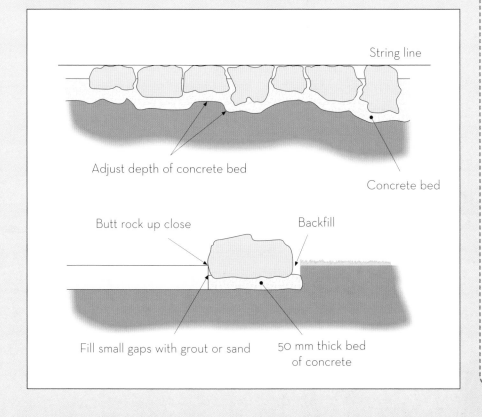

String line

Adjust depth of concrete bed

Concrete bed

Butt rock up close

Backfill

Fill small gaps with grout or sand

50 mm thick bed of concrete

USING MORTARED JOINTS

1 To mortar the joints between the stones, follow steps 3–6 but always space the stones approximately 50 mm apart.
2 Make a fairly stiff mortar mix of 4 parts sand and 1 part cement. You can add coloured oxides to the mortar so the joints blend naturally with the rock.
3 Wearing protective gloves, roll the mix in your hands to make large sausage shapes of mortar. Place each 'sausage' in a joint and use a small trowel to work the mortar in and around the joint.
4 Use a small paintbrush to finish the surface of the joints, then sponge the face of the stone until it is clean.

ABOVE This contemporary feature wall is designed to highlight the effects of light and shadow.

RIGHT A well-constructed paling fence will take the weight of large climbers and trained fruit trees.

FENCES AND SCREENS

Just as a wall on a house provides security against the elements and keeps out intruders, so does a fence or screen define, protect and enhance a garden. It lends order and structure, and directs, contains and divides sections — for outdoor meals, for relaxing or for children's play areas. A fence also provides security and privacy, and screens out unwanted views.

The plants and fences that define the boundaries keep most gardens reasonably private, but sometimes you need to block a gap in the vegetation or at the side of a terrace without restricting natural light or the feeling of space. In these spots a screen is the obvious solution, and if it's designed and built well, it can be a decorative feature in your garden.

You can also use screens to hide ugly parts of the garden, such as a fence, bare wall or service area. These screens can be either solid or open (to let light through). As a general rule, try to make the design of the screen sympathetic to the architectural features of the house.

FENCING STYLES AND FINISHES

The right style of fence can turn a purely functional element into a beautiful statement. Choose fencing materials and treatments to complement the style of your house, and coordinate finishes and colours to match the character of the garden. However, often a fence doesn't need painting. If you use the right materials, you can either leave it to weather or treat it with a suitable wood stain.

Generally, a dark colour tends to recede into the background while a lighter colour will make a fence more dominant in the landscape. Before you choose a fencing colour, carefully consider the material. Dark olive green will make an undistinguished fence recede almost entirely, but a solid paling fence painted black is more obvious than an open fence of timber slats or metal railings painted in the same colour. A fence painted white, on the other hand, becomes an imposing structure that draws attention away from the garden.

A fence can also serve as a backdrop to plantings. You may want to show off a specimen plant or enhance a bed of perennials, for instance. Don't neglect seasonal changes — for example, a fence will become more prominent in the landscape as the deciduous trees planted in front of it lose their leaves.

Some fences, such as the custom-designed metal types, have a sculptural quality all their own, but you can also use a fence or wall as a blank canvas on which to hang a wide range of garden ornaments, such as plaques, wall pots or sculptures.

THE FUNCTIONS OF FENCES AND SCREENS

Different purposes require different types of fences. Most people are conditioned to respect the front fence as a boundary of private property, so it doesn't have to be a high brick wall to keep them from straying into your garden. It may be something as understated as a low picket fence or a brick wall, a chain attached to wooden or stone pillars, or simply a line of brick or stone edging.

Side fences, on the other hand, provide privacy so that you can enjoy your garden without worrying about what the neighbours are doing. Most side fences are taller than the front fence, and are generally simple structures clad with timber palings. You can use coping and overlapping palings to dress up the standard fence and provide a more aesthetically pleasing backdrop.

To keep your garden free of views of neighbouring houses or distant apartment buildings, combine a fence with trees and shrubs.

Fences direct traffic around and through a garden in much the same way as a path. They may direct people to clearly defined entrances and prevent access to other areas. For example, a low hedge or timber fence usually helps keep people away from a garden bed or an area of lawn. Within a garden, there is sometimes a need to define areas, such as a vegetable garden or clothes-drying area, or to hide an ugly feature of the garden, such as an oil tank, dustbins or compost heaps and other service areas.

ABOVE You can soften a metal fence using plantings such as this attractive lavender hedge.

TOP A post-and panel-fence is ideal for a pool or any area requiring privacy.

A lattice fence is the ideal way to obscure such views and direct attention to the area in front of the fence. It also allows air to circulate and move naturally, and it can be painted to either recede into the background or be a prominent feature.

Sometimes, however, privacy and security require larger, more imposing structures. A security fence needs to be at least 2 m tall. A solid fence may prove counterproductive, allowing intruders privacy while they break into your house. Sometimes a high, open fence, metal railings or broad timber lattice maintain security better than a solid masonry wall.

A solid fence can alter the microclimate of a garden. Open fences allow wind to pass straight through but a solid fence forces wind up and over, exacerbating the effect of windy conditions. It also prevents sunlight from penetrating, creating cold, shady conditions on one side or the other.

FENCING MATERIALS

Most fences are made of timber, but metal, stone, brick and concrete are also commonly used. Timber is the most versatile as it can be stained, painted or left to weather naturally. Picket fences are ideal for cottage or country-style gardens and older, brick or white-washed houses. Where a rustic look is required, logs make a good fence and can be creatively interpreted. You can easily dress up a common paling fence in your backyard with cappings and crossbeams.

Stone and masonry fences are solid and permanent. They suit modern, Mediterranean-style and traditional houses. Often the pillars are constructed of stone or brick, connected by timber railing. Versatile and open to various stylistic interpretations, these materials are expensive and should be installed by qualified stonemasons or bricklayers.

Whether made from solid aluminium or Victorian-style iron railings, a metal fence is another type of permanent boundary. Railings need regular maintenance and painting, although modern aluminium copies are powder-coated to last for many years without maintenance. If you're using such materials, make sure you match the styling to the design and period of your house. If you're uncertain, choose a generic design without embellishments. Metal fences are expensive and labour-intensive in construction, so be absolutely sure that you will be happy to live with the results for as long as you are in the house.

WITHIN THE GARDEN

Internal garden enclosures don't need to be as substantial as the side or front fences. Again, simplicity is the key. You may have materials readily at hand. For example, if you want a rustic timber fence for a cottage or country garden, wire and branches make a very attractive dividing fence. The example at left demonstrates the aesthetic benefits of using simple materials. Composed of nothing more than a strong post at either end, a collection of branches and some strong fencing wire, it's ideal for separating the bottom, wilder-looking end of the garden from the home garden where flowers, fruit and vegetables might be growing.

BELOW Fallen branches make a striking rustic fence, which in turn hides a wire barrier.

Low hedges can be used as living fences. Buying 50 or more container-grown specimens plants such as box or cotoneaster is expensive, but you can easily grow them from cuttings.

Within the garden it is less likely that you'll want to completely enclose and block a section of the garden from view, so choose lighter materials for internal fences. Lattice and widely spaced posts that let air and light through are good choices.

Whether you are building a fence or planting one, prepare carefully to ensure you achieve a straight line and an even height. Allow plenty of time for measuring out, and always check your calculations.

ABOVE Lattice is a great way to screen unattractive views and service areas.

PRIVACY SCREEN WITH A VIEW

While this project requires a reasonable amount of skill with woodworking tools, it's a great way to maintain visual fields, light and air circulation. Design the screen so that the angle of the slats is directed towards a view or garden outlook, or so that they block views from outside and towards the private area.

1   Measure the area for the screen. Set 100 x 100 mm posts into the ground, or secure them to the deck so that each panel will be approximately 1800 mm wide.

2   Measure out the top and bottom rails. Using a sliding bevel, mark out the slat rebates on one rail. Use the marked rail as a template for the other one. For maximum privacy, set the rebates at about 45 degrees and 25–40 mm apart. For 100 x 19 mm slats, make the rebates 20 mm wide.

3   Set a circular saw or router bit to a depth of 10 mm and score the rails to create the slat rebates. Chisel out the rebates.

4   Cut the slats to measure. Temporarily fix the end slats to the top and bottom rails and check for square.

5   Take off the top rail and slide the remaining slats into the rebates. Fix on the top rail.

6   Cut mortises into the posts to suit the top and bottom rails, and fix the panel between the posts.

BELOW Working drawings for a privacy screen with a view.

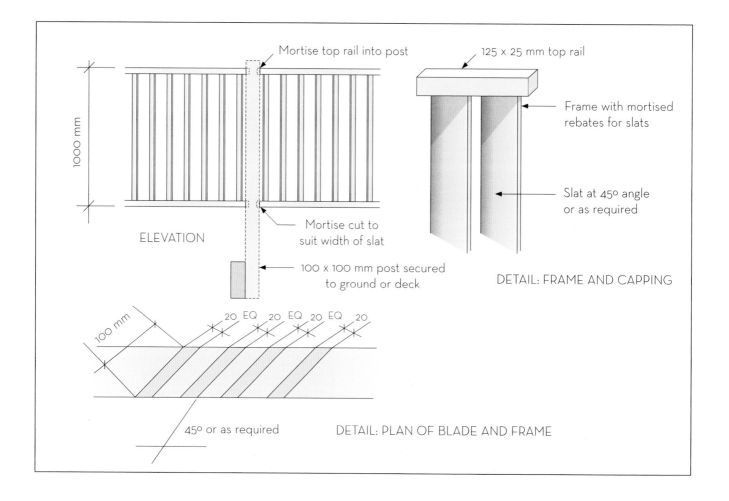

Mortise top rail into post

125 x 25 mm top rail

Frame with mortised rebates for slats

1000 mm

Slat at 45º angle or as required

ELEVATION

Mortise cut to suit width of slat

100 x 100 mm post secured to ground or deck

DETAIL: FRAME AND CAPPING

100 mm

20 EQ 20 EQ 20 EQ 20

45º or as required

DETAIL: PLAN OF BLADE AND FRAME

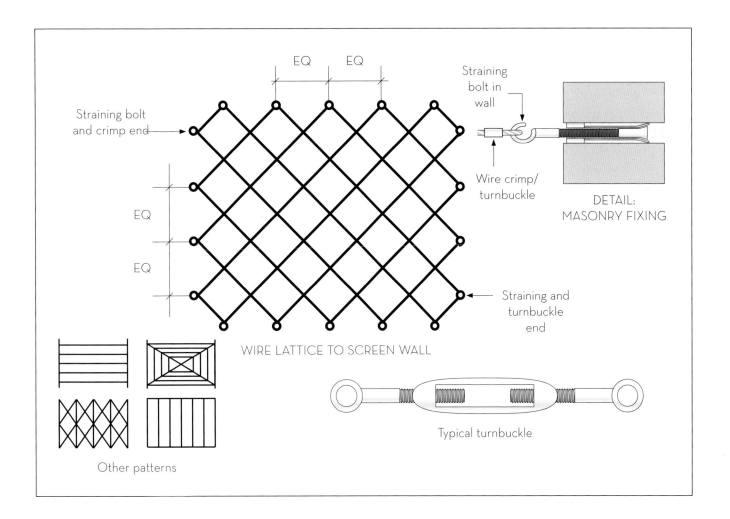

WIRE TRELLIS

You can easily screen an ugly wall or fence with climbing plants. Flowering climbers and twiners make a perfect backdrop in any garden, although it may take years for them to cover the screen. While they establish themselves, however, you can create striking visual effects by building the trellis in geometric or free-form shapes. Vary the geometrical pattern for more interest.

A wire trellis can also be fixed between two posts to make a free-standing screen. For a more formal effect, chamfer the post edges and add a decorative newel knob. Use a similar method for extending an 1800 mm high boundary fence by using taller posts and fixing wire between them.

MAKING A WIRE LATTICE

This lattice can be attached to a brick or masonry wall.
1. Mark out the points for the straining bolts or eyelet screws on the wall, measuring off from a level line to create a regular pattern. Drill and set the straining bolts.
2. Secure the wire to the bottom left-hand straining bolt and feed it through the others to form a criss-cross pattern (see the diagram above). Fix the

ABOVE Making a wire trellis.

SUITABLE CLIMBING PLANTS

- *Actinidia kolomikta*
- *Akebia quinata*
- Boston ivy (*Parthenocissus tricuspidata*)
- *Campsis* sp. and cv.
- *Clematis* sp., cv. and hybrids
- Confederate jasmine (*Trachelospermum jasminoides*)
- Honeysuckle (*Lonicera* sp.)

other end to the straining bolt with a turnbuckle or tension loop (see the diagram on page 107). Complete the pattern, keeping it square.

3   Plant vigorous climbers below the trellis and train them up the supports.

SCREENING A SERVICE AREA

A functional and attractive garden requires a service area. Whether it's for dustbins and compost or a clothesline, you'll need to screen it from view. There are many types of suitable screens but, as always, it's best to link the screen with some decorative element on the house.

MAKING A TIMBER SLAT SCREEN

A timber slat screen suits many garden styles. The slats or battens can be either treated pine or cedar and should be thoroughly sealed with paint or preservative. Use long lengths of timber to avoid joins, and adjust the spacing of the battens to suit the degree of privacy required. Rebate the battens into the posts for a flush finish or fix them to the face of the posts.

1   Set out for the screen with the posts evenly spaced and centred no more than 1800 mm apart. Dig the post holes (see page 353) and compact the base.

2   Set the posts in the holes and prop them upright. Pour concrete into the holes, and check that the posts are vertical.

3   Leave the concrete to set solid, and then cut off the tops of the posts level at 2000 mm. To provide resistance when nailing, leave the props in place until you have finished securing the battens.

4   Set the first batten, leaving 50–100 mm clearance from the top of the post, and check it's level before fixing it in place with galvanized nails or screws. If you are using hardwood battens, pre-drill the holes.

5   Continue fixing battens, using another batten or offcut as a spacer. Check every third or fourth batten for level. Leave 50–100 mm clearance from the bottom.

BELOW RIGHT Constructing a timber slat screen.

BELOW Some alternative designs for timber screens.

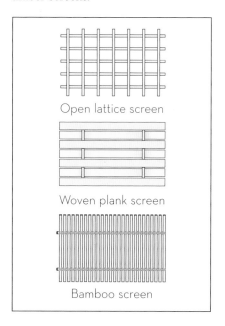

Open lattice screen

Woven plank screen

Bamboo screen

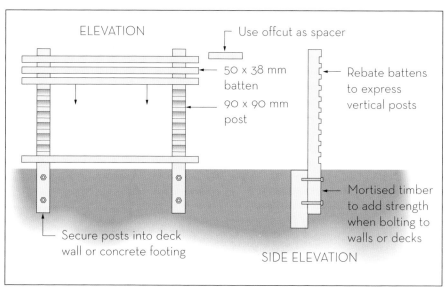

ELEVATION

Use offcut as spacer

50 x 38 mm batten

90 x 90 mm post

Secure posts into deck wall or concrete footing

Rebate battens to express vertical posts

Mortised timber to add strength when bolting to walls or decks

SIDE ELEVATION

PLANTING CLEMATIS

A simple grid structure such as this wire mesh provides ideal support for a climbing plant. Slanting canes encourage the plant to grow towards the grid in the early stages.

1 Before planting clematis, soak the pot in a bucket of water, then lift the plant and allow any surplus water to drain away.

2 Dig a hole twice the size of the root ball, to encourage the roots to grow out, and a little deeper than the plant pot. Refill the hole, firming the soil.

3 Spread out the shoots and position a tie about every 30 cm along the stem. Where possible, push the new shoots between the wires and the support. Water in.

WEAVING A WILLOW SCREEN

A woven organic screen can make a perfect surround for a cut flower garden, or even a backdrop for delicate climbers such as sweet peas.

1 Begin by pushing a series of uprights at least 20 cm into the soil. Make sure you use the thickest and straightest rods as the vertical props.

2 Push the diagonals into the soil, putting the longest lengths into the central section. Leave a 30 cm space between them.

3 Tie the diagonals to the uprights. Where they cross, twist their tops around the horizontals and then tie them in.

LATTICE SCREEN

TOOLS

- Tape measure and pencil
- Marking gauge
- Square
- Tenon saw or jigsaw
- Circular saw (optional)
- Chisel: 25 mm
- Spirit level
- Electric drill
- Drill bits: 6 mm, 10 mm*
- Screwdriver
- Socket spanner (for coach screws)
- String line
- Post-hole auger
- Water level (optional)
- Five G-clamps
- Hammer
- Cork sanding block

* Use a 10 mm masonry bit if you are fixing to a brick wall.

3 Hold the post against the wall, ensure it is vertical and draw a line along the edge of the post.

This versatile screen is supported by a simple post-and-rail frame, which can be fixed to an existing wall at one end or left free-standing. You can also add extra panels if you wish. Use it to screen out a service area or divide one area of the garden from another.

THE POSTS

1 On the front edge of the wall post, mark out and cut the housings for the beam and rails (see the 'Post housings' diagram on page 113 and 'Cutting a housing' on page 353).
2 Mark the centre of the outer face 300 mm from each end. If the wall is timber-framed, adjust the marks to suit the framework. Using a 10 mm bit, drill the holes.
3 Hold the wall post against the wall. If the wall is brick, position the post so the fixings won't go into the mortar joints. Ensure the post is vertical. Run a pencil down the edge of the post so you can see if it moves. Drill through the holes into the wall, using a 10 mm masonry bit or a 6 mm bit for a timber frame. Insert a coach screw with washer, or a masonry anchor, into each hole.
4 Measure 5 m from the wall post and drive in a peg. Nail a cloutnail into the wall post and a second nail into the top of the peg. Tie string to one nail and pull it tight to the other nail; tie it off. To check that the line is square to the wall, measure along the wall 4 m and along the line 3 m. If the diagonal is 5 m, the string is square to the wall.
5 Along the string measure 1200 mm from the wall and dig the post hole (see page 353). Dig the second centred at 2400 mm, the third at 3300 mm and the fourth at 4455 mm. Erect each post so the face lines up with the string. Cut the posts off level with the top of the wall post.
6 On each post, mark out housings as you did on the wall post, measuring from the top of the post. Check the housings are on the same side as on the wall post. Cut the housings, starting at the top.

RAILS AND LATTICE

7 Cut the beam to length and lift it into the housings on top of the posts. Hold it to each post with a G-clamp. Skew-nail through the beam into each post with three 75 mm nails.
8 Cut the rails so the ends are flush with the posts at the opening and insert them into their housings. Skew two 75 mm nails into each post.
9 Place a lattice panel on the frame with the edges against the wall and flush with the top of the beam and the lower edge of the bottom rail. Fix it with 50 mm flat-head nails at 200 mm spacings all round. Fix the other two panels so that the edge beside the opening is in the centre of the post.

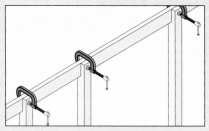

7 Cut the beam to length and use G-clamps to hold it in the housings on the top of the posts.

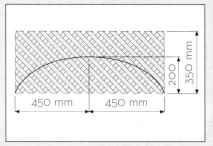

ABOVE Mark out the desired arch on the lattice.

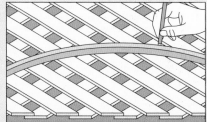

10 Bend a thin piece of timber or tubing to indicate the curve and draw the curve onto the lattice.

LEFT Here the lattice screen is used to separate the living area of the garden from the driveway and the neighbouring house beyond.

SAFETY

Always take these precautions when handling treated timber.

- Wear gloves.
- When machining or sanding, always wear a dust mask as well as goggles that completely enclose the eyes. If you suffer from respiratory problems, wear a cartridge-style mask.
- If you are working indoors, ensure there is good ventilation.
- Wash your face and hands before eating and drinking.
- Never use treated timber for heating or cooking, as the smoke and ash will be toxic.

OPPOSITE LEFT Framework and front view of the lattice screen.

OPPOSITE RIGHT The post housings.

MATERIALS*

PART	MATERIAL	FINISHED LENGTH	NO.
Beam	140 x 45 mm treated pine	4500 mm	1
Post**	90 x 90 mm treated pine	3000 mm	4
Wall post	90 x 45 mm treated pine	2090 mm	1
Rail	90 x 45 mm treated pine	2445 mm	2
Short rail	90 x 45 mm treated pine	1245 mm	2
Top trim	90 x 20 mm treated pine	4500 mm	1
Vertical trim	90 x 20 mm treated pine	1910 mm	4
Bottom trim	90 x 20 mm treated pine	1110 mm	2
Short trim	90 x 20 mm treated pine	1065 mm	1
Wall post trim	45 x 20 mm treated pine	1910 mm	1
Lattice panel***	diagonal lattice	2000 mm	3
Arch panel****	diagonal lattice	900 mm	1

Other: Two 125 x 10 mm coach screws and washers or two 125 x 10 mm masonry anchors; 25 x 2.6 mm cloutnail; 75 x 3 mm galvanized bullet-head nails; 65 x 3 mm galvanized bullet-head nails; 50 x 2.6 mm galvanized flat-head nails; timber peg; concrete; eight 1800 mm long timbers for props; abrasive paper.

* Finished size: 4500 mm long and 2090 mm high. You can adjust both the length and height as required. Use treated pine lattice.
** Use C24 treated pine. Length may vary according to the amount of slope on the site. All posts must finish at the same level as the wall post.
*** Finished width 1200 mm.
**** Finished width 350 mm.

10 Mark out the arch on the arch panel (see the bottom diagram on page 111) and use thin timber or tubing to draw the curve. Cut out the arch with a jigsaw or tenon saw, and sand the edge smooth. Fix it on the frame so the top is flush with the top of the beam.

11 Fix the top trim over the lattice, with the top flush with the lattice edge, using 65 mm nails 300 mm apart. Fix a vertical trim over each post, flush with the sides of the posts. Add the wall post trim and the three bottom trims.

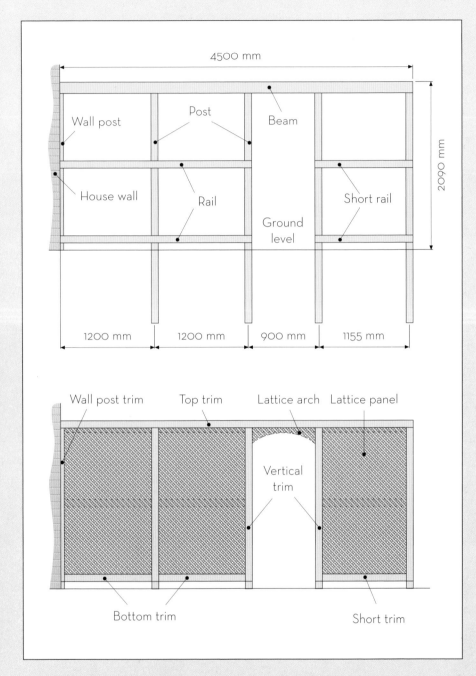

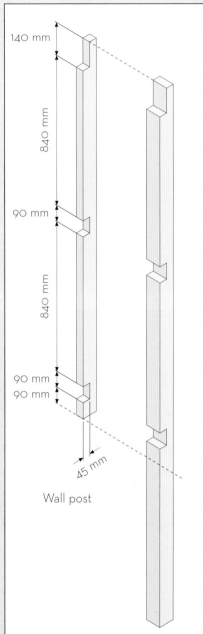

4500 mm

2090 mm

Wall post

Post

Beam

House wall

Rail

Short rail

Ground
level

1200 mm   1200 mm   900 mm   1155 mm

Wall post trim   Top trim   Lattice arch   Lattice panel

Vertical
trim

Bottom trim

Short trim

140 mm

840 mm

90 mm

840 mm

90 mm
90 mm

45 mm

Wall post

HEDGES

A hedge is more than just a boundary to a property, keeping out unwelcome animals and people and providing privacy. It can also be used as the 'skeleton' of your landscape, creating garden 'rooms' for you to decorate, concealing utility areas and unsightly views and acting as a windbreak.

Small hedges form borders along driveways and paths. Tall hedges provide windbreaks and shelter from salt spray and hot, drying, dust-laden winds. Hedges offer more protection than a solid wall because they slow down the wind, filtering the air in the process. Solid walls, on the other hand, provide a barrier, increasing the turbulence in your garden.

Formal or informal, flowers or foliage, there are hedges suitable for all areas of the garden. The traditional garden hedge is close-clipped and neat, but there's a huge number of attractive shrubs that will form low-maintenance, informal hedges.

ALL SHAPES AND SIZES

Before planting your hedge, consider the height, purpose and time span that you've allowed for growth. Fast growers may screen quickly but their vigour will mean more maintenance later on to keep them under control.

- Conifers (for example, *Leylandii* cypress) form a fast-growing evergreen hedge — perfect for a windbreak or a screen.
- Native trees and shrubs, particularly berrying or fruiting kinds, will attract wildlife such as birds to the garden.
- Try yew, box, *Lonicera nitida* (box honeysuckle) or *Euonymus japonicus* (Japanese spindle) for formal low hedges.
- For taller, flowering hedges, choose from escallonia, photinia, *Viburnum tinus* or *Berberis* x *stenophylla*.

PLANTING A NEW HEDGE

The most effective hedges are evergreen, as they provide the most privacy and protection, but some deciduous plants make attractive, although less dense, hedges in the winter. For an informal hedge, plant a row of flowering shrubs close together and prune once a year, after flowering. However, a traditional formal hedge should be pruned at least a couple of times a year in order to grow well and maintain its shape. As a guide, space tall, narrow plants such as holly at 60 cm intervals and spreading plants such as berberis at 90 cm. Plant hedges either in a straight line or in a diagonally spaced, staggered row. The latter technique creates a thicker, denser hedge.

1 Start by marking out the course of the hedge with a string line.

2 Using a spade, dig out the hole for the first plant, and place the soil in a wheelbarrow (take this soil to the end of the hedge line and use it to fill the final planting hole).

3 Remove the plant from its container and position it in the planting hole, making sure the root ball is at the correct depth.

4 Dig out the hole for the second hedge plant, and place the soil from this second hole around the roots of the plant in the first planting hole.

5 Adjust the level of the plant's root ball and firm the soil in the planting hole with the heel of your boot. (Repeat steps 3, 4 and 5 until the hedge is completed.)

6 Finally, remove the string line and cover the soil with a layer of well-rotted organic mulch to suppress weeds and retain moisture.

ABOVE Bamboo creates the right atmosphere for an oriental-style garden.

RIGHT Picket fences are a popular choice for weatherboard cottages and older-style houses.

GATES

Just like a fence, a gate can be highly individual. It can affect the whole mood and feeling of a garden because it's the first thing the visitor sees, creating a first impression that lasts. It may be imposing, grand and ostentatious, or it can be humble, rundown and rickety.

A gate is an entrance that governs our comings and goings. It can be used for a number of purposes — such as safety, security and status — but it can also carry a subliminal message of anticipation and discovery. Even if there's no fence in your front garden, you may still need a gate to shut off a side passage or access to a swimming pool or pond.

The style of your garden will influence the gate design you choose, although the architecture of your house will play an important role with both. You can take two approaches to choosing a gate (and fence). One is to make it stand out. If the fence is a vertical picket, you could choose a gate with a criss-cross or horizontal pattern so it contrasts and clearly denotes the entry point. Alternatively, you could play it down and disguise it, using the same materials and pattern as the fence.

Another factor to consider is the ease of entry. This depends on the size and weight of the gate, which should be in scale with the fence, and the level of security you require. You can increase the level of security by using electronic locking devices that you control from within the house. Obviously, a low gate and fence offer little or no security.

MATERIALS FOR GATES

Any gate is a functional item; to be successful, it needs to work effectively. A gate is subject to more use and abuse than any other garden feature, so whether it's simple, ornate, custom-made or factory-built, it must be sturdy and strong enough to withstand constant opening and closing.

Good hardware is essential. Don't skimp on cheap hinges, latches and locks. Not all gates need a lock, but the hinges and latches need to be strong enough to last for years.

When choosing material for a gate, consider the fencing material. When you buy timber, check that it's straight. If it's warped, the gate will be out of line and sag, and it probably won't close properly. This will put extra strain on the hardware.

You can find a wooden gate to suit just about any style. Picket fences suit country cottages and look good next to flower borders. However, they require regular maintenance, especially if they're painted. For a rustic look, an unpainted timber fence of treated pine will last for many years, but you could oil it to ensure longer life. Mixing materials allows you to obtain interesting effects. For instance, bamboo poles or timber dowels on a timber frame lend a Japanese look to an oriental-style garden.

Metal and iron fences need to be matched carefully to period. Wrought iron has been adapted to many styles, including Victorian terraces, Mediterranean villas and 1950s bungalows, but it's not recommended that you mix and match the styles.

BELOW A lych gate should be strong enough to support climbing plants.

BELOW LEFT Small Art Deco metal gates were a common feature of suburban bungalows during the first half of the 20th century.

LYCH GATES

Lych gates provide shelter over the gateway and make an attractive architectural feature at the front or side of the house. Usually traditional in design, they are best treated as an integral part of the front fence: try to incorporate architectural features that connect them to the house.

BUILDING A LYCH GATE

If you're considering a new front fence, it might be best to start with the lych gate and use it to form the posts for the fence. Position the lych gate over the front path and set it back to form a landing.

1 Set out the post holes, allowing a minimum of 1500 x 1500 mm for the structure's size. The dimensions should reflect the scale of your house.
2 Use treated pine posts and set them 450–600 mm deep in a concrete footing. Brace each post to vertical and leave the concrete to set.
3 Measure and cut the roof beams. Cut housings in the top of the posts and bolt the beams to the posts as shown in the top diagram opposite. Make decorative cuts and overhangs on the beam as preferred.
4 Cut the rafters to length. Temporarily brace the ridge beam in place. Fix the rafters at each end to form the gables, and then the intermediate rafters at approximately 450 mm centres. Add diagonal bracing to the roof.
5 Provide some bracing between the side posts.
6 Set the roof battens at the appropriate spacing for the chosen roof material (450 mm centres for metal roof sheet). Fix the roof material in place and provide overlaps as specified by the manufacturer.
7 Fit the ridge capping in place and trim any overhanging material.
8 Apply the gable sheets to both ends and fix decorative brackets or finials in place.
9 Install the gate, if required, to match the fence. Paint as preferred.

RIGHT The pitch of a lych gate should be the same as the pitch of the house roof. This one also matches the architecture of the house.

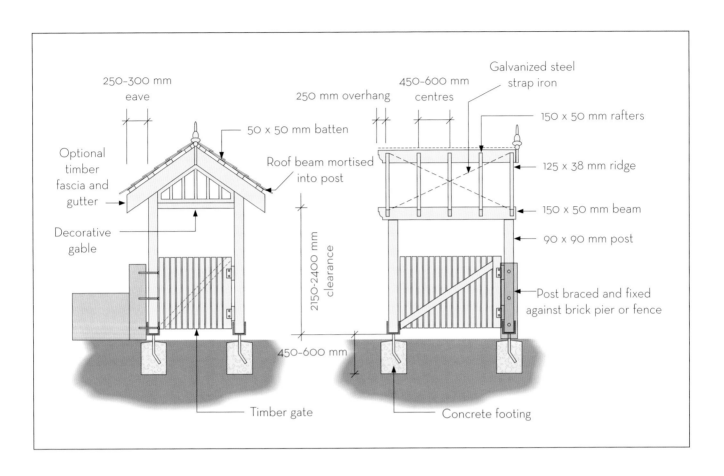

250–300 mm
eave

250 mm overhang

450–600 mm
centres

Galvanized steel
strap iron

50 x 50 mm batten

150 x 50 mm rafters

Optional
timber
fascia and
gutter

Roof beam mortised
into post

125 x 38 mm ridge

Decorative
gable

150 x 50 mm beam

90 x 90 mm post

2150–2400 mm
clearance

Post braced and fixed
against brick pier or fence

450–600 mm

Timber gate

Concrete footing

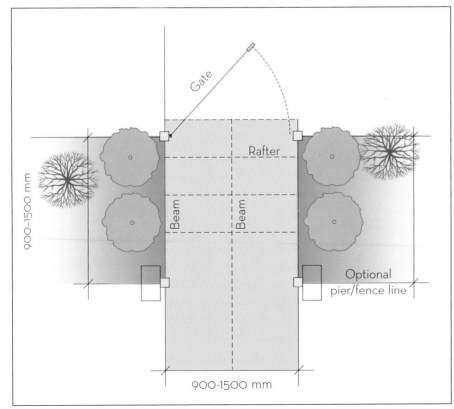

Gate

Rafter

Beam

Beam

900–1500 mm

Optional
pier/fence line

900–1500 mm

ABOVE Side and front elevations for a lych gate.

LEFT A plan for a typical lych gate.

TIMBER DOOR

An imposing wooden door, decorated with ornamental studs and hinges, makes a grand garden entrance. When closed, the robust façade creates an air of mystery, suggesting that whatever is on the other side must be worth seeing.

KNOW YOUR MATERIALS

The oak planks used for this door were once tar-covered railway sleepers, bolted to tracks and pummelled by passing trains. Cut-down sleepers are available from salvage yards. Always buy decorative nails and door furniture that have been coated with rustproof paint. This stops corrosion and prevents tannins in the oak reacting with the iron, which would cause grey stains to appear on the face of the door.

METHOD

1   Cut the planks to the height you want the door and then cut them to width using a circular saw fitted with a fence (a guide bar that ensures that the cuts are straight). The width of the planks depends on the width of the door, and a little maths is necessary to get this right as they aren't of equal width. When put together, all four have to be 3–4 mm smaller than the width of the opening, but the two central planks need to be 20 mm narrower than the edge planks. This ensures that the cover strips (see step 3) that are fixed over the joints between the planks are evenly spaced. To get this right, cut a strip of timber that's the width of the opening, and mark the position of each plank and cover strip to ensure that their spacing is correct. If you are using reclaimed timber, save the soundest planks for the ledges (see step 2) and check for straightness. Where necessary, use a plane to remove any lumps and bumps.

2   The ledges, which are fixed to the back of the door, hold the door together. Their length is the same as the width of the door and they can be any width, although to look more in scale, they should be 20–30 mm thinner than the planks used for the face of the door. Once you have cut them, round their edges with a sander. To create an ancient, heavy look, evenly space five ledges on the back of the door, leaving a slightly larger gap between the bottom of the door and the first ledge. Secure them with two brass screws in each plank (always pilot-drill and countersink the holes first). Although the brass looks bright, it won't take long before it weathers down to the colour of the oak.

3   For the cover strips, cut a plank down into 45 mm strips with a circular saw. You need three to cover the joints on the face of the door and enough to make a surround for the door's edge. Clamp each strip to a workbench and, using a router, cut a C-shaped bevel along both edges

1 Using a circular saw, cut the planks to the required width. Remove any lumps and bumps with a plane.

2 Evenly space five ledges on the back of the door and secure them to the planks with brass screws.

OPPOSITE Ideally, this timber door should be set into a solid wall of brick or timber.

MATERIALS

- Seven oak planks from cut-down railway sleepers (or timber) 22 mm thick, 240 mm wide and at least the height of the door
- 32 x 40 mm brass screws
- 96 x 40mm decorative nails
- 12 x 75mm decorative nails
- Five large decorative iron hinges
- Fleur-de-lis butterfly door latch

TOOLS

- Carpentry tools
- Plane
- Sander
- Hammer
- Router
- Circular saw

of the three central cover strips. Then bevel one side of the two longest edging strips, leaving the top and bottom strips as they are.

4 Lay the top strip in position on the face of the door and check that it's square, then fix it with evenly spaced 40 mm decorative nails (four were used for this project). Always drill pilot holes for the nails first, otherwise the wood will split.

5 Cut the central cover strips to length (they should be the height of the door minus the width of the top and bottom strips). Support the door on timber battens, then butt the cover strips against the top edge strip and fix them with 75 mm decorative nails driven through the gaps and through the ledges. Flip the door over and bend the centimetre of nail that protrudes through the door with a hammer. As the nails are hammered over, the cover strips are pulled tightly into the door. Then flip the door back over and fit the edge strips with their bevelled corner facing towards the centre of the door and finally the strip along the bottom of the door. Pilot drill all nail holes before hammering.

6 Make a cardboard template to locate the positions of the decorative nails between the cover strips and over the ledges. Pilot drill holes through the template before hammering home the 40 mm nails.

7 On old doors, the hinges are always set beneath the ledges. To enhance the old-world look, use five, one screwed beneath each ledge. Another design option is to use two sizes of hinges with three 300 mm hinges in the middle and two 450 mm hinges at the top and bottom of the door. Doing this gives the door a stronger appearance, much the same as the hinges of a treasure chest.

8 Position the door in the opening and prop it on wooden wedges while you screw the hinges to the frame. Any sides that stick can be sanded down once the door is hung. Finally, fit the butterfly latch to the door and the catch on the frame.

ALTERNATIVE MATERIALS AND DESIGNS

If you want to save money, use pine instead of oak. Once you've built the door, give it a coat of oak-effect wood stain to darken it and protect it from the weather. No matter what timber you use, this style of door should be set into an appropriate opening, such as the brick piers used here. If you have only fences, it would work if you disguised the edges with ivy or heavy trellis. Alternatively, cut an opening in a hedge.

3 Clamp each cover strip to a workbench and use a router to cut a C-shaped bevel along both edges of the three central strips.

4 Lay the top edge strip in position and check that it's square before fixing it to the planks with evenly spaced decorative nails.

5 Having cut the central cover strips to length, butt them against the top edge strip and fix them with some decorative nails.

6 Make a cardboard template to position decorative nails between the cover strips and over the ledges.

7 Set large decorative iron hinges, coated in rustproof paint to prevent corrosion, beneath each ledge.

8 Position the door in the opening and prop it on wooden wedges while you screw the hinges to the frame.

RIGHT Here bricks demonstrate their versatility as a material for fencing, paving and retaining walls.

HOW TO CALCULATE AREA

Most paving materials are sold by the square metre.

- For square or rectangular areas, multiply the length by the width. For example, for a courtyard that measures 5 x 12 m, the area is 60 m².
- For a circular area, use the formula πr^2, where π equals 3.14 and r equals the radius of the circle. For a circular paved area with a radius of 4 m:

$$\pi \text{ x } r^2$$
$$= 3.14 \text{ x } 16$$
$$= 50.24 \text{ m}^2$$

- For a triangular area, multiply half the base length by the height. If the area is 4 m wide at the base and 6 m high, the calculation is:

$$(\tfrac{1}{2} \text{ x } 4) \text{ x } 6 = 12 \text{ m}^2$$

PAVING

Paths and driveways — the 'high traffic lanes' — are the most commonly paved areas around a home, but you can also use paving to define outdoor living spaces, such as courtyards, patios and pool surrounds, and add colour and style by introducing patterns and texture. Paving material is especially useful where there are changes of level or drainage problems — for example, it's ideal for damp or shaded ground where grass won't grow. And you can brighten areas overshadowed by large trees or buildings by installing a garden seat or a statue on a firm surface of patterned pavers.

Before choosing paving, consider these points.

- Light colours produce glare in exposed positions.
- Surfaces that are hard-paved (concrete, for example) are easier to maintain than those covered with porous or natural materials like clay.
- Larger flat surfaces are more difficult to drain and maintain than smaller ones.
- Combining materials — for example, large concrete pavers with bricks — gives some variety over large areas.
- An area that is in direct view of a living or dining room should be as attractive as possible. If you can make any links with the internal floor covering, you'll extend the visual space of the internal room.
- For paving near a swimming pool, choose a non-slip paver that will tolerate chlorine and other pool chemicals.

PLANNING YOUR PAVING

As paved areas are an extension of your living space, plan to incorporate natural features such as trees, gardens and exposed rock surfaces so that your project is in harmony with its setting rather than imposed on it.

Begin by drawing a detailed plan of your house and land. Mark the key points, such as entry doors, the garage, gates and specific parts of your garden that require connection via a path. Note the places where you like to relax or entertain, or areas that are shady or constantly damp. Plan to connect the proposed hard-surface areas around your home in an interesting but practical way.

Next, consider the shape and size of your proposed paving and the impact such areas will have on the appearance of your home.

CHOOSING PAVING MATERIALS

Once you have decided where to pave, select the most suitable material for the job. You can choose from a wide variety of materials, including clay pavers, house bricks, concrete pavers, slate, marble and stone. Consider the architectural style of your home, how formal your setting is, your budget and the availability of materials. Non-slip surfaces are essential for paving that will be exposed to the elements or used in areas prone to dampness or moss growth.

CLAY PAVERS

The greater strength and hardness of clay pavers give them an advantage over house bricks and make them ideal for heavy traffic areas, such as driveways. They are also better suited for paving around salt water swimming pools, as salt has a corrosive effect. You can tessellate consistently rectangular clay pavers to create different patterns and, because they are flat on both sides, you can hide any chipped corners on the downward face.

Clay pavers are available in a variety of sizes, but 230 x 115 x 50 mm is the most useful. As its width is exactly half the length, it's possible to create interlocking designs (such as basketweave) as well as standard paving patterns. Clay pavers come in warm, earthy colours, and clay, being a natural material, provides a richness that doesn't fade over time. In exposed situations, dark clay absorbs heat, becoming very hot, particularly in summer. Light colours stay cooler and can make an area appear larger, but in damp, shaded areas or under shedding foliage, staining and moss growth will be an obvious problem.

Choose paving materials and styles to suit the style of your garden.

HOUSE BRICKS

Both new and old house bricks are an alternative to commercial pavers. The rustic appeal of house bricks adds an old-world charm to any setting, particularly if you are able to purchase original sandstocks. House bricks are best suited to courtyards, paths and patios, and should not be used around swimming pools.

Before using house bricks in driveways, discuss their suitability with the supplier. House bricks usually measure 215 x 102 x 65 mm, so in an

ABOVE You can buy concrete pavers in many different styles — these days many are made to look like natural materials such as stone.

interlocking pattern, such as basketweave, the joints are slightly wider than usual as the length-to-width ratio is not exactly 2:1. Slight variations in dimension make positioning more difficult.

With their 65 mm depth, standard bricks require deeper excavation than is necessary when laying clay pavers. Dry-pressed house bricks (or solids) have a frog on one side to assist in the bonding of the mortar bed, so each is left with only one possible exposed surface. Extruded house bricks (or wire cuts) are manufactured with holes running through their centres and must be laid on one edge, making them relatively fragile when they're in use.

CONCRETE PAVERS

The most common paving material, concrete can be nondescript, but it's possible to lay it creatively. For example, concrete paths can be stamped with moulds to imitate cobbles, inlaid with pebbles or be brushed or smoothed for various effects.

Standard pavers made from concrete — some available with spacing lugs on the sides — help make laying simple. Suitable for any paving pattern, the standard concrete paver (225 x 112 mm) is appropriate because of its 2:1 length to width ratio. And they vary in thickness. The thinner 40 mm pavers are ideal for pedestrian-only areas, such as courtyards, terraces and swimming pool surrounds.

Modern, fade-resistant concrete pavers are often made to resemble natural products, such as sawn sandstone, slate, split granite and even terrazzo, with honed and polished surfaces.

The cobblestone has a time-worn appearance, particularly when the edges are rumbled. Approximately 230 x 190 x 50 mm, commercial cobblestones are unsuitable for some patterns such as basketweave.

Irregular, interlocking pavers — suitable for driveways because of their additional strength — are produced in a variety of sizes and patterns. For domestic driveways, a 50 mm thickness copes with normal traffic. For heavier traffic in industrial and commercial situations, it's recommended that you use 60 mm thick pavers.

There are also new concrete products designed to have the texture and colour of natural stone but the strength of concrete. Check with your landscaping supplier to find out what's available.

STONE

Stone is the most expensive paving material but arguably the finest choice for building and style. Any flat-surfaced rock is suitable for use as flagging.

Granite is hard, durable and extremely hard-wearing but expensive. It's usually laid as setts, which are small irregular rectangles or squares laid in a pattern. Granite tends to have an uneven surface and is not good for seating; however, it makes an ideal path on slopes because it provides a firm grip.

Sandstone blocks are sold with one or both main surfaces sawn. Split sandstone is irregular in shape and is suited to a more informal setting. Sandstone is a soft material, easy to cut and lay. New sandstone weathers quickly, and soon starts to look aged. Its natural non-slip surface provides

ABOVE Crazy stone paving.

LEFT This patio features a combination of bricks laid on their ends and slate pavers in different sizes.

an excellent built-in safety element. It's a popular material for steps, courtyards, verandahs, paths and patios, and can be laid safely around chlorinated swimming pools.

MARBLE AND SLATE

Costly and best used in formal situations, marble can be slippery when wet. Marble chips are used in terrazzo floors and paving.

Slate can be split along planes of cleavage to thicknesses of as small as 5 mm. As slate has low porosity, it's generally difficult to stain unless it's laid around a barbecue where it's exposed to oil and grease spills.

Slate is very architectural and a good choice for sunny situations. Its one drawback is that it absorbs heat and can be hot to touch. Frequently used as an edging, it makes an attractive contrast with other materials. You can choose from mottled tones of brown, pink, silver, red, black, gold and red. As darker colours absorb heat, use these for interior or shaded areas. For open exterior paving, lighter-coloured slate is best.

You can buy slate tiles with cut, hand-sawn or chipped edges. Cut-edged tiles are uniform in size and give a formal finish to paving, while hand-sawn slate varies slightly in dimension but has neat edges on both sides. Chipped slate is guillotined, causing chipping on one side. This usually means you can only lay it with the chipped side facing down.

There's a paving material and style to suit every type of garden and budget.

TILES

Tiles range from plain terracotta to complicated tessellated patterns and colours, and vary widely in price. Exterior tiles can be used for driveways and paths, in courtyards, on patios, terraces and verandahs and around swimming pools. Made from concrete or clay, they come in a variety of colours, sizes and finishes.

Concrete tiles made from finely crushed aggregate are fired at extremely high temperatures and are usually quite thick, with a variety of texture finishes that imitate natural products. They have low porosity and high impact resistance and offer a range of tessellating options when laid. Colours usually vary between batches, so try to ensure your order is filled from a single source.

Clay (or ceramic) tiles are popular for interior and exterior floors. Those suited to exterior use include terracotta and quarry tiles. Quarry tiles have a rough surface, making them non-slip and therefore suitable for areas that are exposed to the weather. Tiles made from terracotta have a porosity higher than that of concrete tiles, which makes them more absorbent, a problem around barbecues in particular. Generally, their rough surface and fade-resistant, rich, earthy colours make them a popular choice for exterior use. To maintain the non-slip finish, leave terracotta tiles unsealed outdoors.

GRAVEL

Gravel is versatile and by far the cheapest option, but it must be laid on a level surface. Gravel will shift in heavy rain and needs regular re-grading if it's used on a slight slope.

Pale gravel reflects light and is good in shady areas. White quartz can be used in formal garden plans or as a contrast with other materials such as slate. However, it's not recommended for very young children as they tend to put it in their mouths.

First you'll need to lay a compacted sub-base of 7–15 cm, depending on the soil type and the amount of expected traffic. Then lay 5 cm of 2 mm gravel and roll it well before adding 5 cm of fine, partly washed gravel combined with clay particles so they bind together. Use a heavy roller to compact the gravel and keep it steady.

The disadvantage of using gravel is that you'll need to weed it regularly. Spraying with glyphosate or another weedkiller will help. If trees overhang the gravel and drop leaves, you'll need to rake it so it doesn't become stained and slippery.

COMBINATIONS

Many paved areas combine two or more of the above materials. Before selecting your combination, decide whether you want harmony or contrast in the finished path. Harmonious combinations have similar colours and are of similar origin, such as timber stepping stones and bark chip. Contrasting combinations can be based on colour or choice of materials, such as a white pebbled path edged with red bricks.

When selecting materials for a combined path, avoid a piecemeal appearance by limiting your choice to only two or three materials.

PAVING BONDS

Some bonds are stronger than others so your final choice may depend on the area you want to pave.

STACK
Stack is easy to lay, but it doesn't provide a strong bond, making it unsuitable for driveways.

STRETCHER
Stretcher creates a strong bond, and is useful on large straight areas and curves and in unusual layouts.

HERRINGBONE
Herringbone is a strong style that is particularly good for high-use areas. Plan the layout carefully to ensure you minimize the amount of cutting.

BASKETWEAVE
This pattern tends to reduce the apparent size of paved areas. It's most appropriate in square or rectangular situations.

SPIRAL
Spiral is an active pattern, creating movement from the centre.

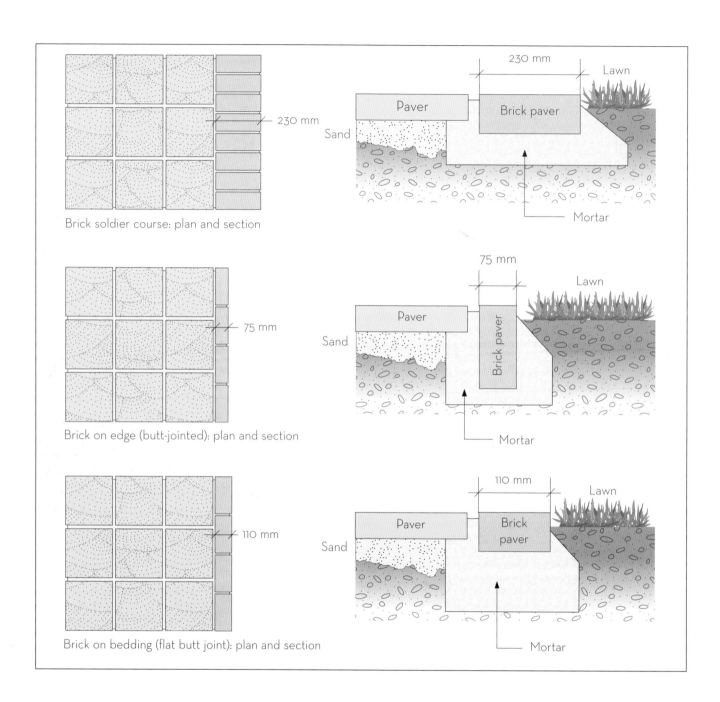

Brick soldier course: plan and section

230 mm

Lawn

Paver

Brick paver

Sand

Mortar

Brick on edge (butt-jointed): plan and section

75 mm

Lawn

Paver

Brick paver

Sand

Mortar

Brick on bedding (flat butt joint): plan and section

110 mm

Lawn

Paver

Brick paver

Sand

Mortar

ABOVE Securing paving perimeters.

PROVIDING AN EDGE

Any paved area requires an edge, which provides a perimeter to contain the paving, retain bedding sands and loose material, delineate other areas (such as garden beds) and even double as a mowing strip at the side of a lawn (see also page 96). This brick edging can be used with any paving material. If you haven't already paved the area, you can lay the edging first, or add it to an existing paved area.

1 Excavate the area for paving, compacting the substrate and foundation material and ensuring the area has adequate cross-fall for drainage. Set up string lines to indicate the final level.

2 Carefully excavate a trench through to the substrate, for the edging.

3 Place a layer of mortar 50–75 mm thick in the base of the trench.
4 Lay bricks on the mortar, either on edge, on end or in a bedding
  course. The way the bricks are bedded will depend on the depth of
  the substrate and foundation. Continue this process around the whole
  pavement perimeter or where erosion could pose a problem.
5 Start from one edge and work around the area, mortaring in the
  edge pavers to the brick edging to complete the pavement surface.

ABOVE Combine gravel with pavers to
accommodate awkward corners.

MAINTAINING YOUR PAVING

Regardless of the paving material you choose, you'll need to clean it
regularly as well as maintain it and fix various problems.

TREE ROOT DAMAGE

Over many years, tree roots can cause paved areas to crack or lift. If you
can't move or prune the tree, introduce a curve or circle to redirect the
paving around the troubled area. If the damage affects only part of a long
length of paving, create a slight, unobtrusive undulation to disguise it and
maintain the existing direction. Re-lay the pavers in the damaged section
and for several metres on both sides.

ABOVE Steam cleaning is a fast, efficient way to clean paving.

SUBSIDING SURFACES

Pavement subsidence is usually due to poor foundation and substrate preparation or to poor drainage, so it's important to prepare a sound foundation or base for the paving in the first place. Make sure you reduce any runoff, which can undermine the edge of the surface, thus eroding the foundation material.

Correct minor sinkages by lifting the surface layer of pavers, bricks or stone and adding extra bedding sand. If the problem is significant, loosen the surface of the base material, rake in dry cement, re-compact the base and replace the pavers.

CLEANING BRICK PAVING

Here are some tips for removing unsightly blemishes on paving.

- Efflorescence appears as a white, powdery discolouration on the surface of new bricks or pavers. Brush it off with a stiff-bristled brush or broom, or remove the deposit, sweep off excess salts and then wash the paving down with a weak 20:1 solution of water and acid.
- Contain growths such as mosses by ensuring moisture doesn't accumulate under paved surfaces. Expose affected areas to increased sunlight by removing or pruning back overhanging plants or trees. Use a spade or stiff-bristled brush to scrub away the bulk of the material, then treat the area with a bleach or fungicidal solution.
- Wear protective clothing when using an acid-based wash for removing stains. A mixture of 10:1 water and hydrochloric acid is appropriate, but the acid can cause discolouration and damage some timbers and metals. As a last resort, lift, turn over and re-lay the pavers.

CLEANING STONE AND TILES

Earthenware tiles are difficult to stain, and exposure to the elements usually keeps them clean. Sealing is the most practical option for barbecue areas or where grease or oil spills are likely to occur. Maintain slate and sandstone pavers by sweeping them regularly and washing them with clean water, or mix 5 litres of water with 250 millilitres of chlorine bleach and use it as a scrub.

MAINTAINING STONE AND UNIT PAVING

Large pre-cast or stone paving units tend to be quite porous and will soak up dirt, grease and moisture. There are various things you can do to minimize the time and effort needed to maintain this material and keep it looking its best.

- Make sure the area is adequately drained, with plenty of cross-fall.
- Don't let leaves settle on it for long periods.
- Keep metal objects or furnishings such as pots from having direct contact with the surface.
- Apply a surface sealant (available from tile shops, DIY or hardware stores) to minimise the porosity of the stone.
- Use bleach or chlorine solutions to clean unsealed pavers about once or twice a year.

Paving in a circular or spiral pattern creates a sense of movement.

TEXTURED SLAB PATIO

1 Once you have excavated and laid the hardcore base, position screed rails at 1.5 m intervals.

2 Put a layer of mortar on top of the hardcore and use a piece of timber, positioned on the rails, to screed the mortar flush with the screed rails.

3 Once you've removed the rails, fill any gaps that appear with mortar, then smooth them off with a trowel.

Since textured slabs do not imitate natural stone, they are ideally suited to gardens with a more contemporary feel. A patio laid with textured, non-slip paving is ideal for a family garden. It's also useful for the area around a swimming pool or in the shade of overhanging trees where moss may grow.

METHOD

1 Mark around and excavate the patio area, allowing for 75 mm of hardcore and 75 mm for the combined depth of the mortar bed and slabs. You can lay textured paving directly onto a screeded bed of mortar covering the entire area to be paved rather than place the mortar in ridges and furrows under each slab. After compacting a layer of hardcore, lay out screed rails across the hardcore base at about 1.5 m intervals, depending on the overall size of the patio. The rails should be lengths of timber as thick as the depth of the mortar bed — about 37 mm. There is no need to fix the rails, as their function is simply to support the timber used for the screeding process.

2 Make up a mix of fairly dry 1:6 mortar and tip it out onto the hardcore. Use a shovel to push the mortar around to a rough level before screeding. With a straight piece of timber laid from one screed rail to the other, screed the mortar to the correct level. Keep screeding the mortar until the whole area is flush with the tops of the rails. (*Note:* It's a good idea to screed out only as much mortar as you think you'll be able to pave over within an hour, or it will dry out and become unusable.)

3 Once you have finished screeding, carefully remove the rails without disturbing the mortar, and fill in the resulting gaps. You can do this by trowelling mortar into these gaps and then smoothing it off with the back of the trowel. Alternatively, gently run a straight edge of timber once more across the mortar to smooth off the filled-in gaps.

4 To show the finished height of the paving, set up string lines around the edges of the patio. Do this by setting up pegs in the four corners and running the string lines around them. Check for level. You can now begin to lay the slabs. It's important to spend time getting the first slab correctly positioned, since it will set the fall for all the others. Lay the slab in one of the corners, so that it lightly touches the two string lines marking the edges, and very gently tap it into position.

5 Continue to lay the slabs in the same manner, building up your pattern as you go. Jointing patterns can be truly random, with different slab sizes laid with no attempt made at an obvious pattern. Some manufacturers print out examples of random patterns for patios of various widths, which is useful for ordering the right quantity of slabs for each size.

MATERIALS

- Hardcore
- Pegs
- String
- Timber screed rails
- Timber straight edge
- Mortar
- Textured slabs of your choice
- Kiln-dried sand

TOOLS

- Groundwork tools
- Paving tools

5 Lay all the slabs in a random style, incorporating the occasional small slab to suit the design.

LEFT Laying slabs of different sizes and shapes creates interest in a contemporary garden.

6 Scrape away any mortar on the edges of the slabs so that you can butt-joint them neatly.

7 When you've finished laying the slabs, spread kiln-dried sand across them all, brushing it into the joints to seal them.

If you don't want to use a pattern at all, then it's best to let the supplier know the size of the area you are planning to pave. They should be able to advise you on the correct quantity of each slab size so that you are not left with too many big or small slabs that cannot be worked in. Whether or not you lay to a pattern, the most important thing to remember about random-style paving is that you should avoid long joints. To do this, try to lay occasional small squares around which the other slabs radiate.

6 Textured paving slabs have crisp, even edges, allowing them to butt up tightly against each other. You can lay them with mortar joints but they look better butt-jointed. Make sure you scrape away any particles of mortar from the slab edge so that the next slab fits tightly against it. If the slabs do not butt together well, there is a danger that the joints will begin to creep, and this will make the laying of subsequent slabs that much harder.

TO FINISH

7 When you've laid all the slabs, smooth off the mortar around the edge of the patio with a trowel. The next day, after the slabs have set firm, you'll be able to walk on them in order to spread fine, kiln-dried sand across the patio, brushing it in with a soft brush to seal the joints. After a few days the sand will combine with general dirt to form a tight seal, binding all the slabs together.

RIGHT Concrete slabs are ideal for paving around a pool or in an entertaining area.

PATHS

In ancient times there were few roads and these were largely tracks of dirt. When it rained, horses and carts churned them into deep furrows and impassable, slippery hellholes. A garden without paths can also be treacherous in the wet, and we wouldn't tolerate slipping in mud these days.

Paths are so basic and essential to our enjoyment and movement that we often forget how important they are. They are one of the most noticeable features of any garden. They have a profound practical and aesthetic value, making the garden accessible, habitable and appealing.

Too often paths are left to the end of the planning stage, but they should be an integral part of the initial design process. While their function is to provide a clean, firm and safe surface to walk on, they are also crucial to the character of a garden. Paths shape the land around us, delineate sectors and help establish views within a garden. Like pointers on a diagram or the grids on a map, they direct our attention to particular things. Choose materials that harmonize with the style and materials of the house itself to create an appealing landscape picture.

ABOVE A path made from stone slabs and fine, compacted gravel.

BASIC CONSIDERATIONS

When choosing materials for paths and paving (see page 125), consider the style and colour of the house and its features, the scale and proportion of the land you are working with, and the required function and suitability of the accessway.

Every garden has different types of paths, with each matched to a task. Choose materials based on the purpose and function of each and consider texture, pattern and colour to avoid visual clashes. Closer to the house, surfaces need to be permanent and hard-wearing. For well-trodden paths leading to and from the front and back doors or to the service areas within the garden, choose hard materials such as concrete or stone. Where foot traffic is light, 'soft' paths — including grass, bark chips or gravel laid directly onto a compacted surface — are suitable. Often these are secondary paths used to border garden beds or take us to areas some distance from the house.

Don't neglect practical matters too, such as glare and the need for maintenance. Cheaper, loose materials, such as gravel, bark and hard-packed, decomposed granite, often require regular cleaning and care and are more easily tracked into the house. Moss grows rapidly on shaded paths, weeds thrive in gravel, stains may mark stone or other surfaces, edgings need cutting and gravel may need weeding or regrading after rain. If you consider everyday care in the planning stage, you can save money and time later.

THE PURPOSE OF PATHS

Within the average garden, paths vary according to their function. For example, generally a path to the front door should be unobstructed by plants and of reasonable width (900 mm) so that you can carry furniture

ABOVE Herringbone is a strong bond that must be planned carefully.

LEFT A randomly laid path suits an informal garden.

OPPOSITE A herringbone paving pattern creates a sense of movement.

and goods along it. In other areas of the garden, paths can range from formal and decorative paths that lead the eye to a feature or focal point to subtle and rustic ones that provide casual access to a favourite shrub or part of the garden.

Paved paths not only direct traffic, they also reduce the amount of dirt and mud carried in from outdoors. As well as leading visitors to the main entrance of the house, they provide protection for plants and lawn. A winding path, for example, often gives rise to a sense of mystery as it leads the eye to the unseen, while a path leading straight to a door can give a sense of welcome.

Some paths are designed to simply direct you from point A to point B — for instance, from the laundry to the clothesline or to the dustbin. You won't want to manoeuvre your way around narrow corners or under overhanging bushes while carrying a heavy load of wet washing or

A well-planned path will last for years.

rubbish. A straight, unencumbered path is the most practical solution for paths leading to service locations within the garden — the garage, the compost bin, the vegetable patch and even the front door. For such frequently trodden paths, it's sensible to choose a hard, permanent surface such as concrete or stone or brick pavers laid on concrete.

As a rule, follow the most direct route to a destination. It's important to distinguish between a path for strolling along and an access path. If an access path winds without a valid reason, it's natural to take the most direct route — usually across a lawn. A worn track is the result. Architects refer to this as a 'desire line'.

A path that takes you around a garden is used by the homeowner maintaining the garden or by the occasional visitor. Because it's designed to weave through the garden, such a path can afford to take turns so you can view plants and features as you go. To make the turns more realistic, place an obstacle such as a large stone, birdbath or a clump of trees in the way so there is a valid reason for the path to veer, otherwise a track will soon appear along the most direct route.

PLANNING

Providing access for vehicles and pedestrians within a garden can often create problems, especially on steep or sloping sites. How these bold elements are positioned and integrated into the landscape is a vital aspect of your garden design. For example, large, unbroken areas of paving can be unsightly in a small garden, not to mention the problems they create because of reflected heat and water runoff. Permanent surfaces such as stone, concrete and brick are more expensive and harder to lay than less permanent surfaces and need more planning. Organize them at the beginning of the garden design process rather than as an afterthought. Look at changes of level: a path may need to include steps, a ramp and retaining walls if it's to be built on a slope.

Slopes should be no more than a gradient of 1 in 20. For driveways, 1 in 8 is acceptable, provided the surface is sufficiently coarse to enable traction. You can roughly calculate the rate of slope by using the following formula, where G per cent is the grade per cent.

G per cent = Rise or fall x 100

HORIZONTAL DISTANCE

Estimate the horizontal distance of a slope (the distance from the start of the slope to the end point) and the rise or fall from the lowest level. You'll need to estimate both without professional tools, but a landscape surveyor will be able to make more accurate measurements.

The gradient is expressed as a percentage, such as 5 per cent for a slope that's 1 in 20. A 10 per cent slope is the steepest path you can have without needing to add a ramp or steps.

Generally speaking, the wider the path the more imposing it is. For most houses the widest path is the approach path to the front door. Here you can afford to splash out a bit as it creates an impressive entrance. A path of 1.5 m allows two people to walk side by side with comfort. Where simple access is needed, a 1 m path is acceptable.

And think about maintenance. You won't want to create work for yourself. Small pockets of lawn hemmed in by paths create tasks.

COST

As a rule, hard materials are more expensive than soft materials. Stone is the most expensive paving material and is probably the hardest to lay well. Consequently, the need for skilled labour lifts the price even more.

You can soften the edges of paths with appropriate plantings.

PROPORTIONS

Paths often lead to or from paved terraces or patios and the materials tend to be the same for both, so you should include them in the same design package. The transition from living spaces to access routes requires careful consideration of the proportions of both path and patio. A skimpy path or tiny patio will ruin the design of your garden.

TYPES OF PATH

Garden paths give you the opportunity to create attractive combinations, such as blending stone and timber or gravel and brick — in fact, any possible combination. Clever combinations can make even humble materials extraordinary. For more information on paving materials, see pages 124–9.

BELOW Constructing a staggered stone path.

OPPOSITE Stepping stones suit a variety of garden styles.

CONSTRUCTING A PATH

The construction of the path will depend entirely upon its use and context, but here are some basic guidelines for ensuring that it's comfortable to use.

- In shady or damp areas, use roughly textured material to prevent slippery patches from developing.
- Don't use smooth materials on sloping paths as they can be slippery, especially when wet.
- Fill any gaps with sand or gravel so that the heels of your shoes don't catch in them.
- Where possible, choose the most direct route for the path and avoid tight curves.
- Provide cross-fall on solid paths so that water will drain off.
- Lay an agricultural drain beside solid paths to help remove the water more quickly and directly. This will reduce moisture intake and the associated algal growth.

BUILDING A STONE PATH

You can adapt this basic method for building a stone path to your situation. As with any path, thorough preparation is critical.

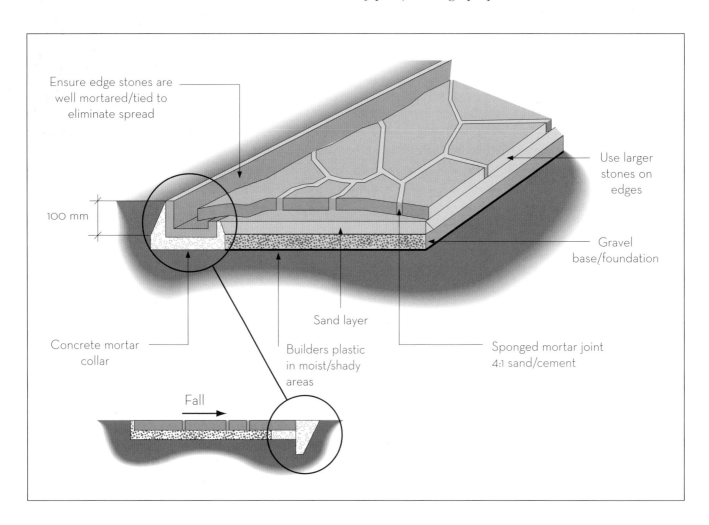

Ensure edge stones are well mortared/tied to eliminate spread

Use larger stones on edges

100 mm

Gravel base/foundation

Concrete mortar collar

Builders plastic in moist/shady areas

Sand layer

Sponged mortar joint 4:1 sand/cement

Fall

1. Excavate the area for the pathway to approximately 200 mm below the garden or lawn surface. Contour the substrate to fall to one or both sides, and allow for a small gutter on the lower side. Ensure that the gutter will drain to a suitable point.
2. Consolidate the substrate with a compactor or fire rake. You can lay a plastic membrane over the substrate to prevent groundwater soaking into the stone.
3. Spread coarse gravel or aggregate in the compacted gutter to the height of the adjoining substrate. You could put an agricultural pipe in the base if you wish.
4. Spread a 50 mm layer of road base or gravel over the remaining substrate and compact it.
5. Spread a 50–100 mm layer of coarse sand over the gravel to form the foundation material for the stone, then roughly adjust the level to suit.
6. Select larger stones to form the outer edge of the path, laying the straightest side of each stone towards the edge. Work each stone into the bedding sand so that it's level and has a cross-fall in the same direction as the substrate.
7. Use the smaller pieces of stone to lay the body of the path, setting them about 25 mm apart; ensure there are no continuous joints.
8. Mortar in the joints and finish them with a sponge.
9. Apply a mortar collar to both edges of the path, being careful not to completely cover the gutter on the lower side. Any water will run off the path into the drain, which will also help prevent the stone from absorbing ground and surface water.

STEPPING STONES

Stepping stones can be set in grass or gravel and be made of stone, concrete or wood. However, they need regular maintenance, so take this factor into account at the planning stage. Irregularly shaped stones tend to look more casual, while square or rectangular stones lend an air of order and formality. Timber makes an unusual path but don't lay it in moist locations.

BRICK AND TIMBER PATH

TOOLS

- Basic tool kit (see page 332)
- Circular saw or chainsaw
- Power drill and bits

MATERIALS

- Old railway sleepers
- 75 x 3.5 mm galvanized lost-head nails
- Coarse bedding sand
- Bricks
- Fine sand
- Cement

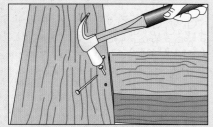

5 Place the cross sleepers in position to create the bays. Fix them together by skewing nails across the joint.

You can create wonderful paths by combining a variety of materials. You can base your chosen combination on texture, colour or size. This rustic path is constructed with old house bricks and railway sleepers.

PREPARATION

1 Make the initial preparations and lay out the path.
2 Set the string lines to the finished height and with an internal spacing of sleepers at 950 mm. To avoid cutting bricks, lay out the pattern on the ground to make sure the spacing fits your pattern.
3 Remove all vegetative material and excavate the ground to the depth of the railway sleepers.
4 Place the edging railway sleepers in position, setting them lengthwise to the two string lines.

LAYING THE SLEEPERS

5 Using either a circular saw or a chainsaw, cut the remaining railway sleepers to a length of 950 mm, to fit across the path. Create 570 mm long bays by placing these cross sleepers in position. The sleepers have butt or square joints, fixed together by skewing 75 x 3.5 mm bullet-head nails across the joint. Use three nails per joint to hold the sleeper framework together. Predrill the holes to prevent the wood from splitting. Using a spirit level, check the surface is level.
6 Prepare a notched screed board from a piece of timber that is wider than the path. Cut notches in both ends so that the screed board sits inside the edging rails to a depth of 68 mm. This depth allows 8 mm for later compaction of the bricks.
7 Fill the bays with sufficient coarse-grained bedding sand for screeding. Pack the sand firmly and screed off the excess with the notched screed board that you made.

ADDING THE BRICKS

8 Lay the bricks in a stretcher pattern (or use another pattern if you prefer). Lay the whole bricks first, and cut the half bricks with a club hammer and bolster chisel.
9 Firm the bricks down with a club hammer and a straight edge that is long enough to cover the width of the path. Move the straight edge down the path, hitting along the top of the wood with the hammer. As the bricks are held in place by the timber edging, there is no need to hold the edge bricks in place during this process.

7 Pack the sand firmly in the bays and level off the excess with the screed board you made.

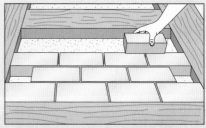

8 Lay the bricks in a stretcher pattern. Fill the bays with the whole bricks first, then cut the others to fit.

9 To ensure the bricks are level with the timber, compact them with a lump hammer and straight edge.

TO FINISH

10 Grout the bricks with fine sand or a dry mix (of 6 parts fine sand to 1 part cement). Use a stiff-bristled broom to sweep the sand into the joints. Sweep away the excess sand, and finish by hosing off with the nozzle set on fine spray so it doesn't move the grout out of the gaps. Carefully work across the surface in a systematic manner, making sure that you don't leave any cement on the surface, otherwise it will cause staining.

ABOVE LEFT This combination of bricks and sleepers looks good in an informal garden, but bear in mind that building combination pathways requires more organization and construction time.

DRIVEWAYS

A driveway is often the first thing a visitor notices. Try to blend the design of your driveway with the architectural style of your house and its garden setting. A straight driveway creates a formal approach to a home, whereas a curved or sweeping driveway appears more inviting.

A driveway must be firm, so the base needs more elaborate preparation than a simple path. It needs to be reinforced, often concreted, and it needs a certain amount of space on either side to allow unfettered access. A driveway should also be slightly higher in the middle so water flows away to the edges. The runoff can be directed towards lawns or garden beds, or it can be collected in a drain or water-retention pit.

ALLOWING SUFFICIENT ACCESS

Some existing houses already have a driveway. Many plain concrete driveways can be enhanced with an access path on one side or by resurfacing with pavers, stone or stamped concrete. The minimum width for a straight drive is 2100 mm. A curved drive should be at least 2700 mm wide. If the drive doubles as a path, allow enough room for a pedestrian to gain access when a car is parked.

Driveways can create other access problems. Unless you include a turning bay in your design, you'll have to reverse your car when leaving or entering the property. Reversing onto a busy road is dangerous so, where

ABOVE and TOP Steep driveways should be built from reinforced concrete, using heavy textures and parallel striations to help increase tyre grip.

RIGHT In a larger garden you can allow for a turning circle.

OPPOSITE Cross-section of a typical driveway construction.

possible, include a bay approximately 5–6 m from the turning side edge of the drive. The length of the bay will depend on the length of your car.

CONSTRUCTING A DRIVEWAY

If possible, a driveway should be sloped away from a garage, but if the driveway slopes downhill towards yours, install a drain at the entrance to the garage. Even on level sites, however, you should take care with driveways. They should be constructed on dry, solid substrate, and always on a foundation of compacted free-draining material, such as road base.

Many suppliers provide information on how to lay paving units, but as it's a labour-intensive job, it's often best left to the professionals.

PREPARING A SOLID FOUNDATION

The best foundation material for a driveway is a concrete bed, preferably reinforced. However, the method below provides a cost-effective alternative if your budget won't cover the cost of concrete.

1 Following any heavy machine work, use a fire rake or similar stiff-bladed tool to expose or dig out any sodden holes or loose rocks. The idea is to bring as much of the area down to solid substrate as you can. If the substrate is rock, then expose as much of it as possible.
2 Use a plate compactor to consolidate the substrate over the area, working over it until it's solid underfoot.
3 Fill any fissures, springs or sinks between the substratum levels with dry concrete mix, then compact the mix and water it in. (This method can also be used to fix sunken driveways.)
4 Prepare the foundation material of road base or crusher dust by mixing in one bag of cement per cubic metre of foundation material to provide extra solidity. Spread it with a rake or by machine.
5 Level the surface with a straight edge to the appropriate level, and use a plate compactor to compact the material.
6 Water the material in lightly and prepare the area for paving.

MATERIALS FOR DRIVEWAYS

The material you choose ultimately depends on the location and your budget.
- Concrete is long-lasting and sturdy.
- Asphalt is ideal for a long driveway.
- Bricks and pavers are neat and economical, but check that they have the necessary load-bearing capacity.
- Larger units are suitable for larger properties.
- Lighter colours make the area look larger as they reflect more light.
- If you use the same colour for the surface as you use on the walls of your house, the area will appear larger.
- Highly textured materials are suitable for steeper inclines.
- Smaller units are more labour-intensive.

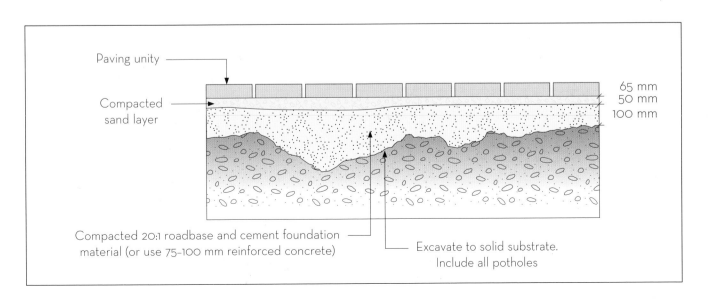

Paving unity

Compacted sand layer

65 mm
50 mm
100 mm

Compacted 20:1 roadbase and cement foundation material (or use 75–100 mm reinforced concrete)

Excavate to solid substrate. Include all potholes

ABOVE A wild or wooded garden needs steps that blend into the landscape. These steps, made from packed earth and logs, provide a gentle walk up a substantial slope.

STEPS

Steps are really paths for slopes, allowing safe passage from one level to another. But steps can also be a design element in their own right. Broad, deep steps look stately and give a generous sense of proportion to a design, while wide steps can double as additional garden seating and be worked into the general design statement as a focal point, something that draws the eye or leads you on to explore the vicinity.

You can also use steps as an architectural feature or as a staging post for container plants, matched to the style of your garden. For instance, for a grand statement you could extend the width of your steps to cover the entire length of a garden terrace.

An alternative for going from one level to another is to use ramps, which have the major advantage of enabling you to move wheelbarrows, mowers and other tools uphill. However, deep, shallow steps also provide access for barrows and take up only a quarter of the space. Steps can be built on a gradient as steep as 1 in 2, whereas the gradient of a ramp should not exceed 1 in 8. For gradients in between these two extremes, try a stepped ramp, which is a step and ramp combination. Low risers and long treads built on a gently sloping gradient make it easier to push or pull implements up the slope.

Steps that have a gentle rise have a leisurely pace and are more comfortable to use. Although steps connect two separate points, they can be allowed to meander a little in order to find the easiest route.

DESIGNING A FLIGHT OF STEPS

Steps have two elements. The vertical part of the step is called the riser and the flat surface is the tread. The relationship between treads and risers is fluid, depending on the function of the step but the tread should always be consistent and of equal size. Walking is a rhythmic exercise. When you walk and climb up stairs, you work up a momentum, but if the size of the step varies with each footfall, your rhythm is interrupted. This makes stumbling and tripping more likely.

A good all-purpose guide is to design steps with a riser of 150 mm and a tread of 300 mm. The depth of the tread combined with twice the height of the riser should add up to 600 mm for each step. The individual measurements of riser and tread can be varied but the proportions should always be the same. Generally, treads should have a 5–10 mm fall to the front to prevent water from pooling, otherwise the step will become slippery and dangerous.

On steep slopes, a continuous line of steps can be hard to climb and psychologically daunting, but you can overcome these twin obstacles by combining steps with landings. Allow for a landing every eight steps. If you want to slow down movement, make the tread wider but reduce the size of the riser proportionately. 'Slower' steps are good in the decorative part of the garden but 'faster' steps — ones that have a shallow tread and deeper riser — are better for approaches to service areas.

For more information on steps, see pages 32–7.

ABOVE Brick risers and stone treads are an attractive combination.

LEFT Circular steps leading to an archway lend a sense of drama and surprise to the garden — you're not sure what you'll find on the other side of the hedge.

DIFFERENT TREATMENTS

The materials used for steps should blend with the materials used for paths. Construct the tread, the flat surface, using the same material you used for paving elsewhere in the garden. The risers can be made from other materials if you prefer. If your paths are made of brick, for instance, the treads should also be in brick but the riser can be made from a squared block of stone. Sturdy timber railway sleepers are often used as risers because their height provides a comfortable stepping height.

There are lots of other combinations to choose from. In a wooded area or shrubbery you might choose logs as risers and packed earth for the treads. Decomposed granite is a good alternative to packed earth as it's almost as firm as concrete but has a pleasant earthy quality that concrete can never imitate. Selected hardwood timbers may be suitable for steps, but most softwood trees tend to rot after a few years. A better alternative is to use pressure-treated pine.

Stone paths are durable and attractive, but they need to be laid carefully with a firm foundation to ensure they don't split or become undermined by water during periods of high rainfall.

ABOVE An outdoor dining area needs shelter from the sun and rain.

OUTDOOR LIVING AREAS

Using parts of the garden for outdoor entertaining or meals is a concept that has become very popular in recent years. It was inspired by the Mediterranean lifestyle, which provides ideas on how to integrate these areas with the rest of the garden and the house.

Outdoor living spaces should draw people to them, and so the elements used in their construction should be attractive as well as provide the necessary form. Selecting the right position for such an area is once again part of the overall design process. Here are some points to consider.

- A sunny position is preferable for most areas. However, you will want to use this area as often as possible and so you'll need shading devices such as pergolas, awnings or deciduous trees in summer.
- Make sure the position has good air circulation but is protected from prevailing winds.
- There should be direct access to the kitchen or barbecue so the journey from cooker to table doesn't take too long.

COURTYARDS

Small gardens and courtyards can be outdoor rooms — places for relaxing on sunny days and for dining out on balmy evenings. Most suburban houses have fairly small gardens, a trend that is set to stay with increasing pressure on development land. But it is possible to create wonderful gardens in restricted spaces and there are many books on the subject.

You can transform a small space into an attractive, usable extension of your home's living space to make an outdoor room. This can be intimate — with lattice smothered in perfumed creepers, for instance — or cheery and portable, which is ideal for those in rented accommodation.

First, decide on the landscape features — for example, raised planters, water features and paved areas — you want to include. Then create your design, integrating these elements but emphasizing decorative shapes and detailed design elements. The design should be practical, but don't limit yourself to bricks and concrete, as the resulting space will probably be hot and uncomfortable. Where possible, use plants and shade structures to provide cooler areas.

Here are some points to consider.

- A focal point makes an outdoor space more inviting. Create a highlight such as a garden seat, potted urn or fountain.
- Lighting helps to create a mood and gives a small garden depth.
- Plant a tree, or build a pergola or raised garden beds to help enclose an area and convert it into an outdoor room.
- Decking and paving, unusual types of foliage and architectural shapes can add interest, definition and substance to small spaces.
- Mirrors, hedges, *trompe l'oeil* and manipulation of perspective can all make a space appear larger than it is.

Remember also to make adequate provision for drainage before you begin landscaping (see page 52). If there is no provision for water collection and runoff, your courtyard will become damp over time.

OUTDOOR DINING AREAS

The size of your outdoor room should reflect the scale of the landscape and buildings, but you should also consider the number of people you'll need to accommodate. The table below tells you how much space to allow for easy circulation around the table, depending on the number of people.

The materials used to construct the area should be chosen to maximize comfort and minimize maintenance, although maintaining a paved area is much easier than maintaining other parts of the garden. For more information, see 'Paving' on page 124.

Use paving, plantings and shelter to create a feeling of enclosure in your outdoor living areas.

MINIMUM SIZES FOR AL FRESCO DINING

NUMBER OF PEOPLE	AREA REQUIRED
4–8	3 x 4 m
6–12	4 x 6 m
12–24	6 x 10 m
30+	8 x 12 m

MOSAIC TABLE TOP

TOOLS

- Router
- Brush
- Pencil
- Ruler
- Protractor
- Compass (see diagram 7 on page 154)
- Stylus (optional)
- Goggles and mask
- Tile nippers
- Mixing containers
- Palette knife
- Rubber gloves
- Rubber squeegee
- Rags and cloths
- Sponges

MATERIALS

- 20 mm plywood*, 1000 mm in diameter
- Water-based sealer suitable for exterior use
- Large ceramic floor or wall tiles: red, dark green, orange, lemon–green, light green, cream, mustard, patterned mix for border
- Tracing paper (optional)
- Carbon paper (optional)
- Multi-purpose tile adhesive
- Black grout
- * A high-grade waterproof plywood is recommended for exterior use.

The top of this striking table is cut from a large piece of plywood, and the wrought iron base and legs were especially made by a blacksmith.

PREPARATION

1 Using a router, cut out a round piece of plywood measuring 1000 mm in diameter. Alternatively, pay extra to have your timber supplier cut out the table top for you.

2 You may already have a table with a glass or wooden top that you can use. Remove the glass and insert the piece of plywood in its place. Otherwise, take the wood to a blacksmith and ask for a 25 mm wide metal band to be made to support the table top. You'll also need 12 small nail holes to be drilled in the centre of the band, spacing them 260 mm apart (the plywood is held in place with nails). Decide on the design of the legs for your table.

3 If you plan to use the table outdoors, waterproof the wood with a water-based sealer. Allow it to dry.

DRAWING THE DESIGN

4 Following the top diagram on page 155, draw the basic design for the table. Alternatively, use a photocopier to enlarge the pattern. Using carbon paper and the stylus, transfer the design to your table. (If you prefer to mosaic a square table, this design can be adapted to fit. Keep the star in the centre of the design, and following the same measurements given in the top diagram on page 155, draw the design using squares instead of circles.)

5 If you are using the diagram to draw the design, first locate the exact centre of the plywood circle and mark it with a pencil. Draw a line through this point from one side of the table to the other.

6 Divide the table into eight even 'pie' sections. To do this, place the protractor on the pencil line and mark off three angles of 45 degrees. Place the protractor on the opposite side and do the same. Following the marked points, rule up the lines.

7 Using a compass and the measurements given on the diagram, draw three circles on the table. If you don't have a compass, use the string and pencil method (see diagram 7 on page 154). Draw a star in the centre of the table.

FIXING THE TESSERAE

8 When working on a large table such as this, it's difficult to prepare all the tiles in advance. Wearing goggles, cut enough tiles to complete one area of the table, then cut more tiles as you need them.

SAFETY

When cutting mosaic tiles, always take the following safety precautions.

- Protect your eyes with goggles or glasses.
- Cut tiles at arm's length to avoid small shards flying up and cutting your face.
- Wear a mask so that you don't inhale dust or glass particles.

LEFT This table will take several sittings to complete, but the results will be stunning. To ensure the surface is level, only one type of tile (rather than a mix of materials) is used. If you like, use an old glass or timber table that needs revamping.

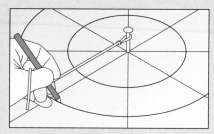

7 Holding the string taut, draw a circle around the board.

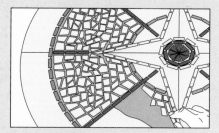

11 Use cream tesserae to fill in the eight segments between the outer and middle circles.

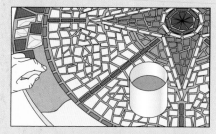

14 Apply the adhesive to one area of the border and fix a mixture of plain and patterned tesserae.

16 Using the rubber squeegee, spread black grout over the surface, ensuring all the cracks are filled.

9 Starting in the centre of the table, fill the inner circle with red tesserae cut into eight wedges. Spread the adhesive onto the table with a palette knife and fix the tesserae in place. Surround the wedges with a row of thin, rectangular red tesserae.

10 Using these thin, rectangular-shaped tesserae, follow the pencilled design to establish outlines for all the geometric elements. Use dark green for the outer circle, orange for the middle circle (note that the orange circle is not continuous, but is interrupted by the green star and the red radiating lines) and lemon–green for the inner circle. Use red for the eight radiating lines and light green to outline the star. Without using adhesive, position all the cut tesserae on the table to ensure that they will fit your pattern. When you are happy with their placement, fix them with the adhesive, working on one section at a time. It may be easier in some areas to butter the backs of the tesserae with the adhesive and press them onto the surface: if you apply the adhesive directly on the table you will obscure your drawn lines.

11 Using irregularly shaped cream tesserae, fill in the eight large segments between the outer and middle circle. Apply the adhesive directly to the surface, working on small areas at a time, and fix the tesserae in place.

12 Fill the small areas between the middle orange circle and the star with mustard tesserae.

13 Use a mixture of wedge and large rectangular-shaped dark green tesserae to complete the star.

14 Use a combination of plain and patterned tesserae to fill in around the border.

TO FINISH

15 Before grouting the table, allow 24 hours for the adhesive to dry. Use black grout to provide contrast with the brightly coloured design.

16 Wearing rubber gloves and using the rubber squeegee, apply liberal amounts of the grout over the surface. Use your hands to push the grout into any cracks that you may have missed. Wipe off the excess grout with the squeegee or with a cloth or rag and allow the mosaic to stand for 5–10 minutes.

17 With a damp sponge, and rinsing regularly, wipe over the surface to reveal the mosaic. This may take several changes of water.

18 Once the mosaic is dry, a light film of grout residue will appear. Use a combination of slightly damp and clean, dry rags to polish the table.

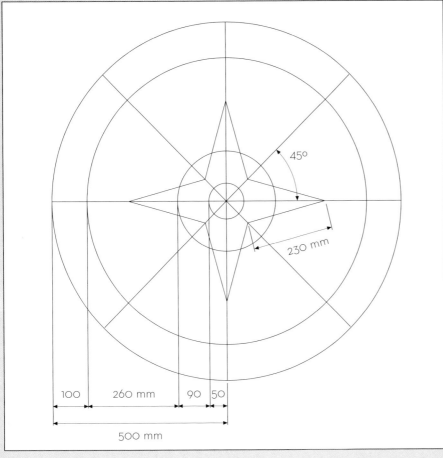

LEFT Insert a nail into the centre of the board and tie a piece of string to it. Measure out the string to the required length and tie a loop in the other end. Slip the loop over a pencil and, holding the string taut, draw a circle on the board. To draw circles of different sizes, adjust the length of the string.

BELOW Outline the basic elements of the design, as shown, and then fill in the areas using tesserae of different shapes and sizes.

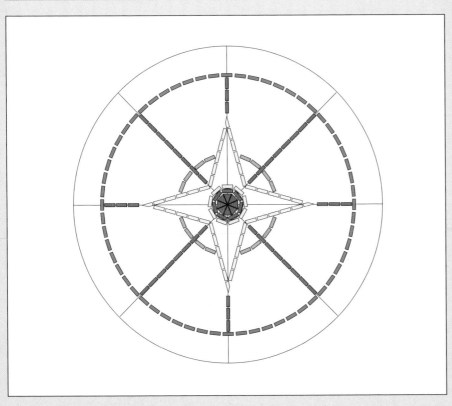

BARBECUES

Before you start building a barbecue, consider which type will suit your home and lifestyle best. A built barbecue can become a feature in the garden landscape and an integral part of your garden lifestyle, but it will require a considerable amount of work to build, so decide whether you'll use it often enough to justify the effort involved. A portable unit may suit your lifestyle better. Consider these points.

- Ideally you'll need a level site that is close to the house. The site will also need to be large enough for the cook and helpers to move safely around the barbecue. If you have to build the barbecue any distance from the house, plan paths or walkways to link them.

- You can build a barbecue that uses solid fuel or one with a drop-in gas cook top. If you have plenty of wood on hand for a solid fuel barbecue, then fuel will cost you nothing.

- The cost of building a barbecue increases in proportion to the size and detail of the construction. Include in your budget the cost of the fuel as well as features such as retaining walls or screens, paving or other surfacing, any shade structure, seating and lighting and power.

- Decide on whether you need lighting in your barbecue area during the planning stage so that electrical conduits can be run beneath any paving or concrete.

- If you don't have the time and basic bricklaying skills to build your own barbecue, be prepared to pay someone to do it for you.

BELOW The chimney on this barbecue can draw smoke from one or both fires at the same time. A cap directs smoke away from the cooking area.

DECIDING ON A DESIGN

The design of your barbecue will depend on how much space you have, the type of fuel and whether you need preparation areas and storage for solid fuel or gas bottles. You'll also need to consider whether to include a chimney and any other structures such as seating, planter boxes, walls or pergolas. Finally, consider how much you can afford to spend.

MATERIALS

The materials you choose for your barbecue will depend on the style of your home, the formality or informality of your garden design, your budget and, of course, the availability of the materials.

Brick barbecues are the most common because of their ease of construction and their ability to tie the house and garden landscape together. If the barbecue is sited close to the house and the house is brick, you should choose bricks that match it. If this isn't necessary, you should select bricks that will be able to withstand the heat of the barbecue, particularly if it is wood-fired. If possible, choose well burnt, dry-pressed bricks and avoid the softer calcium-silicate bricks. Your local brick supplier will be able to advise you.

Stone barbecues are also popular in areas where rock and sandstone can be easily purchased. Rock lends itself to a natural, rustic setting and is an ideal choice for wood-fired, informal designs. Choose carefully, however, as river boulders and limestone can 'explode' when subjected to great heat. Sandstone is a softer, more porous stone and allows for shaping and facing, making it a popular choice in more formal settings. You can buy it in regular geometric shapes in either block or slab form. Sandstone is also available in split, irregular forms.

DIMENSIONS

You'll need to consider the dimensions of not only the unit but also those of the surface areas that will be used for cooking and preparation. You'll also need to include space in your plan for the firebox or gas unit as well as storage for solid fuel, gas bottles and other accessories.

If you are working in brick or cut stone, design the barbecue to suit full brick or block dimensions. This will make laying easier and you'll be able to avoid unnecessary cutting. Brick sizes vary considerably but a standard brick size is 215 mm long x 102 mm wide x 65 mm high. The table on page 156 gives the numbers of bricks you'll need for making up various lengths or heights. Adjust the measurements to suit.

HOTPLATE

The size of the area required for cooking depends on the number of people to be fed. An average sized cooking plate of 930 x 600 mm caters for 12–15 people. If you usually cook for smaller numbers, reduce the plate size to 690 x 600 mm, and then if you occasionally need extra space, you can bring out or hire a portable barbecue to supplement it.

TYPES OF FUEL

The commonly used fuels for firing barbecues are solid fuels or gas or electricity.

- Wood and charcoal fires require patience, as you need flames to heat the hotplate, but you can't cook until they subside and leave a stable hotplate temperature.
- Gas is clean and efficient, and you can accurately control the temperature with the turn of the knob.
- Electricity is also clean and efficient, and provides excellent temperature control. However, plug-in household power has a maximum of 240 volts, so you can only use it to fuel a small unit.

BRICK MEASUREMENTS*

NUMBER OF BRICKS	LENGTH (MM)	HEIGHT (MM)
1	225	75
2	440	140
3	655	205
4	870	270
5	1085	335
6	1300	400
7	1505	465
8	1730	530
9	1945	595
10	2160	660
11	2375	725
12	2590	790
13	2805	855
14	3020	920
15	3235	985

* Including allowance for 10 mm joints. To include half a brick, add 108 mm to the length.

Make sure the plate size will suit the brickwork dimensions. The two plate sizes given on page 155 will fit inside standard brickwork with a 10 mm gap all round for expansion. You can cut the plate to any size. If the steel plate is too thin, it will eventually buckle. A good thickness is 6–8 mm.

PREPARATION AREA

Most barbecue designs include a preparation area next to the hotplate on one or both sides. The size of this area can vary according to your needs and the space available. If the area is going to be used to store and prepare food before cooking as well as serve guests, an area twice the size of the hotplate would be useful.

When designing the preparation area, include an appropriate finish so that it will be easy to clean. Surfaces such as concrete and stone attract dirt and grease over time whereas ceramic tiles, sealed terracotta or slate, for example, can be wiped clean.

WORKING HEIGHT

Consider the height of the preparation and cooking areas. An average height is between 850 and 950 mm, but if the cook is particularly tall or short, you should adjust the height to suit. Thirteen courses of brickwork will give a height of 855 mm, while 14 courses will give 920 mm.

STORAGE

Including preparation areas in your design often creates space for storage below. You can either add doors or leave these storage areas open to the weather. You can install shelves for utensils or equipment or use the space to store solid fuel or gas bottles.

If your barbecue is to be a gas-fired unit, it's safer to store the gas bottle away from the burners and out of the weather. A small opening can be left in the brick jointing during construction so that the gas line can be connected to the burners. Incorporate this into your planning and design stage or drill out a hole later. If doors are to be added to these areas, allow adequate ventilation in case of gas leakage. A gap at the top and bottom will allow air to circulate while protecting the area from the weather.

ABOVE On either side of this barbecue, a brick wall with two arms supports a slatted seat that can double as a preparation area.

SURFACING MATERIAL

Select the surfacing material for the area carefully to provide an easy-care, comfortable and durable surround for the barbecue. Your choice will depend on the style of the house and landscaping, and your choice of material for the barbecue itself. For example, a barbecue constructed of sandstone blocks will often look best surrounded by sandstone flagging.

Popular materials for surfacing the area around a barbecue include: brick pavers of clay or concrete, house bricks, concrete (either plain, stencilled or stamped), exposed aggregate, slate, tiles (terracotta or concrete), sandstone and timber decking. If you use terracotta or slate, note that they provide a non-slip surface only if they are unsealed, but they are then likely to absorb grease from the barbecue. Sandstone is porous and will show stains and discolour over time. It can be sealed, but make sure you check the manufacturer's instructions on a variety of sealants to select the best one for your paving.

Lawn is not a good choice for a barbecue surround, as it tends to wear and remain wet underfoot. Try to avoid loose materials such as gravel as they can be unstable, especially when you're carrying platters of food.

SHELTER

You may need to include some protection from the weather, depending on how exposed the barbecue is to wind and sun. When looking at the alternatives, consider the probable cost, ease of construction (and your level of skill) and how each will complement your house and garden.

Some possible structures to choose from are:

* roofing attached to the house;
* a separate cabana-type structure;
* a pergola or other open timber framework that can be covered with light material such as lattice, canvas, overlapping fibreglass or metal sheeting;
* a trellis structure, perhaps used with a pergola to support climbing plants such as ornamental grape; and
* a screen or hedge of plants.

There are also less permanent forms of shelter, such as umbrellas.

BARBECUE WITH STORAGE

TOOLS

- Bricklaying tools (see page 162)
- Circular saw or tenon saw
- Pencil
- Hammer
- Drill with timber and masonry bits
- Screwdriver
- Cork sanding block
- Router (optional)
- Try square
- Rubber mallet

TYING BRICK WALLS

To tie spur walls into the main wall, cut a notch halfway across and along the brick for the main wall and remove one-quarter of a brick for the spur wall. Alternatively, you can use brick ties.

You'll need basic bricklaying and carpentry skills to build this simple brick barbecue. The cooking area is flanked by terrazzo preparation areas while timber doors conceal the three storage areas below.

MATERIALS*

- Concrete for slab: 0.25 m³ ready-mixed, or cement, sand and 10 mm aggregate
- 100 x 50 mm timber for formwork
- Timber pegs and nails
- Steel reinforcing mesh: 2300 x 800 mm. See page 346.
- Bar chairs for supporting mesh
- 220 full bricks and 30 half bricks
- Portland cement, bricklayers sand, lime and plasticiser for mortar
- Two 860 x 740 mm terrazzo slabs and one 685 x 190 mm terrazzo slab (to fit behind gas unit)
- Two-burner gas barbecue unit with sand tray
- Hot rock tray and rocks
- Gas bottle, regulator and hoses
- * Finished size: 2380 x 710 mm and 897 mm high. Measurements are based on a brick size of 215 x 102 x 65 mm. Purchase the gas unit before starting to build and adjust the measurements to suit. Materials for doors are on page 162.

THE DESIGN

The basic structure consists of a wall with four projecting arms. In the centre bay a two-burner gas unit (divided into hotplate and grill and fuelled by bottled gas) is suspended between the side terrazzo slabs. A hot rock tray beneath the grill and plate disperses the flame, providing an evenly heated cooking surface. A sand tray beneath the unit collects spills from the cooking surface.

On either side of the cooking area are terrazzo slab preparation areas. Below are three storage areas, with space for the gas bottle.

THE BRICKWORK

1   Set out and lay the 2500 x 800 mm concrete slab (see page 340–6).
2   Following the base course set-out diagram on page 163, construct the two end corners and two end arms to 11 courses of brickwork.

LEFT In this barbecue the gas unit is supported on the side slabs. You can ensure a neat fit by purchasing the unit and adjusting the layout before you begin to build your barbecue.

As you work, use the spirit level to check for vertical and trueness on the rake.

3   Fix a string line in place between the corners, using two corner blocks. Also fix a string line across the front of the two end arms. These string lines can be moved upwards as each course of brickwork is completed. Complete the remainder of the back wall and the two centre arms to 11 courses, building the centre arms at the same time as the back wall so that you can check the relative heights as you work. Tie the centre arms into the back wall on the fourth and eighth courses (see the bottom box opposite). Allow the mortar to dry for 2–3 days before proceeding.

SIDE STORAGE AREAS

4   Cut the jambs and headers for the side bays, adjusting them to fit. Cut a 25 mm deep housing in each end of the headers. Rout a 15 x 15 mm rebate along the bottom front edge of the headers for the top of the door to fit against. Glue and nail each header with 50 x 2.8 mm nails on top of the two jambs.

5   Place the frame in the opening, 50 mm in from the face of the brickwork. Using a pencil, mark two drill locations on each side, making sure the hole will be in the centre of a brick. You do not want to drill into a joint. Drill the holes to accommodate 50 mm x 8 gauge countersunk screws. Place the frame in position, making sure it's vertical, and use a pencil to mark the position of the holes onto the brickwork. Remove the frame and use a masonry bit to drill 30 mm deep holes into the brickwork to accommodate plastic plugs. Tap the plugs into the brickwork before replacing the frame and fixing it in position with 50 mm screws.

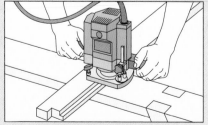

4 Rout a rebate along the bottom front edge of the header to prevent the door from swinging iinwards.

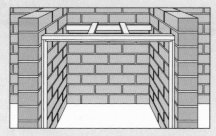

8 Fit the tray support piece to the back wall, sit the tray rails on it and fix them to the door header.

BRICKLAYING TOOLS

- Measuring tape
- String line
- Spirit level
- Builders square
- Spade
- Hammer
- Steel mesh cutters or angle grinder
- Shovel
- Wheelbarrow
- Wooden float
- 75 mm edger
- Green masonry pencil
- Mortar board
- Bricklaying trowel
- Gauge rods (if required)
- Corner blocks
- Club hammer and bolster chisel
- Scutch hammer
- Jointing tool (optional)
- Small brush
- Sponge and bucket

MATERIALS FOR DOORS*

PART	MATERIAL	LENGTH	NO.
Header (side areas)	50 x 50 mm WRC	590 mm	2
Header (centre area)	50 x 50 mm WRC	710 mm	1
Jamb (side areas)	50 x 25 mm WRC	840 mm	4
Jamb (centre area)	50 x 25 mm WRC	670 mm	2
Tray support (back)	50 x 25 mm timber	710 mm	1
Shelf support	50 x 25 mm timber	500 mm	4
Ledger (side doors)	50 x 25 mm WRC	545 mm	4
Ledger (centre doors)	50 x 25 mm WRC	330 mm	4
Brace (side doors)	50 x 25 mm WRC	800 mm	2
Brace (centre doors)	50 x 25 mm WRC	600 mm	2
Tray rail	50 x 75 mm timber	500 mm	2
Cladding (side doors)	88 x 10 mm shiplap	810 mm	14
Cladding (centre doors)	88 x 10 mm shiplap	640 mm	10
Shelf	88 x 10 mm shiplap	590 mm	14

Other: Twenty plastic plugs for attaching timber frame to bricks; 50 x 2.8 mm galvanized lost-head twist nails; 30 x 2 mm galvanized lost-head twist nails; 50 mm x 8 gauge galvanized countersunk screws; eight hinges; four door knobs; four magnetic door latches; abrasive paper; finish of choice.
* Western red cedar (WRC) was used for all timberwork. The timber sizes given are nominal. Adjust lengths to fit your structure.

6 Take two shelf supports. Place them against the side walls in one side bay, about 460 mm above the level of the concrete slab. Once again make sure that the drill location is in the centre of a brick. Drill the holes and fix the supports in the same way as the door jambs. Repeat with the other two shelf supports in the other side bay.

CENTRE STORAGE AREA

7 Cut the pieces for the centre bay framework. The jambs reach to the top of the eighth course of bricks. Repeat the process in steps 4 and 5.
8 Cut the tray support piece to length. Drill holes and fix it on the back wall, 50 mm below the top of the header. Sit the tray rails on the support piece, butting them against the header. Nail them in place.

DOOR CONSTRUCTION

9 The doors are constructed to allow a 3 mm gap all round (the gap at the bottom provides air circulation for the storage areas within). The side doors on this unit are 810 x 545 mm while the centre doors are

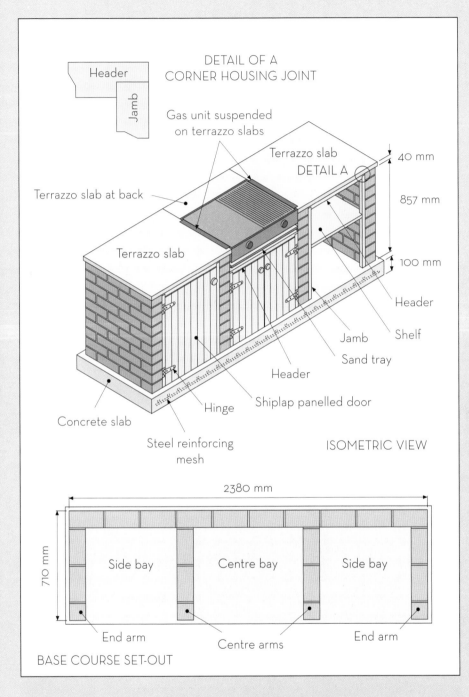

DETAIL OF A CORNER HOUSING JOINT

Header

Jamb

Gas unit suspended on terrazzo slabs

Terrazzo slab at back

Terrazzo slab

DETAIL A

40 mm

857 mm

100 mm

Header

Shelf

Jamb

Sand tray

Header

Shiplap panelled door

Hinge

Concrete slab

Steel reinforcing mesh

Terrazzo slab

ISOMETRIC VIEW

2380 mm

710 mm

Side bay

Centre bay

Side bay

End arm

Centre arms

End arm

BASE COURSE SET-OUT

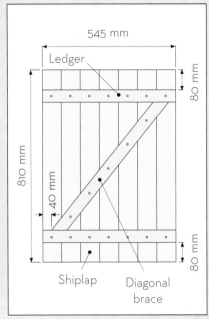

545 mm

Ledger

80 mm

810 mm

40 mm

80 mm

Shiplap

Diagonal brace

ABOVE Inside view of the side door.

LEFT Isometric view and basic course set-out.

640 x 330 mm, but adjust them to fit your unit. Cut shiplap panelling slightly longer than is required. For each door lay out the boards, inside face up, butting them loosely together.

10 Cut the top and bottom ledgers to length. Square up the ends and fix them to the inside of the shiplap. Nail through the ledgers with 30 x 2 mm nails to fix each panel in place.

11 Place the diagonal brace in position: it should be angled from the bottom inside to the top outside and 40 mm in from each side. Next, mark the angles with a pencil and cut them. Fix the brace in place.

MAKING A GOOD FIRE

You might have a barbecue with a solid fuel fire. The secret of a good fire is plenty of air. If the fuel is set on a grate, air can be drawn up from underneath and into the flue and up the chimney, which helps produce a good draught. The opening to the flue should be 2–3 courses high and the top should be level with the hotplate so that smoke is drawn up the chimney. If the opening is too small, smoke will build up and flow out of the front of the barbecue.

Square up the top and bottom of the door and cut to the exact length that you require.

12 Lightly sand and paint or stain the doors. Fit a pair of hinges to each door, centred 100 mm from top and bottom. This ensures that each hinge is fixed where the ledger is located. Fit door knobs at the height of the top ledger for strength. Fit magnetic door latches to complete the doors.

TO FINISH

13 Construct the shelves as for the doors, using shiplap and offcuts for ledgers (a diagonal brace is not needed). Place each shelf in position and fix it with 30 x 2 mm nails.

14 The large terrazzo slabs sit over the side bays while the small one fits behind the gas unit. To fit the slabs, spread mortar on top of the brickwork with a trowel. Ensure there is a good bed that will compress down to a thickness of about 10 mm. Lift each slab and place it carefully in position so that there is an even overlap all around (you will need a helper). Check that the distance between the slabs will accommodate the gas unit. Tamp the slabs into position with a rubber mallet and check for level in all directions. Allow to set and dry.

15 Drop the barbecue unit into position. Slide the sand tray beneath the unit on the timber rails. Connect the gas and light the barbecue.

RIGHT Built from dry-pressed bricks laid in a rustic style, this barbecue includes an area for chargrilling, a removable hotplate, a rotisserie unit and a sink with running water.

OPPOSITE Sandstone is used on the corners and top to great effect on this natural gas barbecue.

ABOVE In the right setting, steps can double as bench seating.

ABOVE RIGHT To protect yourself from the strongest summer sun, position dining settings in some dappled shade.

OPPOSITE ABOVE This timber bench is as much a garden ornament as a place to sit and relax.

SEATS

A garden can be both a retreat and a venue for social gatherings. Make sure there is at least one spot where you can sit and relax.

Types of garden seating vary according to their function. Seats for reading and relaxing are more generous in scale than those for dining, and must be comfortable. Whether you add cushions is up to you, but always try before you buy. If you like relaxing and snoozing in the garden, you'll need some comfortable recliners.

Another type of garden seat is used more as a focal point than as a spot for lingering. Seats within a garden can be used for a short rest, a chance to take in a view or to sort out seed packets or tools before you get back to planting. Here comfort is a less important factor. Stone, tree seats, simple tree trunks and rough-hewn logs all fall into this category.

POSITIONING YOUR SEATING

A recliner for reading, a hammock between two trees, a dining setting for Sunday brunch — each requires different amounts of space and decoration. A breakfast nook is best sited where the morning sun will warm and invigorate you, whereas a dining area for lunch should allow for shade from the midday summer sun.

Good siting is the key to effective relaxation, so take care with your garden design to position your dining and entertaining areas well. Consider the levels of sun and shade at different times of the year as well as exposure to strong winds. In summer, a north-facing position will be cooler than a south-facing one, and deciduous trees are more versatile in a small garden than evergreens. These allow sun in winter and shade in summer.

A PRIVATE SANCTUARY

For contemplation, try to position a seat away from the house. Create a mood by enclosing a corner of the garden with a dense planting on one or two sides or add a light trellis covered by vines. Fragrant plants and perfumed flowers will make this type of seat a haven.

The ground beneath the seat is just as important. If the seat is used frequently, the grass below will become worn. If the seat isn't used often, the grass will become long and untidy. And each time you mow the lawn, you'll have to move the seat. A gravel surface is the easiest to install, but for a popular spot, nothing beats a good firm base, such as that provided by pavers or bricks.

An alternative is to plant aromatic low-growing herbs, such as thyme and chamomile. If you choose to have paving around your bench, remove one or two slabs and plant the herbs in the spaces created; with gravel, simply plant them in small groups, cutting through the landscape fabric under the gravel. Scented-leaf pelargoniums and lavender in pots are also suitable. All these prefer a sunny well drained spot, but there are other plants that would do well if your sanctuary is more shaded. Shrubby roses are a good choice, lilies are romantic and many are perfumed and mock orange (Philadelphus) has a powerful fragrance and delicate white flowers.

TYPES OF SEATING

Garden seats range from the portable to the permanent. Your final choice will depend upon the space you have available, your budget and how often you're likely to use them. Among the portable seats suitable for outdoor use are folding and stackable chairs, such as director's chairs and deckchairs. You should pack these away when they're not in use, or rain and moisture will make the canvas become faded and mouldy. You can leave some small dining chairs available from furniture or DIY stores outside, but most will last longer if you put them away after using them.

Rattan or wicker seats are comfortable and attractive, and you can return them to a sunroom or conservatory indoors when they're not needed in the garden. Bring out cushions and covers when necessary, or for a special occasion, use different fabrics for added colour and variety. All-weather cushions (usually much plainer) are also available.

For small dining settings, the so-called café tables and chairs, modelled on Parisian styles, come in a range of designs. These vary from slatted timber chairs to all-metal ones, often with a wire finish. Most of these are weatherproof, but the quality varies considerably.

Permanent outdoor furniture includes built-in seats made of formed concrete or brick, often covered in mosaic or stone. These are constructed on-site, and some can double as display benches for favourite plants. Heavy timber benches are also more or less permanent. Their weight makes them difficult to move in a hurry and they usually form part of a focal point in the garden.

Steps can also double as seats, but they need to be wide and generous. Depending on the architecture of your house, you can use long beams of timber or a masonry construction. When guests come, add plump cushions for comfort.

FURNITURE DESIGN

Just like a piece of sculpture or a fountain, a good seat is an ornament in a garden. The style of seating you choose should blend with the style of your house and garden. There is a wide range of traditional styles available, such as reproductions of Victorian wrought iron.

Look for well-made furniture that will withstand the elements. Durable timbers such as oak, teak or cedar make the finest outdoor furniture, but treated pine is also long-lasting. Carefully check for rust-proof fastenings and enamelled iron or brass fittings.

Glass is popular for tables, and aluminium, stainless steel and plastic are some of the modern materials available for both seating and dining tables.

PERGOLAS AND GAZEBOS

The built features in a garden landscape are often designed to solve a problem, such as providing shelter from the elements or filling an awkward gap. They have been refined over centuries so that they not only serve their purpose, they also act as attractive features. Like all garden elements, however, these features will deteriorate over time and contribute to maintenance problems. The trick is to build them well in the first place.

PERGOLAS

BELOW This gazebo will be a more attractive feature in a few years' time, once climbing plants have covered the posts and roof.

BELOW RIGHT A pergola design can be used to form an archway, framing a view or marking the transition from one part of the garden to another.

OPPOSITE This solid outdoor structure is reminiscent of some Balinese homes, where the rooms are open to the elements on all sides.

It's probably easiest to think of a pergola as a series of arches. Like an arch, a pergola is often used as a passage to mark your progress through a garden. In strict architectural terms, a pergola is a freestanding structure, but it's often thought of as a type of open loggia. An architect defines this as a covered gallery, often supported by pillars and attached to a building.

Pergolas can perform several functions. They frame views and provide a shaded, cool area for walking. They can lead you to other parts of the garden and can also be useful for providing shade and privacy in situations where a tree is inappropriate. Pergolas can also define a larger open space, where tables and chairs might be located under the shade of crossbeams.

If a pergola is attached to the house, it serves to mark and unite the transition from the inside to the external space, and it can also provide an illusion of space by extending the living areas of your home onto a terraced or patio area. This is particularly the case in the modern garden,

GROWING ROSES ON PERGOLAS

Don't wind roses around the posts of a pergola. Roses need annual pruning and cutting out, and twisted canes can become a nightmare. Instead, tie the canes to heavy guy wires attached to the piers or supporting posts. This is true of other plants, too, but to a lesser degree. Tie plants loosely so the tie does not cut into the bark during the growing season. Where possible, use twine or a similar material that will break down.

which is used more for entertaining and outdoor living than simple show. This type of pergola can also act as a natural air-conditioner if it's covered with vines or deciduous climbers.

Use 'directional' pergolas to lead the eye along its entire length to an interesting focal point. Alternatively, position them so they open out into another section of the garden and a new functional role — perhaps an entertainment area. A pergola is also a good way to introduce a sense of mystery, especially if the destination is not visible from the starting point.

PRACTICAL CONSIDERATIONS

A pergola needs to be sturdy and well-constructed, particularly if you plan to grow vigorous and heavy climbers, such as roses, Boston ivy or wisteria, over it. Achieving the right balance between strength and scale in relation to the rest of the garden can be the most difficult part. Massive brick piers and a light, flimsy series of crossbeams will look clumsy in a small garden as well as limiting your choice of climbers: a simple design is usually the best.

Don't position posts directly in front of windows, and make sure they are high enough to support pendulous plants, such as wisteria, without impeding pedestrians. A good height is about 2.1 m. For pergolas close to the house, dressed timber and treated pine are best. Rounded poles of treated pine are more rustic and look better located some distance from the house; as a general rule, use more refined materials the closer the pergola is to the house. Square posts of 130–150 mm and crossbeams of 100 mm are usually sufficient.

FREESTANDING WALKWAY

TOOLS

- Handsaw
- Power saw
- Jigsaw
- Hammer and nail punch
- 25 mm chisel
- Builders square/ combination square/ sliding bevel
- Tape measure
- Marking gauge
- Power drill with assorted bits
- Spanner (in size to suit nuts)
- String line
- Shovel/spade/mattock
- Post-hole auger
- Spirit level and water level
- Clamps
- Hand plane
- Router (optional)

This versatile design can be an arbour for supporting climbing plants, a grand garden entrance, an entertaining area or even a carport. Simply vary the dimensions. It's supported on treated pine posts embedded in concrete and covered by lattice.

MATERIALS*

PART	TIMBER	LENGTH	NO.
Post	90 x 90 mm treated pine (C24)	3000 mm	4
Beam	140 x 45 mm treated pine (C24)	3000 mm	2
Rafter	140 x 45 mm treated pine (C24)	2100 mm	4

Other: Eight 125 x 12 mm galvanized round-head nuts and bolts with washers; 2 kg of 75 x 3.75 mm galvanized lost-head nails; stain or paint, primer and undercoat; approximately two buckets of coarse gravel; concrete; timber preservative; lattice (optional).

* Finished size: 2400 x 1200 mm (footprint) by 2100 mm high. Adapt these requirements to suit your own needs.

ESTIMATING YOUR MATERIALS

1 Using an architect's or suveyor's plans as your reference, estimate and order the materials you'll need.

PAINTING THE TIMBER

2 Before you start building the pergola, apply one or two coats of paint or stain in your desired colour. It's much easier to paint loose pieces of timber on the ground than an upright structure. Once the assembly is complete, you can touch up the joints and around the cut ends.

PREPARATION

3 Determine a building line for the front of the walkway. Lay a piece of timber across the path to represent the starting line. The path in this project measures 600 mm wide and has a 300 mm allowance for the post positions at each side. To determine the front positions, measure 300 mm to each side of the path on the building line. Place wooden pegs temporarily in the ground at these points to represent the outside

LEFT This simple white wooden structure is supported by four posts, with four rafters resting on parallel beams. A lattice provides some shade.

faces of the posts. Just outside each peg, erect a building profile across the corner, at an angle of approximately 45 degrees. Insert a nail in the top of each profile and stretch a string line between the two, securing it to create a building line.

4   Place a spirit level on top of the temporary corner pegs and plumb to the string line. Wrap masking tape around the string then, with a pencil, create a clearly visible mark on the taped section where the plumb line crosses it.

5   From the temporary corner pegs, measure 2400 mm along the path and drive in a second set of corner pegs. Erect another pair of profiles as described above. Pull a string line down one side of the path, making sure it passes over the masking tape mark. Drive in an additional nail and secure the string line. Repeat this step on the other side of the path. Measure the distance between the string lines at two points to ensure they are parallel, adjusting them as required.

6   Working from the second set of temporary corner pegs, plumb up to the string line and mark it clearly. Stretch another string line across the path from one profile to the other, passing over the two marks. Measure the diagonals between the intersecting string lines to check

HINT

Before starting any excavation, contact the relevant local authorities to request plans of underground pipes and cables running across your property, Make sure you consult your electricity, gas and telecommunications suppliers. Damaging these utilities not only exposes the home builder to the possibility of extreme physical danger, but also usually results in costly repair bills.

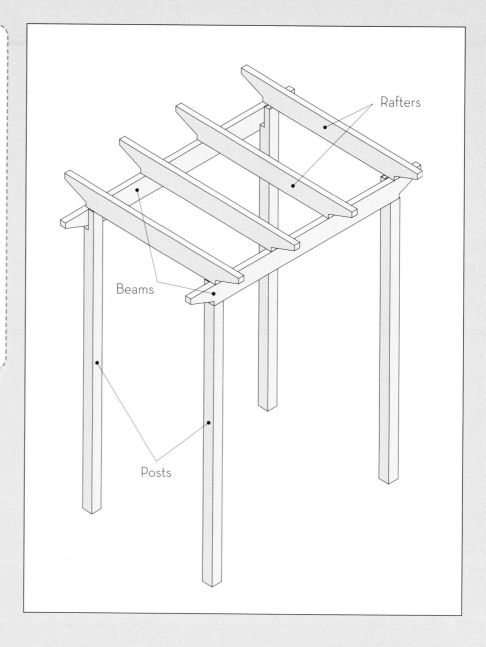

RIGHT Isometric drawing for the freestanding walkway.

Rafters

Beams

Posts

that they are equal and that, therefore, the project is square. Once the set-out is correct, remove the string lines to provide easy access while you're digging the footings.

DIGGING THE FOOTINGS

7 As the string line represents the outside face of the post, the footing must extend beyond this line. The post sits in the centre of each footing. Scratch the outline of the footing on the ground to mark the position of the hole and dig each footing 300 x 300 mm and to a depth of 550 mm. When designing a freestanding pergola as a companion to an existing structure, consider its overall dimensions. To create a pleasing scene, make sure it's in proportion with the original building.

8 To aid drainage, add a 100 mm layer of coarse gravel to the bottom of each hole, particularly if the area has heavy clay-based soil.

9 Replace the string lines and secure them tightly to the nails in the tops of the profiles.

ERECTING THE POSTS

10 Stand each post carefully in its hole, ensuring it's plumb and in line with the intersecting string lines. Work with posts slightly longer than required, trimming any excess away later.

11 Brace the posts temporarily and recheck for plumb. Mix cement and sharp sand with water to form concrete to the consistency of stiff paste, then pour it into the hole. Ram the wet concrete down well to remove any air bubbles trapped in the mixture and ensure the post is held firmly. Before beginning construction, allow the concrete to set for at least seven days and up to a fortnight.

FIXING THE BEAMS

12 In this project, the beams run parallel to the path at a height of 2100 mm. Beginning with those — if any — that stand on slightly higher ground, measure up from the bottom of each post and square a line around all four sides. Use a spirit level, a straight edge and a pencil to transfer the beam marks to the remaining three posts.

13 Place a single cross on the side of each post where a beam will be housed. On the outside of each post, using a power saw and chisel, cut out and neaten a 140 x 45 mm housing just below the beam line to support the beam (see 'Cutting a housing' on page 353).

14 Plan for the beam to overhang the posts by 300 mm at either end. Cut a stepped splay on the bottom edge. Cut the beam to length and shape it, removing any sharp edges by dressing with a hand plane. Place the beam in its housings and hold it in position with clamps. Drill holes through the beam and posts, and secure them with two 12 mm diameter round-head nuts and bolts.

FIXING THE RAFTERS

15 On each rafter, create a stepped splay and a 300 mm overhang to match those of the beam. Place the end rafters in line with the posts and space the two intermediate rafters evenly. Skew-nail each to the top of the beam with 75 x 3.75 mm galvanized lost-head nails.

TO FINISH

16 Remove the temporary bracing and touch up the timber with your choice of paint or stain. This pergola is finished with two coats of white exterior acrylic paint.

17 Add a sheet of white-painted lattice to the roof, if desired.

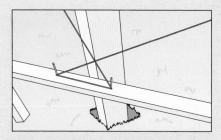

10 Stand each post carefully in its hole, ensuring it's plumb and in line with the intersecting string lines.

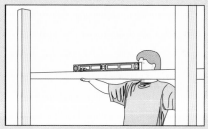

11 Brace each post temporarily with timber off-cuts and, using a spirit level, recheck for plumb.

12 Using a spirit level and a straight edge, transfer the position of the beam to the remaining three posts.

ABOVE Arches draw the eye along the path, creating an element of mystery.

OPPOSITE An elegant gazebo, perfectly positioned in the landscape.

HINT

If you can't visualize the size and impact of an arbour or arch, make a mock-up. Use two large stakes or bamboo poles and lash some supple branches to the tops of each to mark the height and shape of the proposed arch.

GAZEBOS AND SUMMERHOUSES

Gazebos, summerhouses and open-sided garden rooms provide some protection from the elements while adding a sense of style to the garden.

Ideally, any garden structure needs to be big enough to comfortably accommodate several people. (Arbours, on the other hand, are usually designed for one or two.) A gazebo has a hexagonal base and is open on at least two sides. A summerhouse usually has a rectangular or square shape and opens onto a verandah or patio. Both the gazebo and the summerhouse are covered buildings, and should ideally be positioned so they afford views.

THE IDEAL SITE

Positioning is an important consideration. If you plan to regularly use your summerhouse or gazebo for dining, locate them near the kitchen or barbecue. If you mainly entertain at lunchtime, avoid placing it where it will receive full sun at midday — in summer, it will be too hot and will attract flies and other insects. In winter, any sun will be much appreciated and you may not want a fully enclosed position. A site close to a deciduous tree could solve the problem.

The structure itself will be a focal point in the garden, but you should also consider the focal points that will be visible from it. Avoid placing it where it will capture unsightly views, such as the compost heap or the clothesline. If the ideal position for your summerhouse or gazebo doesn't provide a pleasant outlook, consider revamping a section of the garden to make it more attractive.

CHOOSING A DESIGN

Make sure your building complements the setting, and does not fight with it. Start by considering the architecture and period of your house. Both the style and mood of the house should be compatible with that of any garden structure; you can even include details from the house in the design.

For a gazebo, try to match the joinery details used on the house. Most gazebos are constructed of timber with a roof of tiles, shingles or felt. Wrought iron was a popular material for gazebos in Victorian times. If you prefer that look, you can choose from the range of imitation period gazebos made from aluminium.

ARBOURS AND ARCHES

Arbours and arches are built structures that support plants, and are both ornamental features and places to rest. They mark a passage from one section of the garden to another. Although they look much the same, they have different functions.

An arch is used to cover a path and mark the transition from one area to another. The arbour, on the other hand, is a cocooned structure, often backed by lattice or plants. Sheltered and cosy, it provides the ideal location for an inviting seat. It is usually located at the end of a vista, or designed as a walk-through feature with seating on either side.

Both these structures are prominent and will be clearly seen. First consider how one will fit in the 'big picture' view of your garden. You'll need to locate it so that it seems to 'belong', and the best way to create this effect is to make sure it performs a role — such as marking the entrance to the front garden or a section of garden.

POSITIONING AN ARCH OR ARBOUR

Arches frame views and mark a passage from one section of garden to another. Use an arch over a path, possibly in conjunction with a hedge or shrub border, to define sections. Arches are particularly useful for marking the point at which the style or function changes.

If you only have a small garden, where it's inappropriate to divide the garden into sections, an arbour could be the answer. You can place an arbour against a wall or position it at the end of a view to mark a 'full stop' to the vista from the house. The advantage of an arbour is its versatility. The ideal arbour is sheltered in winter but cool in summer, so positioning is important. A south-facing position, possibly on a wall, suits the winter requirement for sun and warmth, but in summer the same position could be far too hot for comfort.

ARCH STYLES

The style of arch you choose will depend on the garden itself, whether it's traditional, contemporary or even ethnic. You can change the basic shape with ornamentation. There are English, Japanese, Mediterranean and Mexican styles of arches. Arches (and arbours) can be rustic, formal, modern, whimsical or high-tech, depending on the design.

Formal designs are often constructed from timber or masonry, but the same materials also suit informal designs. Materials for modernist arches include stainless steel, iron and even glass bricks. Rustic arches use twigs, rough branches or treated pine logs.

WATER FEATURES

Water has a universal appeal. It's cooling in a hot climate and calming in a cooler one. Persian and Indian gardeners mastered the rill or water chute so water flowed constantly through a dry landscape. In East Asia, Japanese and Chinese monks built large lakes to reflect the surrounding landscape, and during the European Renaissance, vast areas devoted to formal terraced water gardens demonstrated humankind's ability to tame nature.

Even in the most humble of gardens, water features can be lively or contemplative. Water produces visual effects, such as reflection and movement, as well as calming sounds that not only soothe the soul but also provide relief from traffic noise. Wildlife is also drawn to its intrinsic life-giving qualities. Water has a firm place within garden landscapes.

Whatever the scale of your water feature, it will provide the perfect focal point for both formal and casual garden schemes. It's worthwhile building it properly, as a well-constructed pond is an asset to any garden.

SITING A WATER FEATURE

Three basic rules will help you decide on a site for your pond. First, it should have sunlight for at least half a day. Excess sun can lead to algal growth, which consumes the oxygen in the pond. However, you can control such blooms by carefully growing water plants that will shade the surface. Second, avoid placing a pond under a tree, as its roots may puncture the liner and even lift a preformed pond out of the ground. Also its leaves and flowers will rot and pollute the water. Finally, locate your pond where it's visible from the house or deck, so it becomes a focal point that everyone can enjoy.

Running water has a restful effect in any garden, whether it's an oriental design (below) or a minimalist courtyard (below right).

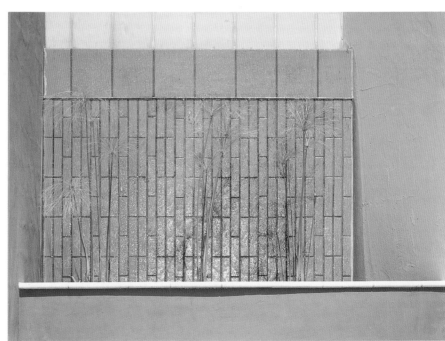

DESIGNING A WATER FEATURE

There are many types of pond — formal, informal, reflecting, wildlife or Japanese styles are just some of the choices. Other types of water feature range from small float bowls for flowers to container gardens, wall fountains or spouts that gurgle water over rocks. Select your water feature according to its function as well as its compatibility with the design of your house and garden. When you draw up your plan, consider the topography, the visual surroundings, available space and siting limitations.

Whatever the style of pond you prefer, remember that a large pool is easier to maintain than a small one. It's less likely to heat up in summer and freeze in winter, and this means that you'll be able to keep the temperatures for plants, fish and other organisms more constant. A good minimum size for a pond would be 2.4 m long by 1.8 m wide with a depth of 30–40 cm. The water surface of a pond this size is 3 square metres, which is a good base size. A gentle slope of no more than 45–60 degrees makes it easier to use pebbles and river stones to disguise the lining.

Before you start digging a pond, make sure that you will be allowed to fill it by your local water comapny. Most will not object, but with very large ponds you may need special permission. In addition, if you have young children, or will have young visitors consider constructing a fence around it to keep them safe.

ABOVE A simple design like this one suits a contemporary garden.

FORMAL REFLECTION PONDS

In the past reflection ponds have been used to enormous effect, most notably in European gardens of the 17th and 18th centuries. There they were used on a grand scale to emphasize the importance of a building or sculptural ornament. You can borrow the formality and symmetry of these gardens for your own garden landscape. A small courtyard or garden can be greatly enhanced by the reflective qualities of water, providing a feeling of space and peace that is very calming.

Formal ponds are generally geometric in shape — perhaps a circle, an arc or a long rectangle. Water plants are generally kept to a minimum in the formal pond. There may be a pot or planting of water lilies in the middle or at either end, but more often the surface of the water is a mirror for the pond's surroundings.

CONSTRUCTING A FORMAL POND

The shape of the pond should be regular, which will also keep the construction relatively simple. The construction of a masonry pond requires careful attention to details, especially with the final waterproofing membrane. Care taken now will help prevent leaks later on.

1 Mark out the outline of the pond with lime or marking paint, being careful to position it symmetrically in relation to other features, such as garden walls.
2 Excavate the soil to a depth of approximately 500 mm (for a 300 mm deep pond).
3 Consolidate the substrate, then spread and compact a 50 mm layer of coarse sand for the base foundation.

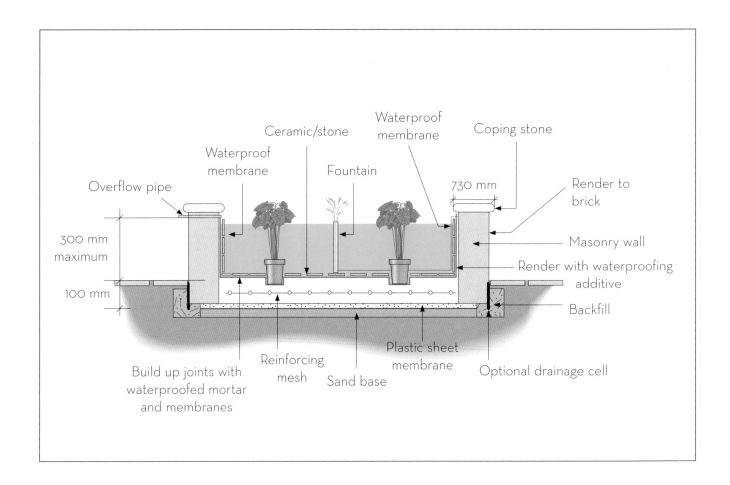

Overflow pipe

Waterproof membrane

Ceramic/stone

Fountain

Waterproof membrane

Coping stone

730 mm

Render to brick

300 mm maximum

100 mm

Masonry wall

Render with waterproofing additive

Backfill

Build up joints with waterproofed mortar and membranes

Reinforcing mesh

Sand base

Plastic sheet membrane

Optional drainage cell

ABOVE Working drawings for constructing a formal pond.

4   Use timber lengths or fibre cement sheets to create the formwork for the concrete base. Excavate about 50 mm extra around the base for workspace. Set accurate string lines to the required heights and ensure the structure is square at all corners.

5   Lay builders plastic over the sand as a damp-proof base membrane.

6   Lay a sheet of chicken wire or mesh for reinforcing. The larger the pond, the heavier the mesh should be. Use an extra-strong concrete mix, with finer aggregate than normal to provide density, and add a waterproofing additive. Pour concrete to a depth of 100 mm and give it a float finish. Let the concrete cure. (See 'Concreting', page 332.)

7   Using solid bricks, construct the pond walls. For larger ponds, use double brick construction to support the volume of water. Add a waterproofing additive to the mortar and reinforce the corner joints with mortar.

8   Set a small diameter pipe into the top of the brickwork as an overflow line and connect it to a suitable runoff point. Set the coping bricks or stones with mortar. Add drainage cell to the rear of the wall if you wish, and backfill behind the wall with coarse gravel, keeping the damp-proof membrane in place.

9   Ensure the bricks and mortar are dry and free from dirt. Apply a minimum of three coats of waterproof membrane to the inside of the walls, allowing each coat to dry before applying the next. It's best to

A water feature can be as simple as a small pond (left) or as grand as a stream with a cascade (above).

use a fibreglass or rubber membrane, preferably one recommended by licensed waterproofers.

10 Touch up the waterproof membrane. Make sure the corner joints are reinforced with the membranes.

11 If you like, tile the inside of the pond. Dark-coloured tiles provide a neat, clean finish and make the pond look deeper.

12 Allow the structure to dry thoroughly before filling it with water. Don't make holes in the slab or walls for electric or reticulation lines; these can be taken under the coping and disguised with plants.

NATURAL PONDS AND CASCADES

An informal pond is usually free-form or more organic in design. Try to blend it with the landscape so that it doesn't look like an imposed element. Use nature as a model — rushes at the edge, randomly placed rocks, reeds, floating plants and lilies distributed casually over the surface. The planting style can range from desert oasis to tropical.

Locate ponds and waterfalls at the lowest part of the garden, where they would be found in nature. Waterfalls that can be seen to start flowing at a point higher than the surrounding ground never look right. If you can't achieve a natural-looking effect, it's better to incorporate a feature such as a fountain instead.

ABOVE A Victorian-style wedding cake fountain doubles as a birdbath.

CONSTRUCTING A POND

It's difficult using concrete and masonry to build and waterproof free-form shapes, so use purpose-made pond liners or prefabricated shells for these ponds. You can add a waterfall to the pond, provided the pond liner continues underneath and diverts all water back into the pond. Even the slightest leak will eventually lead to the pond emptying.

A heavy-duty butyl liner is the best lining for a garden pond. This type of rubber sheeting is relatively expensive but is specially made for ponds. Cheaper products, such as PVC, which are thin and don't have UV stabilization, will need replacing every few years. You can also use concrete for large or unusually shaped ponds, but unless you lay it properly, it cracks, causing leaks to develop.

To help integrate the pond into the garden, add feature rocks to the surrounding landscape and make sure you disguise all non-natural elements such as lead pipes and pond liners with stone or plants.

1 Excavate a free-form shape in the lowest part of the garden to a depth of about 400–600 mm. Remember that larger ponds with an elongated shape will look more natural than small, round ones.
2 Remove any roots or sharp stones or they may eventually puncture the membrane. Cover the base of the excavation with a 50 mm layer of sand to form a soft base for the liner.
3 About 500 mm out from the edge of the pond, dig a trench to secure the pond liner, and add a layer of sand to it.
4 Lay the butyl liner, which should be about twice the size of the pond itself, where possible smoothing it to avoid large folds. Continue it into the trench and backfill the trench with gravel and smooth rubble.
5 Place some natural rocks around the top of the liner to make it less visible, introducing some feature rocks into the body of the pond at the same time.
6 Finish the area with smaller river stones and finer gravel for a more natural effect.
7 Fill the pond and position water lilies, rushes or other water plants. Plant plenty of suitable plants and groundcovers around the pond and rock formations.
8 Once the pond water is clear, you can add some fish. Other creatures, such as water snails, can help keep the pond free of algae. Add natural logs and leaf mulches around the pond to create habitat for wildlife.

A WILDLIFE POND

Any garden, large or small, can have a wildlife pond. Even in the centre of town, insects, birds and small amphibians, such as frogs and newts, will appreciate a water supply, whatever its size. The bigger, the better, of course, and if you have space, you could make a small island in the middle, as a refuge for small birds and mammals.

Make sure one side of the pond slopes gradually, perhaps with a small gravel beach, so that mammals such as hedgehogs can drink safely without risk of falling in. Choose native plants that wildlife will enjoy, such as reeds, comfrey, cuckoo flower (*Cardamine pratensis*) and meadowsweet.

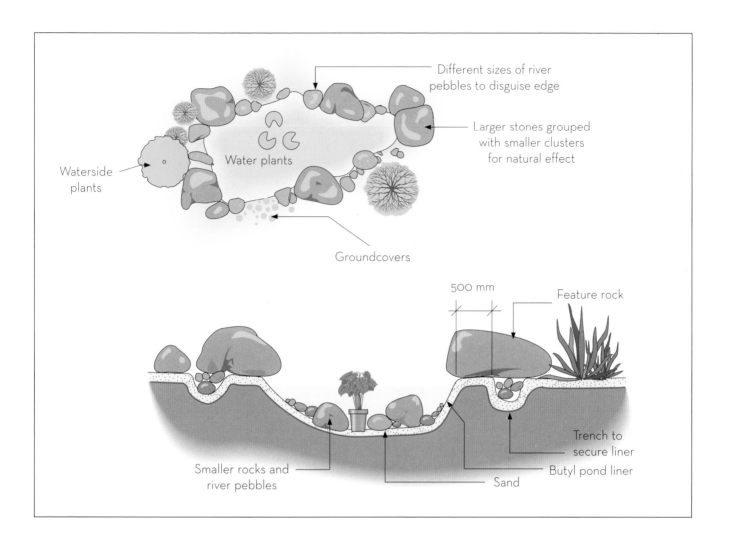

Different sizes of river pebbles to disguise edge

Larger stones grouped with smaller clusters for natural effect

Waterside plants

Water plants

Groundcovers

500 mm

Feature rock

Trench to secure liner

Butyl pond liner

Smaller rocks and river pebbles

Sand

ABOVE Constructing a natural pond.

FOUNTAINS

To remain healthy, pond water needs oxygen, and the process of oxygenating and recycling water provides you with the opportunity to add creative touches. Not only do fountains look and sound good, they also have practical benefits. Any movement in the water helps to oxygenate it, and this means healthier water. Ponds with flowing water have fewer algae problems and are less likely to suffer from a build-up of toxins.

There are fountain styles to suit every garden, from Victorian to modern. There's a wide range of spouts available too, ranging from dainty trickles to bubbling balloons and sheets of water. Pumps are graded according to their horsepower and capacity, so choose a pump according to the volume of water to be recycled. Obviously, large cascades, fountains and streams will require a more powerful pump. A capacity of 5000 litres per hour is fine for most domestic ponds.

If you want to plant water lilies and other surface plants, check that their growth will not be disturbed by a continuous flow or shower of water. If so, choose a fountain spout that drops water into the pond with only a little splashing.

PLANTS FOR PONDS

- *Azolla caroliniana* (fairy moss)
- *Eichornia crassipes* (water hyacinth)
- *Hottonia palustris* (water violet)
- *Hydrocharis morsus-ranae* (frogbit)
- *Iris laevigata* (Japanese water iris)
- *Myriophyllum spicatum* (spiked milfoil)
- *Nymphaea* sp. and cv. (water lily)
- *Ranunculus aquatilis* (water buttercup)
- *Utricularia vulgaris* (bladderwort)

PLANTS FOR POND EDGES

- *Acorus calamus* (sweet flag)
- *Calla palustris* (bog arum — bog plant)
- *Caltha palustris* (marsh marigold)
- *Canna* sp. (Indian shot or canna)
- *Heloniopsis orientalis*
- *Lobelia cardinalis* (cardinal flower — marginal plant)
- *Pontederia cordata* (pickerel weed)
- *Restio tetraphyllus* (tassel cord rush)
- *Zantedeschia aethiopica* (arum lily)

OTHER WATER FEATURES

Large-scale ponds are not the only water features that give pleasure. Often the sound of trickling or splashing water is all that's required to create a calm, restful atmosphere, and so a small fountain, water sculpture or even a birdbath may serve the purpose.

A large pot filled with water and planted with water lilies makes a great focal point, especially in a Japanese-style garden. In fact, any water-tight container can be used to form an interesting water feature. However, if you want to convert a household container to hold water, make sure you start with a clean, dry and intact surface before waterproofing it. You'll need to paint on at least three coats of waterproofing membrane, allowing each coat to dry before adding the next.

If you have a small garden, here are some ideas for creating an effective water feature:

- Large Chinese pot
- Old washtub or laundry tub
- Half wine barrel
- Japanese deer scarer
- Birdbath
- Water sculpture
- Shallow bowl with floating, cut flowers

TYPES OF WATER PLANTS

Plants for a water garden fall into three different categories. Each has a part to play in pond ecology.

Marginals grow on the edges of ponds. You can create a shelf for marginals 25 cm below the surface or else gently slope the sides of the pond as you build it. Place potted water plants on the ledge or plant them among rocks. Bog plants are similar to marginals but are usually situated further up the bank; many prefer drier conditions in winter. All provide protection and nesting sites for fish and small water creatures.

RIGHT An elegant ceramic pot makes an attractive feature in a small pond.

PLANTING A POND

If you select a range of water plants for every level of your pond, there should be very few problems. You'll be able to find good stocks in specialist water garden nurseries.

1 Several days before you introduce any plants to the pond, fill it with water to allow any sediment to settle and the temperature to stabilise. Where possible, position the planting containers, leaving them part full of soil and ready for planting. Use unimproved garden soil, or special aquatic potting compost.

2 Position the plant so that its root ball sits on the layer of saturated soil in the pot (have a piece of pipe) and press the plant firmly into position. This is particularly important, as some plants may float if they aren't firmly anchored. Add a layer of gravel to stop soil particles from floating to the surface.

3 Make sure the plants are at their correct depth in the pond. If they're too deep, they will die from lack of oxygen. To keep plants growing at their ideal depth, place bricks in the water and use them as stands for plant containers. (Before you place the bricks in the pond, soak the bricks in water for several days to wash out any chemical residues.)

The second category of water plant is submerged or oxygenating plants, which grow at the bottom of the pond. They can be left to grow in containers, or you can tease out the roots and anchor them in mud and gravel. These plants add oxygen to the water and remove excess nutrients that would otherwise encourage algae to grow.

Finally, floating-leafed plants, such as water lilies, help to shade water. This, too, is necessary for regulating water temperatures and preventing algae from thriving. Some plants of this type float on the surface, while others have tubers or roots tied to the pond bottom.

FISH AND WILDLIFE

Fish are attractive in water features. Goldfish are the most popular and are easily available. Colourful and hardy, they're always the centre of attention. What's more, they thrive on a diet of commercial fish food. If the pond is sufficiently large, it will generate food, so even if you forget to feed your fish, they won't starve. A disadvantage of fish is that they can dig among plants and cause root disturbance.

HOW MANY FISH?

Overstocking your pond with fish can lead to polluted water, algal growth and spread of disease. For every square metre of pond surface, allow a maximum of 10 fish, each about 5–8 cm long. Unless you are willing to install filtration systems and have a very large pond, avoid koi carp. If you keep these fish, you'll need to do a lot of cleaning.

SPIRAL POOL

TOOLS

- Groundwork tools
- Building tools
- Gloves

MATERIALS

- Steel pin or bamboo cane
- Soft sand
- Geotextile underlay: 3.5 x 3.5 m
- Butyl liner: 3.5 x 3.5 m
- Pump and filter
- Hoses and fittings
- Reinforcement mesh: 1 m²
- Membrane: 4 x 1.1 m
- Chicken wire
- Broken slate
- White cobbles
- Conduit
- Slate: Check the availability of slate with your local tile shop or landscape supplier, as you may need to order it in advance. Many suppliers keep broken slate in crates on site and you can just pick the pieces you want. Transport them in boxes that are easy to handle.
- Stone: During the quarrying process, stone naturally attracts a layer of dirt, so wash all pebbles and cobbles before you place them in your water feature.

This spiral pool has the calm serenity of a natural body of water. Its interest lies in the pattern that you create within the pool, whether it's a formal geometric design or a more organic style.

METHOD

1 Choose the area in the garden for your pool — you will need at least a 3 x 3 m plot of relatively flat soil. Take a steel pin or bamboo cane and push it into the centre of the plot. Attach a builders tape, or a string line that is marked with a radius of 1.2 m, to the cane or pin, and scribe a circle, laying sand as you go. When the circle is complete, you'll have the markings for a pool with a diameter of 2.4 m. Bang in and level a series of pegs around the circumference to give you a reference after you have finished your excavations.

2 Now remove the cane and begin the excavations. The idea is to create a shallow pan that gently slopes to a depth of 400 mm. Once you've dug out the main pan, excavate a central sump hole measuring 600 mm wide and 400 mm deep. This hole will contain the pump that will slowly move the water to a filter system, which is needed to keep the water clear. Start the main excavation from the edges and gradually grade it down to the centre. Keep standing back to check the evenness of your work, and when you are happy with the overall shape of the pool, check that the surrounding edges are level with the pegs. Then excavate the central sump hole, making sure the walls remain intact.

3 Before you lay the protective geotextile underlay, remove any large stones or sharp objects from the site. Lay the underlay over the whole area and, starting in the sump hole, carefully fold the material into the hole. Then work your way out to the edge of the pool.

4 Now place the butyl liner over the pool and fold it into the sump hole. Start by laying the liner over one side of the pool. Take off your shoes so you don't rip or puncture the liner. Next, fold the liner into the sump hole. Continue to fit the liner over the remainder of the pool until it completely covers it.

5 Place the pump in the sump hole and attach the hose to the pump outlet, fastening it with a jubilee clip. Now you need to position the hose and power cable flat against the liner so that the broken slate can disguise them. The hose will need a flow adjuster to control the quantity of water flowing into the filter (alternatively, you can buy a pump with a built-in flow adjustor). This should be situated at the edge of the pool for access, but can be disguised later.

You now need to place a grill over the sump hole. Using bolt cutters, cut a grill measuring 1 m² out of a sheet of reinforcement mesh. Also cut four lengths of membrane about 1.1 m in length — these will cushion the grill when it's laid over the sump hole. Place the membrane

1 Once you have measured the correct radius, rotate your tape, laying sand as you go to create an entire circle.

3 Once you have removed any debris and sharp stones, lay the protective geotextile underlay.

on the liner so that it will lay under the sharp edges of the grill, then carefully place the grill over the sump hole. Finally, place a layer of expanded metal or chicken wire on top — this will prevent the slate from falling through the holes.

6   Next cover the whole pool area with a membrane. This will protect the liner from the sharp slate and will also prevent the pump from being clogged up with silt and sediment. Wearing gloves, wash the slate and then lay it over the pool at a depth of 50 mm, trying to keep it as even and flat as possible. When you have completely covered the area, take a step back so that you can make sure there is no membrane showing through.

5 Once the grill is in place, place a layer of chicken wire on top.

TO FINISH

7   Fill the pool with water until the slate is covered. Now connect the pump, ensuring that all cabling is ducted in rigid plastic conduit 450–600 mm below ground level until it reaches the switch box. Turn on the pump and adjust the filtration unit so that the flow back into the pool doesn't disturb the view of the pool. Using washed white cobbles, lay out the spiral pattern. Starting with a large cobble at a central point, lay a continuous line of stones in a spiral.

ABOVE LEFT White cobbles create a spiral pattern on a bed of broken slate.

ABOVE With the aid of tropical
plantings and large rocks and boulders,
this free-form pool resembles a lagoon.

SWIMMING POOLS

Open-air pools are a challenge in the colour stakes. If they are close to the house they become part of the hard landscaping surrounding the building. If sited further away, they can be completely screened but they are still part of the garden.

Pools need lush plantings around them to soften any harshness between the pond edge and the nearby garden. You can choose bold architectural foliage to complement your pool's design or create a softer effect using plants such as wisteria.

It's a good idea to think long and hard about the colour finish you want for the side and bottom of your pool. Blue mosaic tiles have been popular for years because they make a pool look deeper, but you could consider something more unusual, such as green or even black.

A formal swimming pool, rectangular in shape, will dominate the garden and become the focus of attention. The garden planting will radiate out from it and so it should complement it. In a subtropical setting for example, blue water and orange plants, such as the dramatic strelitzia, look fabulous.

A simple rectangle of blue water works well when it's surrounded by green; simple chairs and a canvas umbrella are all that's needed to emphasize the relaxed look.

Panels with slats provide both privacy and air flow around the pool.

POOL EDGES

The edging of a swimming pool can be either submerged or raised. When paving the pool surrounds, use an adhesive designed to withstand the constant lapping of water against the edge.

Whether you prefer statuary, pots, urns or birdbaths, there is an endless variety of styles to choose from.

GARDEN ORNAMENTS

The style and mood of a garden are usually established by the planting themes and structures, but some gardens can appear to ramble, without any focal point, or they may seem featureless if the planting is sparse.

Garden ornaments can, therefore, play a vital role in providing punctuation in the garden, drawing the eye, so that you pause before continuing to look at another form or planting style. Ornaments such as decorative pots allow you to extend the garden onto a patio or verandah, while others make sculptural, nostalgic, historical or artistic references that help to define the garden as your own.

As with any other garden element, you should consider scale, proportion and context before you position a garden ornament. Some ornaments, such as terracotta pots, look best in groups of threes; others, such as urns, lend themselves to pairs in a symmetrical layout.

CHOOSING AND PLACING ORNAMENTS

Before you place an ornament in the garden, consider its ability to withstand the elements. For example, delicate timber statues or bird boxes will not last unless they are heavily treated or painted.

Place ornaments with a base, especially those that contain water, on a level base of compacted sand or similar material, and make sure that those attached to, or suspended from, trees or posts are level, otherwise they'll look lopsided. Always check with a spirit level.

If you want an unusual garden ornament, consider one of these: a machinery part, garden chair, disused gate or cane pyramid trellis.

POTS AND CONTAINERS

Whatever the size of your garden, you can use containers to decorate every surface. But if you have only a limited space, planting in containers is the obvious solution. In fact, gardening in containers is similar to traditional gardening; however, you do need to be aware that, unlike plants in the traditional garden, container grown plants are heavily dependent on you. You will need to provide extra nutrients regularly and, given that containers dry out very quickly in hot weather, make sure that they receive regular and adequate quantities of water.

Also, fast-growing plants will rapidly outgrow their containers, and you'll need to either repot them every year or so, or once they reach the optimum size, prune the roots, which will slow down growth. Otherwise, pruning, propagating, supporting and general maintenance are the same as for soil-grown plants.

CLIMATE CONTROL

If you have a balcony garden, you'll have to deal with the problem of exposure to prevailing winds. Wind will dry out pots and hanging baskets very quickly, so you need to provide some form of protection. On a balcony, a reinforced glass screen will provide protection without obscuring the view or blocking out the sun.

In a small garden, your choice of plant material depends on the amount of sunlight available. This will vary according to the aspect as well as to the height and proximity of neighbouring buildings. The ideal aspect is a southerly one, which is warm and receives plenty of sun, but you may need some form of protection from the strong midday summer sun.

ROOT BALL RATIO

Try to choose the right pot for the plant and keep everything in proportion. The best container for any plant is one 5 cm larger than the diameter of the root ball and 10 cm deeper. After a year or so, depending on the amount of growth, you will need to repot the plant into a larger container. Don't plant a small plant in a much larger container: plants do best in pots only slightly larger than their root ball. Check that the roots are not growing through the base of the pot. If they are, repot.

With their frothy floral displays, these classical urns look like huge vases.

ABOVE This sculpted pot contains
a small water garden.

SUITABLE PLANTS FOR CONTAINERS

You can grow almost anything in containers, from edible plants such as
herbs and vegetables to water-loving ones. You can even grow trees, but
they will never reach the size they would in an unrestricted situation. You
may need to root prune trees and shrubs every few years.

Slow-growing trees and shrubs mean less work and, similarly, drought-
tolerant plants will cut down on the chore of watering in summer. Make
sure you use a compost that is suitable for the plants you want to grow,
and choose waterproof containers for any water plants. Finally, plant
those plants with the same watering and sun requirements together.

If you have a bigger garden, pots and containers provide the ideal
opportunity to grow plants that would not normally flourish in your soil.
Rhododendrons, for example, like acidic soil; if you live in an alkaline area,
the easiest way to grow lime-hating plants is in containers filled with
acidic compost.

Here are some examples of dwarf and smaller-growing specimens.

- Many citrus remain small in pots. There are dwarf varieties of peaches
  and dwarf forms or pillar-like varieties of apple.
- Small-growing pittosporums are ideal for containers, as are camellias,
  particularly small-growing varieties. Remember that camellias must be
  grown in acid compost.
- Some ideal shrubs for containers are abutilons and brugmansias,
  Camellia x *williamsii* varieties, hardy fuchsias, hebes or shrubby
  veronicas, *Hydrangea macrophylla* varieties, *Leptospermum
  scoparium* varieties, rhododendrons and azaleas.

AESTHETICS

Many of the design principles that apply to a traditional garden also apply
to a container-based garden. Make sure that you have a good mix of
evergreen and deciduous plants; build up displays, using staging if
necessary, to provide colour and interest at several levels; and choose
some good foliage plants to provide either a solid green backdrop to the
flower colour or relief from it. You can clip evergreens into formal shapes
to provide structure in a container display. Box, privet, myrtle, holly,
rosemary and lavender are all ideal, although any evergreen with relatively
small leaves will do.

Use annuals to experiment with colour schemes and change the
personality of your courtyard, patio, balcony or garden. Containers are
also useful for bulbs that die down during their dormant season, as you
can tuck these out of sight and bring them back when they are in bloom.

CHOOSING CONTAINERS

There is a vast range of container styles to choose from, but for a
harmonious display you'll need to pay attention to the size, shape and
materials of the containers. A mismatched selection of pots can look
messy and unattractive. The container is at least as important as the
plant, and just as much on view, so do not skimp on quality.

HOW HEAVY IS THAT POT?

Weight is an important
consideration when potting
a garden for a balcony or
roof terrace. Take into
account not only the
container but also its
contents, which will be
heavy when wet. Before
using weighty containers
on a balcony or roof
terrace, consult a structural
engineer for advice on
what to purchase and
where to site them.

Terracotta and stone are the most attractive options, along with metal and good-quality wood. Plastic, while lightweight and convenient, tends to look flimsy, and some colours are so bright that they dominate the planting scheme. Wire containers, such as those used for hanging baskets, are a good lightweight alternative to plastic, although you will have to line them with moss to ensure that the compost stays in place. When planting out these containers, add water-saving crystals to the potting mix, as they dry out quickly. In hot weather, hanging baskets require watering twice a day.

CHOOSING A SIZE

Container sizes vary from huge half-barrels to tiny wall pots, and you can find both freestanding containers and those specially designed to hang from either walls or brackets. You can also recycle all kinds of household relics, from old metal colanders to bread bins.

If you are planning to grow edible plants in containers, allow for the appropriate depth, since plants that are eaten for their roots will need space in which to develop them. Some purpose-made containers can be purchased for specific plants. For example, strawberry planters make economical use of space. The terracotta container has a series of small planting pockets, so you can grow the maximum yield of strawberries without taking up much floor space.

Growing bags containing special compost for tomatoes and other nutrient-hungry plants are another option, but these aren't attractive in a small garden where they're likely to be viewed from every angle.

ABOVE An urn on a stone-capped wall suits a formal garden.

ABOVE LEFT The repetition of topiary box provides structure.

GROUPING POTS

A group of pots looks particularly effective in a small courtyard. If you vary the size and scale of the containers, you'll improve the look of the plants. Staggered planting heights allow you to enjoy the flowers of all the plants, which might otherwise be hidden behind each other. You can buy containers in a range of sizes; several sizes in a single material look good together.

MINIATURE PLANTER

Several of these miniature planters make a feature on stairs or along a verandah edge. They are simply constructed with plywood sides set into angle timber and decorated with plywood decorations in heart shapes.

TOOLS

- Pencil
- Fold-out or steel rule
- Tape measure
- Square
- Jigsaw
- Block plane
- Cork sanding block
- Tenon saw or mitre saw
- Two adjustable clamps or G-clamps
- Chisel
- Hammer
- Eight small G-clamps or hand-held spring clamps

MATERIALS* (MAKES 6)

PART	MATERIAL	LENGTH	WIDTH	NO.
Wide side	6 mm exterior plywood	170 mm	170 mm	12
Narrow side	6 mm exterior plywood	170 mm	158 mm	12
Leg	31 x 31 mm external angle timber	200 mm		24
Slat	19 x 19 mm timber		158 mm	12

Other: PVA or epoxy adhesive; abrasive paper: two sheets of 120 grit; six plywood hearts; six plywood stars; 25 mm x 1.25 mm panel pins; heavy-duty plastic; finish of choice.

* For six planters you will need two 915 x 610 mm sheets of plywood. Finished size 185 mm square, height 200 mm. The timber sizes given are nominal.

METHOD

1 To make the sides, take a sheet of ply. Using a jigsaw, cut two lengths, each 915 x 170 mm, so that they both have a factory edge (mark these for later identification); this will be the top edge of the planter. Plane one cut edge of the remaining ply and cut another piece 170 mm wide. The planed edge will be the top. Cut two lengths 170 mm wide from each side of the remaining sheet, again marking the factory edges.

2 Choose the best sides of the ply for the face, and using a sanding block and 120 grit abrasive paper, sand them smooth. Sand the external angle timber and cut the legs to length. From the ply strips, and using the jigsaw, cut the 12 wide sides and the 12 narrow sides, keeping them in separate piles with the factory edges together.

3 Position a wide side into two of the angles, with the planed edge at the top and flush with the top of the angle, leaving a 30 mm overhang below for the legs. Glue the side in place and clamp together with a small clamp in each corner, using heavy-duty plastic to prevent sticking, and keeping the top edges flush. Clean off excess adhesive and leave to dry. Remove the clamps. Repeat until the wide sides are glued.

4 Take two glued frames and cut away any dried adhesive from the joining edges with a sharp chisel. Apply adhesive to the edges of

ABOVE Each miniature planter is decorated with a simple wooden motif.

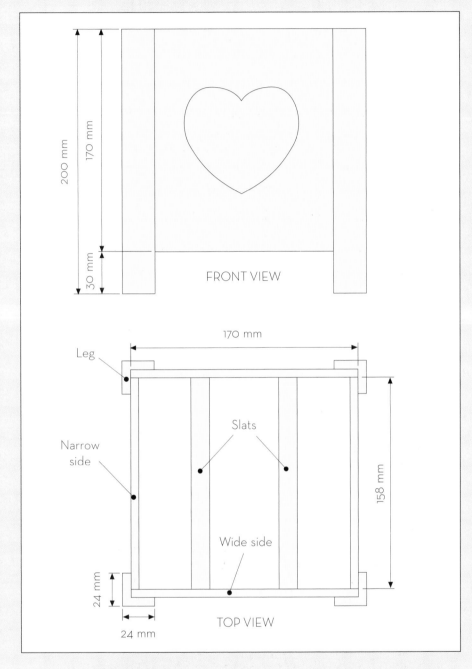

200 mm
170 mm
30 mm

FRONT VIEW

170 mm

Leg

Slats

Narrow side

Wide side

158 mm

24 mm

24 mm

TOP VIEW

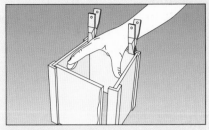

4 Glue the narrow sides to the frames, using spring clamps to keep the narrow sides in place.

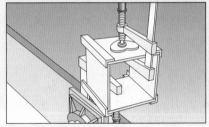

5 Apply adhesive to the back of the plywood shape. Centre it on the box and clamp it in place.

two narrow sides and to the joining edges of the frame. Glue together, using small clamps or spring clamps to hold the narrow sides in position. Check for square, then clean away excess adhesive.

5 Position the plywood hearts and stars on two opposing sides of each planter, ensuring they are centred. Apply adhesive to the back of the shapes and clamp them in position.

6 Position the bottom slats flush with the bottom of the planter and fix them in place with adhesive and nails. Support the bottom edge of the ply with a small offcut when nailing. Clean up the adhesive. Leave to dry.

7 Sand with 120 grit abrasive paper. Apply the finish of your choice.

ABOVE A conventional birdbath made of moulded concrete is both functional and attractive, whatever the style of your garden.

ATTRACTING WILDLIFE

The continuing urban sprawl places biodiversity — the numbers and populations of species — under threat, but we can all do our bit to ensure that wildlife has a chance of survival in our gardens. Natural habitat provides birds and other creatures with food and water, but it is being whittled away. The home gardener can play a big part in recreating and replenishing this habitat. By carefully planting and managing open spaces, you can encourage birds to relocate into your environment. This can often mean the difference between localized extinction and survival for species.

There are many advantages for us as well. A garden without birds and other life forms can be a sterile place. Birdsong adds lyric texture, while the flit and flurry of birds is the purest form of natural rhythm. Insects, too, such as butterflies and moths, as well as bumblebees, add colour and movement as they dart across the lawn. You may have hedgehogs cleaning your garden of snails, insects and other pests. All are easily overlooked, but their value is inestimable.

As long as you leave harmful insecticides on the shelf, birds also do a wonderful job of clearing your garden of insects. Bluetits, for example, love to feed on greenfly and caterpillars, and a young family will make noticeable inroads into even a large infestation. Attract birdlife to your garden by providing them with birdbaths and birdhouses.

BIRDBATHS

Water is the source of life, and birds need a reliable source. It makes sense to add a birdbath, which can be a highly ornamental focal point in your garden. There are styles to suit both formal and informal gardens.

Birds will flock to any shallow water source. You will always see birds, both small and large, taking advantage of the sprinkler, and fountains are ideal, provided the flow of water is gentle enough. Most birds are not good swimmers, so a deep pool is not advisable. For bathing, birds need only to stand in a few centimetres of water so they can splash their feathers. For drinking, provide a place for them to perch or sit. If there is a range of different-sized birds using the facility, add a rock so it sits out of the water or suspend a branch across the centre of the birdbath.

As with most focal points, try to match the style of your birdbath with the style of the house and garden. A traditional design suits a traditional or formal garden but rarely a modern courtyard. For a contemporary setting, you can choose from birdbaths of glass, ceramic, mosaic or carved stone. These same materials are fine, too, for traditional gardens. It just depends on the pattern, design and look of the individual piece.

BIRDHOUSES

You can encourage the right birds to stay by planting native plants and supplementing nesting sites with artificial ones — birdhouses to replace the hollows in native trees that once formed the natural nesting sites.

In the United States, the birdhouse is a traditional garden adornment with an appeal and popularity that stretches back to the days of the Pilgrim Fathers. Early farmers, eager to encourage migrating martins, swallows and other insect-eating birds, set up houses for them. These sociable birds build their mud houses on cliff faces so the houses were often elaborate multi-level affairs. All across the United States, this tradition survives and a thriving folk art has grown.

Elsewhere, birdhouses have a significant role as focal points and features. They can be highly ornamental, and some gardeners use them as garden art. They can be modern and colourful, or cool and classical, painted white, painted in bright shades or in heritage colours that match the house. Bird-feeding stations, too, can be highly decorative and sculptural elements as well as practical feeding aids.

Birdhouses encourage birds to nest in our gardens. The competition for available nesting hollows is fierce and many birds have great difficulty finding safe, suitable nest holes. These days there is a shortage of stems from old trees as we tend to be fastidious about clearing away dead or dying branches where hollows naturally develop.

Face the opening of a birdhouse away from the prevailing weather so that the birds can enjoy as much shelter as possible. Hang a birdhouse from a tree or tie it to branches. Wherever you choose to put it, make sure it's elevated. Some birdhouses for smaller birds can be attached to posts and placed in garden beds.

BIRDHOUSE MAINTENANCE

Keep the birdhouse relatively clean.

- Place a couple of handfuls of wood shavings or sawdust on the floor to help control the moisture level.
- After each breeding season, when the fledgling birds have left, clean out any unwanted pests. Depending on the species of bird, remove any old nests before cleaning the inside with warm water and a mild detergent.
- Finally, wipe out the birdhouse with a cloth soaked in disinfectant to keep bird parasites under control.

LEFT This birdhouse is made from wall slats stripped from cedar lining boards, but slats from old lattice would also be suitable.

CHILDREN'S GARDENS

Making a garden child-friendly can be quite simple, and it will be rewarding when you see the smiles on your children's faces. All you need to do is incorporate features that fire their imagination and give them a sense of fun and adventure. Nowadays, we tend to worry about letting children play in public parks and open areas on their own, so providing them with a safe and fun place to play in your own garden is a good alternative to constantly going down to the park when you have things to do at home.

SMALL GARDENS

Take lawns. They're easy to maintain, observe and supervise. And if they're large enough, they allow children to play ball games such as cricket and football in their own back garden. However, you could forget the prairie of lawn from fence to fence and go for something completely different. Instead, envisage a garden that stimulates innovation, creativity and resourcefulness in young minds.

Most new housing estates leave little space for gardens and hence play, so think creatively about your garden design. Children need to share a

RIGHT Young children need open space so that they can run around and play games.

small garden with adults. If your garden is little more than a courtyard, try to accommodate both adults and children by blending paving and grassed areas with some gentle shrubbery and paths in between.

Children need hard surfaces on which to ride bikes or scooters, and grass for rolling and tumbling, while you'll want entertainment space. Dedicate a square or circle of lawn and pave around it with concrete pavers about 1 m wide. Make sure they are well-laid, as little feet can trip on uneven surfaces. This paved area can become a personal Olympic running track or a velodrome for tricycles. In a small garden it can double as an entertainment venue for adult parties with a 'corral' where you can keep an eye on the kids. It also saves the lawn from excessive wear and tear. Grow some soft, scented plants such as lavender nearby so the fragrance is released every time someone brushes it.

ABOVE LEFT A treehouse can be the focus of lots of fantasy and adventure.

TOP TO BOTTOM Camellias are attractive but tough shrubs for a children's play area, while tender *Rondeletia* sp. and olive (*Olea europaea*) can be used to define the adult's 'corral'.

ABOVE *Pyracantha* sp., a plant with thorny branches.

COPSES AND SHRUBBERIES

If you have a little more space, surround the paved areas with a planting of tough trees and dense shrubs to provide swings for intrepid explorer, pirate or astronaut games. Children respond to places built on their scale. Think about building platforms on several levels, dens, tunnels and hideaways, secret nooks for fantasy and adventure. Try planting shrubs and trees in copses and groves. As plants merge, they form glens and dells full of secret trails and wonderful ideas for games.

Weeping trees make great dens, but take a while to grow — your children may have flown the nest before the den is complete. However, if you already have a suitable specimen with branches reaching down to the ground, install pint-sized furniture and mulch inside the canopy with pine bark chippings. Consider removing the inner, lower branches of large mature shrubs such as rhododendrons so children can creep among them.

A secret track, about 0.5 m wide, between the fence and the garden borders makes a great green playground for adventure games. Plant soft-leafed, smooth-barked shrubs, trees and climbers to produce dense growth among which children can play hide and seek.

TUNNELS

A private domain is every child's dream. A 'tunnel' that's too low for adults to crawl through is ideal. Willow canes are widely available and can be woven together (see page 109) to form living hides, igloos and tunnels. Make entrances about 1.5 m high and anchor them into the ground. Alternatively, use bamboo canes or hazel stems lashed together for extra strength. Bury the ends or tie them to stakes at the entrance (you'll need two frames, one in front, one at the rear). Then attach some tough canvas, igloo-fashion. A curtain over the entrance will make it even more private.

A SOFT LANDING

The area directly beneath and around swings and other play structures often receives a lot of wear and becomes compacted with time. A fall can have a severe impact on a young body, so choose soft surfaces that won't injure them.

Preparing a soft and forgiving base and surround is quite easy, and it will save your children quite a few bumps and scratches. The key to this surface is in the depth, for the deeper and looser the material, the softer the landing. Here are some suitable materials.

RUBBERIZED SURFACE

If you install playground equipment, a rubberized surface could be the best solution. It's required for commercial or public children's playgrounds, but is suitable for home play areas as well. It is an impact-absorbing material designed to protect the body and cushion the impact of a fall. Some products come in several colours and can be cut and pasted together to form interesting patterns and effects.

SYNTHETIC GRASS

For formal play areas, you could use synthetic grass. It's made from a polypropylene fibre woven onto a rubber latex backing, which in turn is laid on a rubberized mat. It's ideal for areas where equipment makes mowing difficult or where foot traffic is too heavy for real grass.

To install synthetic grass correctly, you need to put down a compacted layer of road base, followed by a layer of crusher dust, which is levelled and angled so water will run off it in heavy rain. The rubberized mat goes down on top of this and the synthetic turf is then adhered to the mat. As with paving, fill any gaps with sand. Initially synthetic turf can feel scratchy, but after a wearing-in period it generally settles down to have a softer feel.

PINE BARK CHIPPINGS

An alternative soft surface is pine bark chippings, laid 300 mm deep. This is a byproduct of wood chipping and timber harvesting. It is sometimes used for mulching, but it's also ideal for soft paths and play areas. Chippings are also the best surface to use along 'play paths' within garden beds or between shrubs.

Mulch any conventional playground area with swings and roundabouts with pine chippings or wood shavings to give a soft, safe landing for your children's falls. Cover any paths around shrubs with the same materials to prevent soil compacting and to allow worms to improve soil condition.

SURFACES TO AVOID

Avoid hard and uneven surfaces where children play. Don't use pebbles, as young children tend to put them in their mouths and older ones will scatter them everywhere, regardless of what grade you use. Also, falling on gravel can cause some nasty grazes.

Ideally children's play equipment should sit on some sort of soft fall material, not just on grass.

RIVER STONES

River stones have been used creatively in the Princess of Wales Memorial Garden in London's Kensington Gardens. There, large rounded boulders are set in a concrete base and arranged in the shape of a crocodile, one of the characters in *Peter Pan*, the theme of part of the garden. Children step on the stones, and the differences in size help them to balance and navigate uneven surfaces without worrying about the stones becoming dislodged or wobbly.

OPPOSITE TOP This durable sandpit is made from treated pine, then finished with paint. Unlike the sandpit described on this page, it's designed to sit on top of a level area from which the turf and topsoil have been removed.

OPPOSITE BOTTOM Cross-section of a typical sandpit construction. Just adapt it to suit your needs.

Setts, cobbles and stepping stones are often uneven, and even when they have been laid expertly, the tiny ridges can unsettle young feet, making them trip. Sharp rocks and brick edges should also be avoided.

If using treated pine or hardwood sleepers to define the boundaries of a sandpit or play area, ensure that the edges are chamfered or rounded off so the sharp right angle is softened.

PLAY EQUIPMENT

When you're planning what play structures to include, consider practicality and safety first. Any structures must meet the safety guidelines set by building regulations. Sturdy structures will stand the test of time and provide your children with years of enjoyment, as long as they're properly maintained.

It's also important to locate play equipment carefully — for example, a sandpit should be in a position that receives some sun during the mornings and afternoons, and some shade during the summer months.

BUILDING A SANDPIT

A sandpit is easy to build, but your children won't play in it unless you position it in an attractive area of the garden and keep it dry and free from dirt. The key to building a great sandpit is installing drainage and comfortable surrounds (edging material), which should be smooth and serviceable, and covering it when it's not in use. Bull-nosed bricks or pavers, dressed timbers or smooth sandstone are all suitable. If possible, replace the sand every year.

For this sandpit we used timber sleepers, but you could also use treated timber.

1 Dig the pit to a depth of at least 600 mm (more if possible), and fill the base with gravel to a minimum depth of 150 mm. Include an agricultural drain if necessary.
2 Cover the gravel base with heavy-duty canvas or another kind of permeable geotextile fabric, overlapping the edge of the pit by at least 300 mm. Secure the hemmed edge with pegs. The shade cloth will keep worms, beetles and other organisms from tunnelling through and spoiling the sand.
3 Finish the edge of the pit with timber sleepers. Drill holes through the sleepers and secure them to the ground with stakes. Ensure the sleepers are free of splinters.
4 Fill the pit with fine sand.
5 Make a lid or cover from Perspex or fibre cement sheet set into a timber frame. This will help keep leaves and water out of the pit and prevent cats from using the sandpit as a toilet.

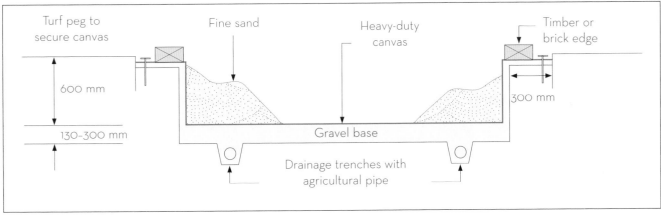

Turf peg to secure canvas

Fine sand

Heavy-duty canvas

Timber or brick edge

600 mm

300 mm

130–300 mm

Gravel base

Drainage trenches with agricultural pipe

BASIC PLAYHOUSE

TOOLS

- Square
- Straight edge
- Tape measure
- Pencil
- Clamps
- Circular saw
- Handsaw
- Jigsaw
- Smoothing plane
- Hammer
- Nail punch
- Notched trowel
- Spirit level
- Screwdriver
- Portable electric drill
- Drill bits: 3 mm, 10 mm
- Utility knife
- Cork sanding block
- Dust mask
- Safety glasses
- Hearing protection

This traditional playhouse has self-bracing walls made from plywood, while the roof is a simple king post truss construction covered with hardboard. It has a door and a window in each side wall. It should provide your children with years of pleasure.

CUTTING OUT

1 Using a tape measure, pencil and straight edge, mark out the floor, sides, front and back on the plywood. Check that the pieces are square. Clamp a straight edge to the board and use a circular saw to cut out the parts. Mark and cut out the other pieces.
2 Plane the edges of each piece to the finished size and ensure all are straight and square. Select the best face of each; mark it as the outside.
3 Using a tape measure and straight edge, mark out the windows on the side walls (see the diagram on page 204). Drill a hole in one corner of each opening and cut out with the jigsaw. Smooth the edges with abrasive paper.
4 Mark and cut out a 40 x 50 mm notch in the top corners of the front and back panels and a 470 x 880 mm doorway in the front. Cut the floor to 1150 mm wide except for the porch (see the top diagram on page 206).

THE FLOOR FRAME

5 Turn the floor upside down and lay out the bearers on it. Starting at one end, position the joists between the bearers at intervals of 500 mm.
6 Nail galvanized metal brackets in each corner of the floor frame. Ensure the frame sits flush with the outside edges of the floor board, excluding the 25 mm overhang at the front and sides of the porch.
7 Turn the frame upright and apply adhesive to the top, using ample amounts around each intersection. Place the floor onto the frame, ensuring it is square, and nail it in place. Seal the underside of the structure with an exterior finish.
8 Choose a level location for the playhouse, so the porch faces the sun. Place house bricks at each corner and in the middle of the long sides to raise the frame at least 75 mm off the ground. Use a spirit level to ensure the brick piers are level. Position the floor frame on the bricks.

ATTACHING THE WALLS

9 Place adhesive along the sides of the bearers and edges of the floor board and firmly press the side walls against them. Ensure that the bottom edge of the walls is flush with the bottom of the bearers and that the wall projects 12 mm at the back. Brace the walls in place.

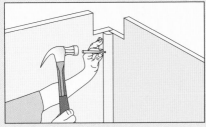

12 Glue a length of interior trim inside each corner and secure it with some panel pins.

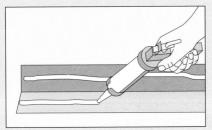

13 Place two-part acrylic adhesive on each exterior trim and press the pieces into place over each outside corner.

10 Attach the back wall to the floor frame in the same way. It should sit between the side panels with the corners flush. Nail the sides to the back.

11 Glue and nail the floor plates to the floor frame on each side of the door position and inset 12 mm from the front ends of the side walls. Glue and nail the front between the sides and flush against the floor plates. Glue and nail the door jambs against the ends of the floor plates and the edges of the doorway.

12 Glue a length of interior trim A inside each back corner. Secure the trim with panel pins. Punch them below the surface and fill with putty. Attach the lengths of interior trim B in the front corners as before.

13 Apply two-part acrylic adhesive on each exterior trim and press it into place over the outside corners. Hold the trim until the adhesive sets.

THE ROOF

14 Place the roof beams on a level surface and position the end beams between them at each end. Ensure the frame is square, then nail

ABOVE LEFT The playhouse can be moved to the shade in summer or left in the sun during the cooler months.

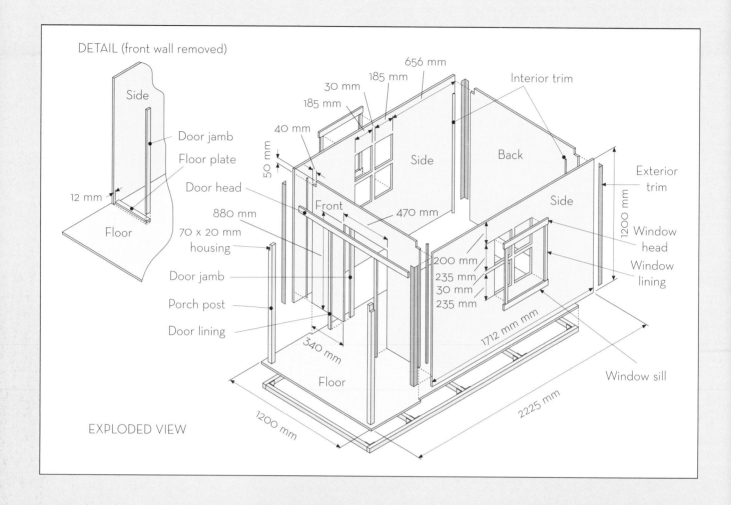

DETAIL (front wall removed)

Side

Door jamb

Floor plate

12 mm

Floor

Door head

880 mm

70 x 20 mm
housing

Door jamb

Porch post

Door lining

340 mm

Floor

EXPLODED VIEW

656 mm

30 mm

185 mm

185 mm

40 mm

50 mm

Front

Side

Back

Interior trim

Exterior
trim

1200 mm

Window
head

Window
lining

470 mm

200 mm

235 mm

30 mm

235 mm

Side

1712 mm mm

Window sill

1200 mm

2225 mm

ABOVE Working drawings for the basic
playhouse project.

right-angle brackets in each corner. Attach temporary braces in two
corners to hold the frame square.

15 In the centre top of each king post, cut a housing 35 mm wide and
70 mm deep. Centre a king post on each end beam and fix it in place
using right-angle brackets. Set the ridge in the housings in the king
posts. Apply adhesive and fix it in place with 50 mm screws. Cut
45 degree splays on both ends of each roof brace and screw them in
place between the king post and bottom of the ridge.

16 Position five rafters on each side of the roof frame, one at each end and
the others evenly spaced. Remove the rafters. Plane 45 degree splays
on the ridge and beams to provide a seat for the rafters. Reposition the
rafters and screw them in place using 30 mm screws. (Drill holes for the
screws at the ridge end of the rafters to prevent the timber splitting.)

GABLES AND ROOF SHEETS

17 Position the gables on the ends of the roof frame. Mark the roof slope
on the back of the gables and cut them to shape. Plane the edges
smooth. Apply adhesive and fix them with 30 mm nails.

18 Position the packers on the splayed edge of the ridge midway between
each rafter. Nail them to the ridge.

MATERIALS*

PART	MATERIAL	FINISHED LENGTH	WIDTH	NO.
Floor	12 mm plywood	2225 mm	1200 mm	1
Side	12 mm plywood	1712 mm	1200 mm	2
Front	12 mm plywood	1150 mm	1113 mm	1
Back	12 mm plywood	1150 mm	1200 mm	1
Window lining	12 mm plywood	500 mm	25 mm	4
Window head	12 mm plywood	470 mm	50 mm	2
Window sill	12 mm plywood	470 mm	50 mm	2
Door lining	12 mm plywood	880 mm	25 mm	2
Door head	12 mm plywood	1150 mm	50 mm	1
Gable	12 mm plywood	1200 mm	688 mm	2
Roof sheet	5.5 mm hardboard	2376 mm	920 mm	2
Floor bearer	70 x 45 mm treated timber	2200 mm		2
Floor joist	70 x 45 mm treated timber	1070 mm		5
Door ledge	50 x 25 mm timber	470 mm		2
Door brace	50 x 25 mm timber	950 mm		1
Door jamb	50 x 25 mm timber	880 mm		2
Floor plate	50 x 25 mm timber	340 mm		2
Packer	50 x 25 mm timber	469 mm		8
Roof beam	75 x 38 mm timber	2376 mm		2
End beam	75 x 38 mm timber	1072 mm		2
King post	75 x 38 mm timber	450 mm		2
Ridge	75 x 38 mm timber	2376 mm		1
Roof brace	75 x 38 mm timber	600 mm		2
Rafter	100 x 25 mm timber	900 mm		10
Porch post	50 x 50 mm timber	1063 mm		2
Door cladding	T&G boards**	880 mm		4
Interior trim A	19 mm quarter angle	1063 mm		2
Interior trim B	19 mm quarter angle	1044 mm		2
Eaves stiffener	19 mm quarter angle	2376 mm		2
Exterior trim A	25 x 25 mm plastic angle	1150 mm		2
Exterior trim B	25 x 25 mm plastic angle	1063 mm		2
Roof trim	25 x 25 mm plastic angle	2376 mm		1
Gable trim	25 x 25 mm plastic angle	920 mm		4

Other: Epoxy-resin adhesive; two-part acrylic adhesive; 24 small galvanized steel right-angle brackets; 30 x 2 mm helical-thread nails; 30 mm panel pins; 30 mm x 6 gauge countersunk screws; 50 mm x 10 gauge countersunk screws; timber putty; abrasive paper; two 75 mm T-hinges with 20 mm screws; 40–45 mm doorknob; house bricks; exterior grade finish of choice.

* Finished size: 2400 x 1400 mm and 1700 mm high without brick piers. Four 2400 x 1200 mm sheets of plywood were used.

** Use tongue-and-groove lining boards. Boards 130 mm wide with double 'V' rebates were used.

DIY
MAJOR PROJECT

RIGHT Set out for the floor frame.

BELOW RIGHT The roof structure.

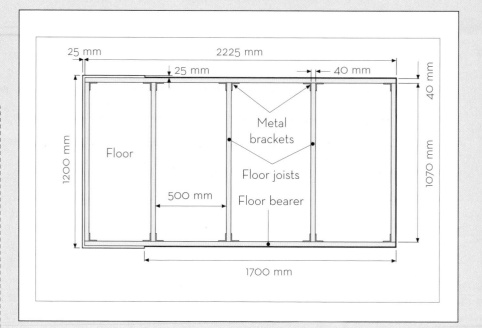

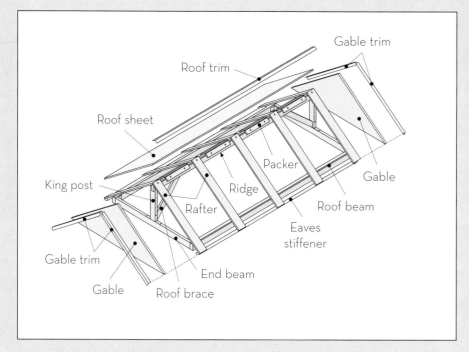

19 Attach the eaves stiffener to the ends of the rafter overhangs using panel pins. Punch them below the surface and fill with putty.

20 Make sure that the roof sheets sit snugly on the frame and that the finished edges line up. Using a notched trowel, apply some adhesive to the rafters, packers and eaves stiffener on one side of the roof frame. Then turn the frame over and lay it on the roof sheet. Next, weight down the rafters and leave until the adhesive sets. Repeat with the other roof sheet, then plane along the ridge to make a neat edge for the roof trim.

21 Glue the roof trim along the ridge to cover and seal the joint in the roofing. Cut the ends of the trim with a utility knife to fit neatly with the gable ends. Position the gable trims and cut them to fit where they meet the roof trim at the ridge, then glue into place.

WINDOWS AND DOOR

22 Glue the window linings to the exterior wall on each side of the window and secure them with panel pins. Punch the pins below the surface and fill the holes with putty. Attach the window head and windowsill at the top and bottom of the linings in a similar manner.

THE DOOR

23 Position the door linings so they overlap the opening by 10 mm. Glue and nail them in position. In the same way fix the door head in position, ensuring that it sits flush against the top of the linings. Sand the edges of the doorway and the door jamb smooth.

24 Apply adhesive to one side of the door ledges and nail the tongue-and-groove door cladding to them. Glue and nail the door brace between the ledges on a diagonal.

25 Mark out a decorative design on the door. Cut out the design with the jigsaw and then smooth the edges with abrasive paper.

26 Screw the strap of the T-hinges to the door ledges, then screw the butt of the hinges to the jambs. Attach the door knob.

TO FINISH

27 Before fixing the roof to the walls, smooth all surfaces with abrasive paper. Use fine abrasive paper on the plastic trim. Apply an undercoat and finished gloss coat of paint. Allow the paint to dry well.

28 Lift the roof into place, ensuring the roof beams rest in the notches of the front and back walls with an 80 mm overhang at the back. Use 30 mm screws to fix them through the side walls near each corner.

29 In the top of each porch post cut a 70 x 20 mm housing to take the roof beam. Plane the sharp edges from the posts.

30 Hammer a helical shaft nail into the base of each post, leaving a 10 mm projection. The posts should sit near the front corners of the porch. Drill 3 mm holes for these nails in the porch floor so that the posts will fit under the beams. Fit the posts in position, with the nails in the holes. Screw the posts to the roof beams with 50 mm screws and skew-nail them to the floor.

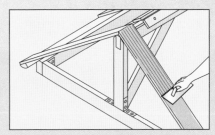

20 Use a notched trowel to apply adhesive to the timbers in one side of the roof frame.

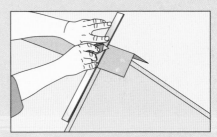

21 Glue the plastic roof trim along the ridge, then cut the ends flush with a utility knife.

PLANTING YOUR GARDEN

For enthusiasts, gardening is one of the most enjoyable and satisfying pastimes. The rewards are great — creating a harmonious garden picture of colour and form, growing delicious produce and providing habitat for wildlife. If you're new to gardening, it can seem a little confusing at first, but with careful planning and the right preparation, you'll soon be enjoying the fruits of your labours.

In this chapter we tell you how to choose the right plants for your soil, climate and aspect; how to plant, progagate and prune; and how to use colour, shape, form and texture in the garden to create a style that suits you and your lifestyle.

FINDING A STYLE

Garden designs range from the minimalist, which is mainly focused on form and architecture — for instance, the formal shrub garden — to those with an unrestrained character, full of colour and variety.

A minimalist garden typically features hard materials or water cover over much of the horizontal surface, leaving relatively little for the gardener to do. To achieve an harmonious look, this style of design requires skill and careful planning; it is a style that tends to suit formal buildings and shaded inner-city gardens.

At the other end of the spectrum, the cottage garden style relies more on herbaceous perennials, grown together in glorious profusion. For this style of garden to succeed, you'll need to develop your gardening skills. The nature of the plantings will be determined by the local climate, the aspect of your garden and the type of soil.

Reading and learning about your garden will provide you with invaluable information. Draw inspiration from books and magazine articles as well as open gardens and garden shows. Keep a notebook of your ideas and a record of your successes and failures and, above all, enjoy the adventure of gardening.

ABOVE From lush woodland plantings (opposite) to cottage gardens (above left) and striking architectural plants, there is a gardening style to suit all tastes and budgets.

TOP Well-chosen bog plants will enhance a damp, shady spot.

ABOVE Lavender grows in climates similar to their Mediterranean origins — cold, wet winters and hot, dry summers — so plant them in a sunny, open position in well-drained soil.

CHOOSING THE RIGHT PLANT

In gardening it's very important to ensure that the plants you choose will flourish in the environment you're offering them. Fortunately, even the most modest garden has some naturally varying conditions — spots in full sun and shade as well as dry or moist areas. However, the soil has certain characteristics that to some degree will determine what you can grow.

SOIL PH

Although many plants aren't too fussy, some will simply refuse to flourish if they're planted in the wrong conditions. For instance, plants that grow naturally in coniferous areas of the world have learnt to adapt to high levels of acidity, and if they're not given similarly acid conditions in your garden, they'll eventually curl up and die. Azaleas and rhododendrons relish acid soil and damp conditions. Other plants, having learnt to cope with the thin limestone-based soils of their native countries, will not flourish in soils with a high level of acidity.

So one of your first tasks should be to determine the acid balance in your soil (see opposite) and ensure you grow plants that enjoy these conditions. You can improve or alter the soil conditions yourself, but it's a slow process and unless you're willing to put in the work, you may be better off limiting your choice of plants to what will grow there naturally.

DAMP CONDITIONS

Very few gardens have natural boggy areas, but if you want to grow moisture-loving plants, it's not difficult to create a pool or a bog garden. Damp-loving plants vary from those that prefer really deep water to those that simply prefer moist conditions. If you have a pool, create more than one level so that you can accommodate both deep-water and shallow-water plants. Water lilies, for example, generally need about 1 m of water, while marsh marigolds prefer shallow water about 15 cm deep. If you create a small bog garden, using a rubber liner to act as a water-retaining membrane, you can then grow a wide range of moisture lovers. (For more information on water gardens, see page 176.)

DRY CONDITIONS

Your garden will almost certainly have areas where the conditions are drier than elsewhere — for example, at the foot of walls, and on the sheltered side of any tall building. If you don't choose the appropriate plants for these conditions you'll have to spend a lot more time watering these parts of the garden.

Plants that enjoy dry conditions tend to have smaller leaves, which are waxy or hairy to prevent water loss. Species that grow on hillsides in the Mediterranean — for example, herbs such as rosemary and lavender — fall into this category, as do the more extreme desert plants, such as sedum and agave.

LEFT Once established, a garden featuring azaleas and rhododendrons is very low-maintenance. These mostly evergreen shrubs flower flamboyantly and also add year-round foliage and structure to your garden.

TESTING THE SOIL

To find out whether your soil is acid or alkaline, use a standard soil-test kit, which you can purchase from nurseries and garden centres.

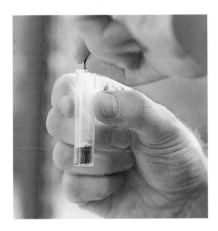

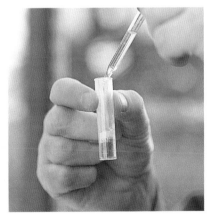

1 Remove a small handful of soil from the area to be tested and place it in the test tube. Then add the soil-test powder included in the kit.

2 Next, add distilled water to the level marked on the side of the test tube. Secure the lid and shake the test tube. Wait for the liquid to change colour.

3 Compare the liquid to the pH colour chart supplied. A yellow or orange liquid indicates an acid soil, while a bright green liquid indicates a neutral soil.

ABOVE You can create an attractive border without using colour. Texture and form are just as important, as these bamboos demonstrate.

ABOVE RIGHT Silver birch (*Betula pendula*) has beautiful bark in metallic tones, making it a feature in winter when the branches are bare.

PLANNING THE PLANTING

To create an attractive planting plan, you need to consider the three-dimensional effects of plants as well as scale, colour, texture and the changes that will happen over the different seasons and in the long term. Orchestrating these different elements requires skill and careful planning.

Any successful planting scheme incorporates a variety of material. Ideally, you should grow plants with a range of heights, forms and foliage types. With their single stems and canopy of foliage, trees will create areas of shade, add privacy and provide a much needed habitat for wildlife. However, remember that tree roots run to the extent of the canopy and that you should never plant large trees close to house walls in case they damage the foundations, drains or service pipes.

Shrubs range from low-growing, spreading varieties, which will act as useful ground cover, to plants as high as 6 m, and these can form part of the framework of your garden. Choosing a mixture of evergreen and deciduous shrubs will help to ensure that your garden is attractive all year round, so it's worth checking if your favourite plants will look good out of season. For example, do they have attractively coloured bark, autumn foliage colour or perhaps scented winter flowers?

PLANTING STYLE

The style of planting you choose will be determined not only by the space available, but also by the amount of spare time you have for gardening. Good low-maintenance plantings include shrub borders, ground covers, especially mat-like spreading types, and foliage perennials such as ferns, bamboos and grasses.

PERENNIAL BORDERS

If you have the time, consider creating a traditional perennial border. It will stretch your talents as a designer as you strive to orchestrate a display of appropriately sized plants in your chosen colours as the seasons unfold. You'll need not only an artist's eye to plan the colour scheme but also the patience to work out the eventual height and spread of each plant, so the border rises in height towards the back, ensuring that each plant is seen in all its glory.

Contemporary garden design has embraced the use of grasses in herbaceous borders. Proponents of these mixed plantings — designers such as Beth Chatto and Piet Oudolf — have created an interest in a much more relaxed style, which allows nature a freer hand. This kind of planting tends to concentrate on large blocks of colour in toning shades; the plants are chosen for their similarity in height and form, creating a gentle sweep of colour across the garden.

However, it's important to remember that no planting scheme will work well unless you have chosen the right plants for the conditions in your garden. Obviously, a dry, sunny border requires a very different mix of plants compared to a damp, shady area.

BELOW In this large wetlands garden, designed by Piet Oudolf, perennials in toning colours make an harmonious picture of colour and texture.

ABOVE When drawing your garden to scale, start with any structures such as walls and arches as well as existing trees and large shrubs.

ABOVE RIGHT When you're designing your garden, it's a good idea to approach it as if you're decorating a room in your house: collect samples of plants and hard landscaping features such as pavers and gravel, and make sketches to work out your colour schemes.

OPPOSITE The fresh combination of yellow and white in this garden has more impact because blocks of the same plants have been used.

CREATING A PLANTING PLAN

If you're planning to plant a new garden, or replant an existing one, you'll need to draw up a plan. This can cover the whole garden, or just a portion of it. If you plant up one part, make sure that the scheme blends well with the remainder of the garden. If the change between sections is too abrupt it will make the garden feel uncomfortably restless.

STARTING TO PLAN

The key to drawing up a planting plan is to keep it simple. On a sketch of your garden, drawn to scale, map out the structural planting first — the large trees and shrubs as well as any vertical elements, such as hedges, pergolas and arches. Once you're happy with the position of these elements, consider the infill planting.

Most people find it hard to take the mental leap from a flat plan to the three-dimensional reality of a garden. One solution is to take photos of different areas of the garden, and enlarge them on a photocopier. Then, using a felt pen, sketch the proportions of the outlines and shapes of the new planting on the photos.

Take the time to plan your planting carefully: make a note of not only flower colour but also leaf form, flowering season and the likely height and spread of each plant. It may be helpful to make a rough sketch of the forms and shapes of the plants you intend to grow. Write the flowering time on the drawing and colour it appropriately. If you want to grow a plant mainly for its foliage, use the foliage colour as the main guide.

To work out how many plants to include, take note of the eventual height and spread of each plant. If you allow two-thirds of the space indicated on the label, you'll get it more or less right. To fill the gaps in the first couple of years, plant fast-growing annuals or perennials, which you can remove easily. On the whole, use larger plants for infilling, as their character, size and colour often better suit the overall look of the scheme.

ABOVE Before you start planting, organize all the materials you'll need.

ABOVE RIGHT Check potted plants before you buy them. The potting compost should be just held together by the roots, not packed with them like this one.

WHAT TO BUY

When you're deciding how to plant up your garden, first work out a realistic budget for the plants, then consider the time frame in which you can do the work. It may be practical — in terms of cost and time — to spread the planting over several seasons.

BUYING PLANTS

If you're stocking a garden from scratch, plan for (and then buy) the largest elements first. The best sources of large plants are reputable nurseries, where the stock is raised by the owners, or good garden centres with a high turnover of stock. The bigger the plant, the more expensive it will be, so obviously you won't want to waste money on diseased or damaged trees or shrubs. Check each plant for health and vigour as well as a good balanced shape. Look for strong and bushy plants.

But the plant's natural habit will, to some extent, govern its form. Before you buy, check out the illustrated section of any good plant reference guide so you can get an idea of how the plant will look. It's always best to plant in the cooler seasons of the year, when there is less risk of the plants drying out. If you plant in autumn, the plants will have a full season in which to establish a good root system before producing new growth in spring.

If you're planting herbaceous perennials, buy them in groups of odd numbers: each group will form a feature, and the effect on the garden will be more harmonious and balanced than if you plant a much wider variety of single plants.

CHECK LIST FOR BUYING PLANTS

It's probably easier to look out for things to avoid. Here are a few problems you may encounter when choosing plants.

- The first thing to do when purchasing a plant is to scrutinize it closely for any sign of insect or larval activity. A number of pests can take hold and quickly overwhelm young plants, especially if they are already weakened by lack of water.
- Damaged leaves are most likely to be caused by pests such as mites, aphids or slugs, but could also be due to poor soil where nutrients are in short supply. If the plant is severely damaged, choose another.
- Yellow leaves can be the result of a number of problems, such as nutrient deficiency and fusarium wilt, which causes the plant to wilt and die.

TOP LEFT Healthy herb seedlings with plenty of lush growth, ready for planting out.

TOP TO BOTTOM Damaged leaves are usually caused by insects; yellow leaves can be a sign of nutrient deficiency; and insect pests may be hiding on the undersides of leaves.

ABOVE Don't buy bulbs in this state. Once bulbs start to shoot, they have used up much of their stored reserves of energy and growing capacity, and they are unlikely to give a good flowering display.

TOP In this cottage garden, alliums have been planted with columbines and geraniums; the delphiniums in the foreground are about to flower.

PLANTING TECHNIQUES

Once you've finalized your garden design and planting plan and also prepared the site properly (see 'Landscaping your garden', page 11), you're ready for the fun of planting.

PLANTING PERENNIALS, ANNUALS AND BULBS

You can combine perennials, annuals and bulbs to form beautiful displays. Perennials add colour and structure to the garden and form the basis of a planting scheme, while annuals are one-year wonders that offer instant colour and form. From tiny jewels to show-stopping giants, bulbs require relatively little effort and produce a remarkably good show, mainly in spring and summer.

PLANTING PERENNIALS

The ideal time to plant out hardy perennials is either autumn or spring. However, planting in autumn gives perennial plants the opportunity to establish themselves before the following flowering season.

As a general rule of thumb, make the planting hole about 13 cm larger in diameter than the root ball. If the soil is dry, fill the prepared hole with water, then mix a small quantity of bonemeal, or a similar fertilizer, into the base of the hole. Position the plant so that the crown is level with the surface of the surrounding soil, then backfill the hole. Finally, carefully firm the soil around the plant with the heel of your boot or shoe, taking care not to mound soil around the stem above the crown.

PLANTING ANNUALS

When planting annuals that have been raised under cover in containers, use the same method as for perennials, but this time dispense with the bonemeal fertilizer at the base of the planting hole. If the annuals have been grown in biodegradable pots, you can plant these as they are.

PLANTING BULBS

As a general rule, plant bulbs to at least twice their depth — for example, plant a bulb measuring 5 cm from top to bottom at least 10–13 cm deep. For taller-growing bulbs such as gladioli, use supports to keep them upright. Shorter bulbs with heavy flower heads, such as hyacinths, will also need supporting; you can make an attractive cage from bamboo canes or willow stems tied with raffia. Improve heavy, poorly drained soil, which may cause the bulbs to rot, by mixing in horticultural grit before you plant.

REPEAT FLOWERING

If you want your bulbs to flower in their second year, you must fertilize and water them once flowering is over. This provides the necessary nutrients for the bulb to produce the following year's flowers. Do not remove the leaves until they're dead, as they are needed to produce food for the plant.

PLANTING BULBS

Make sure you plant bulbs to their correct depth. These gladiolus corms should be planted to a depth that's three times their own height.

1 Gently squeeze the gladiolus corms to check that they're firm and solid. If they're soft, it means they've deteriorated.

2 Position the corms in random groups of odd numbers over freshly dug, weed-free soil. Dig a hole to a depth that is three times the height of each corm.

3 Plant each corm so that the growing tip is uppermost. Press gently into the soil. Cover the corm with soil, and then firm the soil into place.

LEFT A simple two-tiered planting scheme. When the tulips die down, the pansies will help to disguise their yellowing leaves.

HOW CLIMBERS PROGRESS

Climbers can be divided into three groups — clingers, twiners and scrambling plants.

Clingers, such as ivy, don't require support: they attach themselves with aerial roots or sucker pads.

Twiners, such as clematis and jasmine, will twist their long, flexible stems around a support.

Scrambling plants climb by using hooked thorns along their stems; rambling roses, for example, will grow to 9 m or more.

CLIMBERS AND WALL SHRUBS

Plant climbers and wall shrubs with care in positions where they will be able to extend themselves comfortably. You may have to provide them with an appropriate support.

Like trees, climbers need space for their roots, and most need some help in the period after planting to encourage them to grow in the right direction, up the supports you've provided. Since climbers are usually planted close to a support such as a wall, where the soil may be dry and lacking in nutrients, some extra preparation will give the plants a good start and help them to establish.

Walls, pergolas, fences, trees and old tree stumps will all provide a useful backdrop or support for climbing plants. You can also grow climbers over shrubs or another climber, but take care that the more vigorous plant does not smother the weaker one. Some climbers are extremely vigorous, and unless the support is very strong, the combined weight of foliage and flowers may break it. Included among these hefty giants are the large rambling roses, such as 'Bobbie James' or 'Rambling Rector', which will easily reach 10 m and need a large tree for support.

With its delicate stems and beautiful flowers, clematis can be grown over shrubs, giving you flowers for a longer period than just those of the shrub. Although most climbers prefer a wall in full sun, a few, including the golden hop (*Humulus lupulus* 'Aureus') and *Hydrangea anomala* subsp. *petiolaris*, do well in shadier areas.

PLANTING CLIMBERS AND WALL SHRUBS

A planting hole for a new climber or wall shrub should be at least 13 cm larger than the diameter of the root ball and deep enough for the base of the stem to be level with the surrounding soil. Clematis should be planted slightly deeper, as they are susceptible to wilt (see page 109). If this happens, and the plant is deeply planted, it may grow again from the roots, so don't dig up an apparently dying clematis plant for at least one season. Give the young plant a strong supporting framework and tie the leading shoot into this to encourage it to grow in the direction you want.

CLIMBING FAVOURITES

Clematis are beautiful climbing plants but also gross feeders and they must have a cool root run. Train *Clematis montana*, suitable for large gardens, on a pole, trellis or tree supports; let *C. alpina* and *C. flammula* scramble over walls or arbours.

Some other favourites include: passionfruit (*Passiflora edulis*), an evergreen climber with delicious fruit and stunning flowers; Virginia creeper, such as *Parthenocissus henryana,* a deciduous tendril climber of great autumn beauty; wisteria, an extremely vigorous and long lasting climber with deciduous leaves of many leaflets and long sprays of mauve flowers in early spring; bluebell creeper (*Sollya heterophylla*), a delicate twiner, only borderline hardy, with cane-like stems, small green leaves and profuse flowers like bright blue stars; and tender purple wreath (*Petrea volubilis*), a slender twiner with large, heart-shaped leaves and sprays of star-like lilac and purple blossoms.

LEFT Climbing roses need strong support. Here 'Madame Grégoire Staechelin', 'Constance Spry' and 'Complicata' are underplanted with seaside daisy.

VINE EYES AND WIRES FOR WALLS AND FENCES

First, check that the fence you're using is in good enough condition to hold the weight of the climber you wish to grow. You can put in place extra supports, such as netting, once the climber is established.

1 Using the shaft of a screwdriver as leverage, screw in a long-shanked eye. Attach eyes at intervals along the length of the fence.

2 Take a length of galvanized wire (which is resistant to rust and so suitable for outdoor use), loop it through the eyes and secure.

3 Using pliers, tighten the wire until it is taut and then proceed to tighten the eyes along the length of the fence panel.

ABOVE In this charming walled potager, willow stems have been woven into vertical structures to support climbing beans.

SUPPORTS FOR CLIMBERS

Where space is at a premium, vertical gardening (growing plants upwards rather than sideways) allows you to incorporate new features that overcome space limitations. You can try arches, tripods and wigwams in both classic and informal styles. These support the plants and let them develop fully without taking up much room in the garden or on the patio.

If you want to grow climbing plants through supports, there are a number of important factors that you'll need to consider before you decide what to plant.

Try to choose a structure that will suit the plants it will support; this is especially important for plants that have twining stems or tendrils. The support should be thin enough for the plant to twine and grip happily — usually about the thickness of an ordinary bamboo cane. If the support you've chosen has a larger diameter than this, you'll need to use extra ties or training in addition to the structure itself.

Also, if the supports are too thick, the climbing plants will tend to cling to each other rather than to the support. Slender supports, such as hazel and willow twigs or bamboo canes, are ideal for supporting plants like sweet peas. They are strong enough to support the weight of the plants and thin enough to become totally obscured by foliage and flowers as the plants become established and cover the support.

Don't plant a rampant climber, such as Russian vine or *Vitis cognetiae*, unless you're prepared to keep it under control: neglected, unpruned climbers can pull down fences, strangle trees get into guttering and cause arguments with your neighbours.

LEFT and ABOVE A sweat pea 'wigwam' provides a glorious scent and is an ideal way to use climbers in a limited space, such as a courtyard garden. After you've planted the seedlings, position the wigwam over the centre of the pot.

PLANTING A WIGWAM

1 Select a suitable container. If required, make some drainage holes in the base. Line the base with sheets of newspaper to stop the compost running out of the drainage holes. The paper will rot away within a couple of weeks. Add the compost to the required level.
2 Place the wigwam into position, pushing it into the compost.
3 Using a piece of wood as a scribe, mark a line in the compost around the outside of the wigwam legs.
4 Remove the wigwam frame and gently plant the sweet peas into the compost. Replace the wigwam frame in its original position and press it firmly into place.

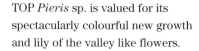

TOP *Pieris* sp. is valued for its spectacularly colourful new growth and lily of the valley like flowers.

ABOVE Photinias make wonderfully dense evergreen hedges, but if you leave them unclipped, the plants will produce panicles of spring flowers.

ABOVE RIGHT A tapestry of colourful foliage, flowers and form.

SHRUBS AND TREES

Whether you raise your own trees and shrubs or buy them from a garden centre or nursery, you'll need to transfer them into their permanent positions. In order to give the young tree or shrub a good start, it's helpful to understand its specific requirements.

In terms of cost and their contribution to the garden, trees and shrubs are quite an investment. They form the framework or structure of your garden, provide shade and privacy, and add value to your property. It pays to ensure that they get off to the best possible start, so plant them carefully. Check that the chosen shrub or tree is appropriate for the conditions in your garden: some prefer a certain soil type and condition. For example, don't plant acid-loving plants, such as camellias or pieris, in a shallow chalk soil as they will always struggle, producing poor growth or yellow leaves. You should also ensure that the chosen plant is not likely to cause problems with your foundations.

DIGGING THE HOLE

Dig a tree's planting hole wide and deep enough to accommodate not only the existing root ball but also the roots as they gradually push further and wider in search of nutrients. Once you've planted the tree, make a well around the trunk to hold water.

If you don't take the trouble to plant a tree properly, you'll prevent the roots from searching out the necessary nutrients and moisture. The tree will go into a state of semi-dormancy and there will be less growth in the short term.

PROVIDING SUPPORT

Plant a tree as you would a perennial, but provide a support for the stem (see below) so that it doesn't fall over and move around too much in high winds. Any rocking movement can destabilize the roots.

PLANNING AHEAD

A mixture of evergreen and deciduous trees provides the best framework for a garden. Even a small garden needs at least one small tree in order to provide some vertical interest. Knowing the ultimate size of the tree before you buy it will save you a lot of time, trouble and money later. If you plant a young tree too close to other trees and shrubs, you'll have to replant it within the first 5–10 years of its life. So try to visualize the tree's height and spread in about 20 years time and plan accordingly.

ABOVE The exquisite silk tree (*Albizia julibrissin*) flowers in late spring and summer. These deciduous trees rarely grow more than 8 m and are trouble-free in the garden.

SUPPORTING YOUNG TREES

Young trees need support until they become established. Use three stakes and secure them with ties in a 'figure-eight' loop. To position each stake, follow these step by step instructions.

1 Position the stake at 45 degrees to the plant's stem or trunk and approximately 25–30 cm above ground level.

2 Tie the tree to the stake, making sure there is a space between the plant and the stake to prevent any rubbing.

3 Ensure the tie is about 4 cm below the top of the stake to prevent the stem from hitting it.

CREATING A LAWN

A lawn is a long-term project, so it's important to prepare the soil well before sowing seeds or laying turf. First, remove any perennial weeds and stones from the site. Then, make sure the area is level, as lawns are notoriously difficult to mow if they are uneven.

LEVELLING THE GROUND

There are various ways to level the ground, depending on the size of the area. For large areas, the simplest solution is to knock wooden pegs, marked with black pen to indicate the height, into the ground, each to the same depth. Then run string between the pegs at the desired height and adjust the soil surface so that it's level with the string. If you're laying turf, allow 5 cm for the turf's thickness on top of the desired height.

DRAINAGE

Another factor to consider when planning a new lawn is drainage. Lawn grasses grow best on well drained, light soil. If your garden is waterlogged and the soil generally composed of heavy clay, you'll need to drain the area first, and you should also incorporate generous quantities of sand

LEVELLING A SITE

You'll find it's so much easier to mow a lawn if the ground is level. Here's a simple method for levelling a site before laying turf or sowing lawn seeds.

1 Mark out the area with canes and a clearly visible string line.

2 Using a hammer, knock wooden pegs into the soil at 2 m intervals.

3 Use a level and a 2 m straight-edged board to check that the tops of the wooden pegs are level. Rake the soil between the upright pegs accordingly.

LEFT Grass roots spread rapidly, but in order for them to penetrate to their maximum depth, they need a regular and plentiful supply of moisture.

and organic matter into the soil itself. To drain a waterlogged site, install a simple soakaway system (see pages 52–7). Add bulky organic matter to very light soils to maximize their water-retaining properties.

PREPARING THE GROUND

Once you have levelled the ground and dealt with drainage issues, you'll need to make the surface firm. Simply tread on the ground, making sure you have covered the whole area. Once it is firm and level, rake the ground to create a fine tilth. Leave the area fallow for a few weeks, then hoe off any weeds that have germinated during this time. Finally, apply a proprietary lawn fertilizer, following the manufacturer's recommended rate of application.

GROWING GRASS

You can either sow a new lawn from seed or you can lay turf. Turf produces instant results but seed is cheaper, so in large gardens, sowing seed is probably the better option. Seed is also the practical option for repairing small bare patches in a lawn. For larger areas, you can replace sections of turf or reuse existing turf in combination with sowing seed.

SOWING SEED

First, check the rate of application for the grass you're using. The seed supplier will provide you with the recommended rates, generally 28–40 g per sq m. If you sow too thinly, the lawn will take longer to establish; if you sow too thickly, the seedlings will compete with each other. Sow large areas by machine, which dispenses the seed evenly; sowing by hand is fine for smaller areas.

THINGS TO CONSIDER

Before deciding whether to have a lawn, think about the wear and tear it will be subjected to. Will it be used by children and household pets or splashed with water from a swimming pool? If the lawn is to be a play area, then you should consider the texture, wear tolerance, hardiness and recovery rate of the grass variety you choose.

ABOVE Lawn grasses grow best in moderately acid to neutral soil. If the lawn is sparse but there are lots of weeds, you may have soil that is too acid. Test the soil, and if the pH is below 5.5, apply lime, then water it in.

PREPARING TO SOW

Mark out the area to be sown in squares of around 2 x 2 m so that you can sow each one before moving on to the next. Work out the quantity of seed for each area and, using a cup or small pail, scatter the seed in one direction and back again to cover the whole area. After sowing, lightly rake the surface to cover the seed, and water it regularly to stimulate germination. Once the seedlings reach about 5 cm in height, you can cut the lawn to roughly half this height with a rotary mower.

LAYING A NEW LAWN FROM TURF

You can lay a new lawn from turf in almost any season, except during frost, droughts or very wet weather. Buy good quality turf from a reputable source. It's usually sold in small rolls, about 30 cm wide by 1 m long. To save waste and unnecessary expense, make sure that you estimate the area correctly before you order. Organize the ordering and delivery of the turf at a convenient time, since ideally, you should lay it the day it's delivered. Inspect it when it is delivered to ensure it is in good condition. If you do have to store the turf for more than a few days before using it, unroll it and lay it surface up in a shady place and cover with plastic sheeting. If you keep the turf like this for more than 48 hours, water it.

Lay the turf with staggered joins, as you would a brick wall. Use the nearest straight edge as a guide and work in rows. In dry weather, water it well, and continue watering daily until the turf becomes established.

SOWING A LAWN

Seed takes longer than turf to establish a lawn, but if it's sown in spring or autumn and you prepare the soil well, it will produce a good-quality result.

1 Rake the prepared soil again to form a finely tilled seed bed, removing any large stones and using the rake to break up any remaining lumps of soil.

2 Mark out the area into equal squares. Weigh out the seed for each square.

3 Sow the seed evenly with your hand at about knee level, half in each direction. Finish by lightly raking the area.

LEFT Before you lay the turf, set up a taut string line to use as a guide.

LAYING TURF

Turf provides an almost instant effect, although it may be several weeks before it's fully stable. As you work, stand on a length of flat board to avoid damaging the newly laid turf.

1 Starting from one corner, lay the first row of turf alongside a plank or string line that has been pulled taut to get a straight edge.

2 From the same corner, lay the second row at right angles to the first. Set each piece so that the joints are staggered, and firm them into place.

3 Spread a dressing of sandy loam over the turf, brushing or raking it into any gaps to prevent the edges of the turf from drying out and shrinking.

ABOVE A basic propagation unit should include seed trays and pots, a pressing board for firming the seed-raising mix, a pair of secateurs, a sharp garden knife and labels.

ABOVE RIGHT A propagating case helps to ensure that seeds germinate and cuttings take root.

PROPAGATING PLANTS

Many plants can be reproduced or propagated relatively easily. The simplest forms of propagation — raising plants from seeds, taking cuttings, layering or dividing — are easy for even an amateur to master, and they'll provide you with an inexpensive supply of new plants as well as a great sense of satisfaction.

Some plants are incredibly simple to propagate, while others have to be coaxed into reproduction with the right conditions, such as optimum warmth, light levels and moisture. Some plants, particularly annuals, grow very quickly from seed, creating a magnificent display of flowers within a few weeks of planting. Others, such as most trees, will take years to grow into a plant of reasonable size and you'll be better off obtaining these as bare-rooted plants via mail order or as container-grown specimens.

PROPAGATION METHODS

Plants naturally reproduce themselves from seeds, but it's also possible to create a new plant just from a cut portion (a 'cutting') of the leaf, stem or root. Other similar methods of propagation include division, grafting and layering. All these methods are types of vegetative propagation.

The method of propagation you choose largely depends on which is the most successful and reliable. Although most plants will grow well from seeds, the process can be slow and occasionally the plants do not breed true to type, so that the seedlings differ substantially from the parent plant. If it's particularly important to you that the offspring closely resembles the parent, vegetative propagation is the best option because the new plants are exactly the same as the parent plant. But whichever method of propagation you choose, the first thing you must ensure is that the parent plant looks strong and vigorous, as its state of health will affect the quality of its offspring.

PROPAGATION EQUIPMENT

For small-scale propagation, a small table by a window or a wide window ledge is adequate, although a propagating case (in effect, a mini greenhouse) will certainly improve your chances of success: it will help to control the two factors that most influence successful germination — warmth and moisture. A propagating case is also recommended for use in a greenhouse.

You can, of course, construct your own propagation unit. One simple but effective method is to cover trays with sheets of glass or plastic film. Another is to cover pots of cuttings with cut-down clear plastic bottles.

SAVING SEEDS

Summer and autumn are the seasons for collecting the seeds of a large range of plants, from annuals to hardy perennials. So don't be in a hurry to pull up annuals and cut down perennials — let them set seeds first.

SAVING SEEDS

Although some plants such as honesty and poppies sow themselves, you'll usually need to collect seeds of many others if you want them to appear again in your garden.

1 Wait till the flower heads have set seed, then use a pair of secateurs to cut them.

2 To dry the seeds, lay the flower heads on a tray lined with paper, then leave it in a warm place for a few days.

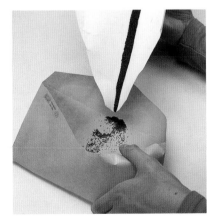

3 Gently shake the flower heads to loosen the seeds, then store them in an envelope or paper bag over winter. Plant in spring.

ABOVE To scarify hard seeds, rub them with abrasive paper.

TOP Collect seeds on a dry day and make sure they're fully ripe. The seed is ready to be collected when the pods or seed cases begin to crack. Seeds are most likely to germinate if they're relatively fresh, so store packets of seed in a cool, dry place and don't keep them for more than a year.

SOWING SEEDS

Most of the plants we grow from seeds are annuals (plants that grow from seed to flower in one growing season) or biennials (plants that do so over two growing seasons). Another group comprises plants that are frost tender, but are actually perennials in their native countries where the climate may be warmer. Members of this group are grown as annuals in colder climates and can be propagated by sowing seeds or by taking cuttings.

When raising plants from seeds, it's important to realize that the seed itself is a tiny powerhouse containing all the genetic material for the plant. This form of evolution has created the most successful method of reproduction. For germination to take place, most plants have very specific needs that are, in effect, a replica of their natural habitat. Seeds from the Mediterranean regions, for example, will germinate at temperatures of 15–21°C, but those from tropical regions will need higher temperatures; in cold climates they'll probably require artificial heat.

For successful germination, provide the seeds with a controlled environment, such as a greenhouse or heated propagator. Novice gardeners usually fail to get seeds to germinate because they don't care for them consistently. Regular watering, well aerated and free-draining compost, warm, stable temperatures and adequate light are all essential.

PREPARING SEEDS

Some seeds have a very hard outer casing, and you'll find germination takes place much more easily if you lightly score this casing before you sow the seeds. This is called scarifying, and it allows air and water to enter the seed, essential for germination to take place. For example, to scarify sweet pea seeds, rub them with some abrasive paper.

Seeds enclosed in fleshy fruits or berries need more vigorous treatment. First mash the fruit, then place it in a jar filled with water and give it a good shake. Remove the pulp that floats to the top and dry the seeds before storing them in paper bags or planting them out.

Certain seeds need to be stimulated out of dormancy before they will germinate. Some cold climate plants need an artificial cool time (called stratification). In nature, this adaptation prevents them from germinating until the last of the cold weather is over so that late frosts and snow don't harm the young seedlings.

SEED-RAISING MIX

The ideal growing medium in which to germinate seeds under cover is made up of two layers. The base layer comprises potting compost (choose one specifically for seeds) and the upper layer horticultural grit or vermiculite, which is free draining. The great advantage of this two-layer system is that the seeds are sown in the free-draining layer of grit, but the potting compost in the layer below provides the nutrients required once the rooting process begins. The alternative is to simply fill the container in which the seeds are to be sown with proprietary potting compost. Soil-free mixes are popular for this purpose.

SOWING SEEDS IN TRAYS

A large number of the plants used for summer beds are half-hardy annuals, and their seeds will not germinate in garden soil until early summer, so sow them under glass in spring.

1 Fill a seed tray with a seed-raising mix. Firm gently until the mix is 1 cm below the rim. For very fine seeds, sieve a second thin layer over the surface and firm lightly.

2 Sow the seeds over the surface as evenly as possible: sow half the seeds in one direction, then turn and sow the remainder in the opposite direction.

3 Cover with a thin layer of compost, grit or vermiculite. Firm gently and water lightly, then cover with a sheet of glass. Add some newspaper if shade is required.

HOW TO SOW

Once you've collect the pots, compost and other equipment, you'll need to establish an area with good light in which to grow the seeds. The average temperature should be around 15°C and should not drop too far below this at night; so germinate seeds in a heated propagating case in a greenhouse or on a windowsill. Once you have sown the seeds (see steps 1–3 above), keep the containers well watered, making sure they don't dry out or become waterlogged. Use a watering can with a fine rose.

WHEN TO TRANSPLANT

A seedling is ready to be transplanted or potted on into individual pots when it has developed its first true leaves. Seedlings develop seed leaves first. These swell on germination to force the seed coat to split open, but the true pair of leaves that appear next indicate the plant is strong enough to handle life outdoors.

HARDENING OFF

Place the seedlings in a cold frame outdoors, then progressively increase the ventilation over 10 days or so until the seedlings are fully acclimatised. This is called 'hardening off'. If you don't have a cold frame, put the seedlings outdoors during the day only and bring them in again at night. When the nights become warmer, leave them outside overnight before transplanting them into their final outdoor positions.

BROADCASTING SEEDS

Broadcast sowing is a useful technique for hardy annuals, salad vegetables such as radishes and spring onions, and green manure crops such as comfrey and mustard.

1 Rake the soil to form a fine tilth, removing any large stones and breaking down large clods. Pour a few seeds into the palm of your hand.

2 Broadcast or scatter the seeds evenly over the soil from a height of about 30 cm.

3 To incorporate the seeds into the soil, lightly rake over the seed bed in at least two different directions. Label the seed bed.

DRILL SOWING

This is a good technique for sowing various annuals and perennials, as well as most vegetables, because it allows you to remove any weeds between the drills more easily.

1 Prepare the seed bed as for broadcast sowing, then mark out the rows with a taut string line.

2 Using a stick, make a groove in the soil along the string line.

3 Sow the seeds thinly by hand, a set distance apart. Using a rake, cover the seeds with soil. Gently pat and firm the soil over the seeds with the back of the rake.

ABOVE Sometimes you might sow seeds too thickly. If this is the case, once they germinate, carefully thin out the seedlings by hand, leaving the strongest.

LEFT An harmonious border densely planted with a mixture of annuals and perennials.

SOWING OUTDOORS

Once the soil warms up in spring, you can sow the seeds of many hardy plants, including hardy annuals, directly into their flowering positions. If you sow seeds directly into the soil, then you need to make sure that you create a very fine tilth by raking it over carefully to remove any lumps of soil or stray pebbles. Such lumps prevent the seeds from reaching the light, thereby reducing the number of seeds that will germinate.

Most seeds should be covered with twice their depth of soil, so the finer the seeds, the closer to the surface they should be sown.

BROADCAST OR DRILLS?

Annuals aren't too fussy about the nutrient content of the soil and will thrive in poor ground, but all seeds need a free-draining, fine-quality soil, with stones or pebbles removed. If you sow the seeds broadcast (literally spread about, rather than in any order), the danger is that then you won't be able to distinguish between the seedlings and young weeds. If you sow in neat rows, or drills, it's easier to see which plants you want to remove and which ones you want to preserve. Remember to label your rows carefully, otherwise you may not remember what you sowed where.

Sowing seeds outdoors can be a hit-or-miss operation, as the vagaries of the weather can easily destroy an entire crop of seedlings. For this reason, it's a good idea to plan for random infilling, so that your overall design isn't marred if the plants fail to flourish in some areas.

WHAT YOU NEED FOR SOWING OUTDOORS

- Fine quality soil without pebbles or stones
- A sunny site without the shade of trees or large shrubs
- A handy water supply close at hand
- Labels or markers

Cuttings can be taken at various points from the parent plant.

- Stem cuttings are cut straight across the stem just below the tip — this point is usually where the current season's growth begins.
- Heel cuttings are created by pulling off a side shoot so that it brings a sliver of the stem (the heel) with it.
- Basal cuttings are prepared from new shoots growing from the crown of a plant, mainly hardy perennials. Remove these cuttings when they are about 5 cm high, and as close to the crown as possible.

TAKING CUTTINGS

The process of taking cuttings allows you to grow a replica of the parent plant. Depending on the type of plant, you can take cuttings from the shoots, roots and leaves.

SOFTWOOD CUTTINGS

These cuttings are taken from the tips of new shoots in spring and early summer. They root more easily than other types, so use this method for plants that are difficult to propagate from mature cuttings. Humidity, warmth and moisture are very important during the rooting period, so use a closed propagating case.

SEMI-RIPE CUTTINGS

Take these cuttings in late summer or early autumn from the current year's growth. They won't root as readily as softwood cuttings, but they have a better survival rate.

HARDWOOD CUTTINGS

These are taken in autumn or winter when the shoots are about a year old, and are rooted outdoors or in a cold frame. They won't root readily unless you apply hormone-rooting powder to the wound. Root formation can be very slow, but most cuttings will root by the next spring.

LOOKING AFTER CUTTINGS

Providing the cuttings with special care in the early stages will encourage new roots to form. To do this, you'll need special potting mix (a mix of equal parts of peat or peat substitute and sharp sand), warmth, light and moisture. Use some kind of transparent cover, such as a cut-down clear plastic bottle, to prevent the cuttings from drying out before they've made roots. You can use a heated propagating case for rooting cuttings.

Since some cuttings can take up to six months to root, you may be tempted to pull them up and inspect them before the process is complete. The plants will have rooted when one or two small new leaves appear on the stem; that's the time to pot on the cutting.

POTTING AND PLANTING OUT

When the cuttings have developed an independent root system, you can pot them. A 9 cm pot is about the right size until each plant is growing strongly enough to be planted out. However, very small cuttings planted directly into borders are easy to pull up by accident when you're weeding the bed, so tend your plants for another year before planting them out. Once the cuttings are growing strongly, nip out the growing tips to encourage side shoots.

TAKING SOFTWOOD CUTTINGS

A wide range of plants — including buddlejas, forsythias, weigelas and many others — will root very quickly and easily from softwood cuttings. Many of them will form new roots in just a few weeks.

1 Collect the stem tips and store them in a moist plastic bag. Fill a container with an open, free-draining mix and firm it down, tapping the tray to level it.

2 Trim the stem base to below a node (leaf joint) and remove the lower leaves.

3 Dip the stem into rooting powder and insert into the compost to just below its lowest leaves. Water well.

TAKING HARDWOOD CUTTINGS

This technique is suitable for propagating a range of deciduous trees and shrubs, as well as bush fruits. It's probably the simplest and cheapest method of propagating from cuttings.

1 Add a dressing of general-purpose fertilizer to the prepared ground. Lay black polythene and insert the tines of a fork through the plastic into the soil.

2 Remove healthy current season shoots from the plant. Trim them into 25 cm lengths, making the top cut above a bud, and the bottom cut below.

3 Apply rooting powder, then push the cuttings, base first, through the holes in the plastic into the soil below, so that the bottom two-thirds are in the soil.

TAKING ROOT CUTTINGS

You can propagate the roots of many herbaceous plants and alpines as well as a number of trees, shrubs and climbers. Do this in winter, or whenever the plants are dormant.

1 Dig up the roots of the plant, then wash them. Cut thick roots into sections 5–8 cm long, with a flat cut at the top, and a slanting cut at the bottom.

2 Insert the root cuttings by gently pushing the slanted ends into a pot of growing mix so that the top of each cutting is level with the surface of the mix.

3 Cover with grit. This will allow air to reach the top of each cutting without letting it dry out. It will also ensure good drainage.

TAKING LEAF CUTTINGS

You can propagate some plants by cutting and planting their leaves in a pot or tray of compost. Cape primrose (*Streptocarpus* sp.) is shown here.

1 Lay the leaf upper-side down and use a sharp knife to cut along the leaf close to the thick fleshy midrib, to leave two sections of leaf blade. Discard the midrib.

2 If you are dealing with particularly long leaf strips, cut them into halves or thirds so that they'll fit comfortably into a tray or pot of growing mix.

3 Insert the strips so that the cut surface is just below the top of the compost. Lightly firm the compost, water and then leave in a warm place.

ROOT AND LEAF CUTTINGS

Some plants produce very short stems and shoots, which can make taking cuttings very awkward, so you may need to take other parts of the plant, such as the roots or the leaves. The sections of root or leaf are placed in or on an appropriate growing medium so that they can develop new roots and shoots.

ROOT CUTTINGS

Plants that produce shoots directly from their roots can be propagated from root cuttings — sumach (*Rhus*) and acanthus are good examples. These cuttings are normally taken while the plant is dormant, in late autumn or during early winter.

How you take the cuttings depends on the root system of the plant. Cut thicker roots into sections 5–8 cm long, but thinner roots into longer sections, up to 10 cm long. Remember to make a different cut at each end so that you know which way up to plant them — for example, make a straight cut at the top (nearest the stem) and a slanting cut at the base.

Fill a tray or pots with a mixture of peat or peat substitute and vermiculite. Insert the slanting ends into the compost. Cover with grit, then water well. Alternatively, cover the cuttings with sand.

With thin roots that are too delicate to insert upright, lay the roots on the surface of the growing mix. Cover with grit, as before, then water well.

Root cuttings can be propagated in a cold frame. Pot when new shoots appear in spring.

LEAF CUTTINGS

Some plants — notably African violets (*Saintpaulia* sp.), Cape primroses (*Streptocarpus* sp.) and begonias — can be propagated from their leaves. The new plants will develop either from the base of the leaf (the leaf petiole) or from one of the veins that run across the leaves. Use a mixture of roughly 2 parts potting compost to 1 part sharp sand. The sand will make rotting less likely.

Propagate African violets by removing a couple of leaves from the parent plant with the stalk attached. Then insert the stalk of each leaf into a small pot of the compost so that the base of the leaf touches the mix. Cover the pot with an upturned clear plastic bottle or plastic bag and leave it in a warm place, out of direct sunlight. Small plantlets will form at the base of the leaves. Once they grow large enough, remove the plantlets and pot them on individually.

You can propagate some succulents, such as crassulas, in the same way by removing a couple of leaves from the parent plant, but make sure you allow a day or so for the wound to callouse over before inserting each leaf into the growing mix.

You can also propagate larger leaves, such as those of Cape primroses, by taking sections of the leaves and planting them in compost. Plantlets will form where the cut surface of a vein is in contact with the compost. To keep the leaf cuttings moist and in a humid atmosphere, cover the tray or pot with a clear plastic bag. Alternatively, all types of leaf cuttings can be rooted in a propagating case.

You can propagate begonias (above) and acanthus, a striking structural plant (top), by taking root cuttings.

SIMPLE LAYERING

This is the most basic form of layering. If the shoots root successfully, you can separate them from the parent plant so that they can grow independently.

1 Select a suitable shoot and remove any leaves within 30 cm of the tip. Gently bend it down to soil level and mark the spot on the stem.

2 Cut a 4 cm 'tongue' halfway into the stem at this point. Dig a shallow hole, so that the side nearest the parent plant slopes at 45 degrees.

3 Lay the wounded section into the bottom of the hole. Peg into place with a wire hoop. Cover with soil.

LAYERING PLANTS

Layering is one of the easiest methods of propagation for the beginner, and has the added advantage of being more or less foolproof. Layering is primarily used as a way of propagating a wide range of shrubs, trees and climbers as well as some soft fruits.

With layering, new plants are encouraged to grow from the stems of the parent plant while they are still attached. This propagation technique makes use of the natural tendency of some plants to produce new roots (known as adventitious roots) where a wound occurs in the cambium (the layer immediately under the bark) of the plant.

You can exploit this habit by cutting through the outer part of the stem and ensuring that this wound is placed in contact with the soil, which is then kept sufficiently moist. You can then carry out layering, either by pegging down a cut shoot or by wrapping the cut area with sphagnum moss, contained in a clear plastic bag. There are several different methods of layering, each suitable for use with plants displaying particular characteristics.

SIMPLE LAYERING

This technique works well with shrubs or trees with flexible stems. Using a sharp knife, cut a tongue into the wood tissue about halfway through, then peg the cut side so that it's in contact with the soil. A small mound of compost placed at the contact point will encourage rooting.

SERPENTINE LAYERING

This method is used for climbers such as clematis or wisteria. Several cuts are made along the shoot and then the shoots are pegged down, so that a number of new plantlets will form.

TIP LAYERING

This method of layering is used for the genus *Rubus* (brambles), including blackberries, which form new plants where the tips of the shoots touch the soil. These plants will often do this without help from the gardener. All you need to do is ensure that the tip of the shoot is buried shallowly in the soil.

AIR LAYERING

This is a useful layering method to use with plants with stems that are not particularly flexible. You can use either the basic layering cut or the stem-girdling technique for air layering (see the picture at right). With this method, the secret of success lies in the creation of a sealed pocket of growing medium around the cut area of your plant, which then encourages new roots to form.

STEM GIRDLING

This method involves damaging the stem of the parent plant in various ways to encourage new roots to form. These methods include twisting wire around the stem, splitting the bark and cutting the stem.

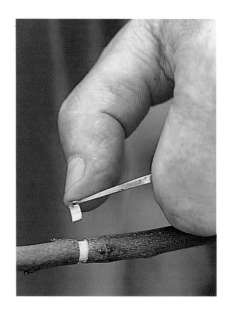

ABOVE A narrow ring of bark is removed to encourage roots to grow around the damaged area. This is one of several methods of stem girdling.

AIR LAYERING

For this method you'll need a small, clear plastic bag, a sharp garden knife, a matchstick, a couple of garden ties and a small amount of sphagnum moss.

1 Cut off the bottom of a plastic bag, then slide it over the leaves. This will keep the leaves out of the way while you cut the stem.

2 Further down the stem, make an upward cut halfway into the stem. Slide the plastic bag down the stem so that the wounded area is in the centre of the bag.

3 Tie the bottom firmly around the stem. Pack the bag with moist sphagnum moss. When the bag is full, firmly tie the top of the bag.

ABOVE One of these Dutch iris bulbs, in the middle section at the right, has two offsets or bulblets. Gently break off the offsets from the parent bulb and plant them separately.

DIVIDING PLANTS

You can increase your stock of perennials simply by breaking up the clumps of adult specimens. With bulbs, simply remove the young bulbs from the parent bulb and pot them to grow into new plants.

PERENNIALS

You can take basal cuttings of perennials (see 'Taking softwood cuttings' on page 239), but you can also divide clump-forming herbaceous perennials. This not only creates useful new plants, but also revitalizes an existing one, because the centre tends to die out as the new growth pushes outwards from the crown. You can divide small clumps of not particularly fibrous-rooted plants relatively easily by digging up the entire plant and then pulling it apart in your hands.

For stronger-growing plants with an established root system, you'll need to apply brute force to split them. The usual method is to insert two forks back to back through the clump, and work the tines of the forks apart to lever away the roots.

It's usually best to divide plants in autumn, once they have become dormant, as the plants then have a chance to rest before the new growth starts in spring. Replant the divided plants, either in pots or directly into their flowering positions. Most divided plants will flower again the following year.

DIVIDING PLANTS

Dividing plants not only provides you with new stock but also ensures that the plants remain vigorous and free-flowering.

1 Using a garden fork, lift the plant out of the soil and hose it clean, removing as much soil as you can.

2 Push two hand forks into the clump, back to back, then pull them apart to split the clump into sections. For tougher clumps you'll need full-size garden forks

3 Break down each section into individual plants with several roots and a few shoots to each piece, then replant these.

SCOOPING BULBS

Beside division, you can also propagate bulbs by other methods. One of these is called scooping. Using a sharp-sided teaspoon, scoop out the central part of the basal plate (the area the roots grow from), leaving the outer rim intact. Dust the ends with fungicide, then lay the bulbs on a bed of sand with the cut end exposed to the air. Keep the bulbs dry until the cuts callouse over, and slowly increase the humidity so they don't dry out completely.

After 12–14 weeks, bulblets should form around the edge of the basal plate. In early winter, plant the bulb upside down with the new bulblets just below the surface. Leaves will form in winter, but don't separate the bulblets until the leaves die down in summer. Store or replant separately when they are big enough to handle. It takes about 3–4 years for the bulblets to reach the flowering stage.

Some plants produce runners with small plantlets on the end, or in the case of piggyback plant (*Tolmiea*), little plantlets at the base of the leaves, which you can remove and plant up.

BULBS
Division will benefit any bulbs that flower poorly, and it's an easy way to produce more plants. The best time to do this is when they become dormant, but this time will vary, depending on the flowering time of the particular bulb. Exceptions to this rule are nerines, snowdrops (*Galanthus* sp.) and winter aconites (*Eranthis* sp.), which are best divided 'in the green' — just after their flowering period has finished but before the leaves have had a chance to die down.

When dividing bulbs, remove any small offsets (which form the next generation of flowers) from the parent bulb. Plant any offsets that are nearly the same size as the parent bulb in their permanent positions in the garden. Plant smaller ones in pots to grow on, as these will not flower until they have reached maturity.

Some bulbs, including some lilies and alliums, produce small bulbs on sections of their stems. You can remove these, treating them in exactly the same way as you would the offsets that form on the bulb itself.

PLANTS WITH RHIZOMES, CORMS AND TUBERS
There are four main types of storage organs — bulbs, rhizomes, corms and tubers. True bulbs are underground storage organs, which are formed from leaf bases and modified leaves. Tubers are swollen stems and roots, while corms and tubers are both swollen stems that produce leaves each year. You can propagate the latter three by cutting the rhizomes, corms or tubers into pieces so that there is a growing bud on each piece. Among the plants that can be propagated in this way are irises and dahlias.

ABOVE The four types of storage organ (from the top): corm, rhizome, tuber and bulb.

ABOVE Once you've mastered the art of grafting, you'll be able to propagate your favourite woody plants.

ABOVE RIGHT Suckers appear when the rootstock of a grafted plant starts to produce shoots from the area below the graft union. If you leave the suckers unchecked, they'll start to compete with the grafted plant. Remove suckers at an early stage by simply pulling them out.

GRAFTING PLANTS

A fascinating way to reproduce plants, grafting involves joining two separate plants together so they grow as one. It's a useful method for plants that are very slow or difficult to root from cuttings, or that do not grow well on their own roots.

The lower part of the graft (the rootstock) will form the root system of the new plant, and for the graft to be successful it should be as closely related to the top part (the scion) as possible. For example, a basic rootstock for grafting roses can be propagated as a hardwood cutting from a wild rose or a sucker from a garden rose. The scion is a section of stem taken from the plant that you wish to propagate. If the graft is successful, the two plants will grow together almost seamlessly and give the appearance of being a single plant.

Over the years, a number of different types of graft have evolved for individual plants or groups of plants, but many of these are complicated and, in a number of cases, totally unnecessary. It's possible to propagate most plants with just one or two of the simplest grafts. All you need is a sharp, good-quality knife, and plenty of practice beforehand. If you want to have a go at grafting but don't have a specialist knife, use a basic general-purpose knife to make the cuts.

Some woody plants can be difficult to propagate by the conventional means of taking cuttings (see page 238). Some of the best known plants that are commonly grafted are roses (in which a vigorous rose adds strength to a less vigorous new variety, for example) and a variety of fruit trees, such as apples and pears (where a dwarfing rootstock, say, will result in a small tree).

ROSE GRAFTING

For this technique you'll need: a cutting from a rose rootstock, a sharp knife, secateurs, a semi-ripe
shoot from a rose cultivar, an elastic band, a pot and potting mix and a plastic bag.

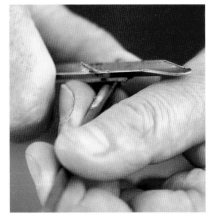

1 Take hardwood cuttings from
   one-year-old shoots of a rose
   rootstock. Start them in a warm
   greenhouse in midwinter —
   remove the lower buds, then heel
   the cuttings into a soil bed. These
   will be ready for grafting in spring.
   Prepare the rootstock by cutting
   the length down to 15 cm.

2 Make a single shallow, upward-
   slanting cut 4 cm long at the top
   of the rootstock, thereby exposing
   the plant tissue responsible for
   healing (known as the cambium),
   which allows the stock and scion
   to heal together.

3 Select a semi-ripe shoot about
   8 cm long from the rose cultivar.
   Remove all the leaves apart from
   the uppermost one, to form
   the scion.

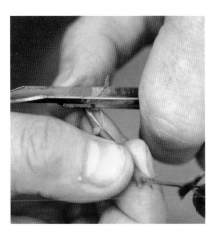

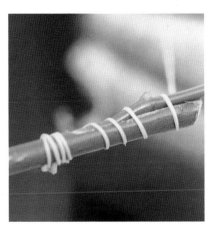

4 Make a single downward-slanting
   cut approximately 4 cm long on
   the bottom section of the scion,
   just behind a bud. This cut will
   expose the cambium.

5 Gently place the two sections of
   plant together, so that the cut
   surfaces match. When they are
   correctly positioned, carefully
   bind the graft with an elastic
   band. This will hold the graft
   firmly until the two sections join.

6 Place the graft into a pot of
   growing mix. Water it well, cover
   it with a polythene bag, and place
   the pot on a warm windowsill
   until the graft has taken.

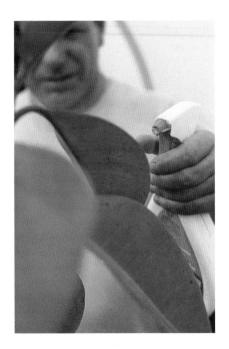

ABOVE Spray foliar feeds directly onto the leaves, paying special attention to any areas that need help.

FEEDING PLANTS

Before feeding your plants, decide whether you wish to use only organic fertilizers, which are obtained from the 'natural' waste of plants and animals and include rotted leaves and plants, or manure and discarded bedding. If you're happy using manufactured fertilizers, there are suitable ones for every plant and situation. The bulk supplied by the bedding helps to improve the soil structure, and it also dilutes the quantities of nitrogen in the manure itself. Add bulky plant foods, such as straw compost (see opposite), in autumn to give them time to break down over winter. Begin a feeding programme with fertilizer in early spring, when most plants are emerging from winter dormancy. Then feed them throughout the growing period. Established plants including shrubs require top dressing once or twice yearly with a slow-release fertiliser, such as growmore. Plants that put on a lot of growth over the growing season, such as clematis and vegetables, need more regular feeding, perhaps once a month or more often. Pots and hanging baskets may need even more frequent feeding. It is best to feed when the soil is damp, or to water once the fertiliser is applied to ensure that the plants can make full use of the food they are being given.

Liquid feeds made from the leaves of comfrey or nettles are popular with organic gardeners. The exact nutrient content of such concoctions varies according to the way they are made, but they generally provide a boost. An alternative, made with animal manure, is sometimes known as blackjack.

FEEDING EDIBLE PLANTS

Edible plants need particular nutrients at specific stages of growth, especially when producing fruit. In spring, hoe a base dressing that contains nitrogen and phosphorus into the top few centimetres of soil. At the secondary stage of growth, give the plants a boost with a top dressing of similar nutrients. When the plant is producing fruit, you can give it another boost using a liquid feed containing plenty of potassium. Use an organic preparation, such as blackjack, or a proprietory feed, such as tomato fertilizer, which is a useful pick-me-up for all types of plants.

FOLIAR FEEDS

These liquid feeds are useful for adding a quick burst of nutrients when your plants are in full growth. Liquid feeds are usually easier to apply than granular fertilizers, and the plants often respond quite quickly to such treatment. You can buy a concentrated foliar feed in liquid or powder form and then dilute it according to the manufacturer's instructions.

Spray leaves in either the morning or evening, but not in full sun, as they may scorch. Most feeding will be needed prior to flowering or fruiting. The composition of feed will be determined accordingly — for example, fruiting plants need more potassium than flowers. Don't apply the feed during wet weather or when rain is forecast, as it may be washed away before it gets to work. You can direct foliar feeds to areas of the plant that need an extra boost.

MAKING STRAW COMPOST

Old straw makes excellent mulch or just bulky organic matter to incorporate into the soil. It will help improve drainage, moisture retention and general fertility.

1 Cover the base of the area with 30 cm of loose straw. Soak the straw with water.

2 Lightly sprinkle nitrogenous fertilizer over the straw. Add another 30 cm layer of loose straw to the stack, water it and add more fertilizer.

3 As the straw decomposes, it becomes covered in a white mould. Eventually it resembles well-rotted manure.

MAKING BLACKJACK

Blackjack, made from rotted animal manure, is an excellent, nutritious plant pick-me-up, which is very useful during flowering or fruiting periods.

1 Mix together rotted animal manure, some soot, which provides nitrogen, and wood ash, which contains potassium.

2 Put the mixture into a plastic net bag, then seal the bag carefully. Suspend it in a barrel of water for several weeks.

3 Decant it as required into a watering can, diluting it to the colour of weak tea. Then water it on your plants.

Winter honeysuckle (*Lonicera fragrantissima*) needs regular pruning to keep it tidy.

PRUNING

This gardening technique causes more confusion than any other. The whole point of pruning is to improve the plant's shape or its fruiting or flowering performance as well as to control growth. In order to do this, it really helps to have some understanding of basic botany. Once you grasp the general principles of pruning, you'll be able to apply your newly acquired techniques to a range of plants in your garden.

Another reason for pruning is to remove any damaged or diseased parts before any viral or infectious disease can take advantage of the exposed tissue. These shoots are best removed close to the main stem in a cut that is angled outwards, to allow any water to drain off.

CONTROLLING VIGOUR

If your main goal in pruning is to control a plant's excessive growth, you might like to consider the suitability of the plant for its setting. Why grow a giant plant that puts on large amounts of growth each year if you don't have the space to let it grow naturally? An overgrown hedge of *Leylandii* cypresses with their tops chopped off is a pitiful sight, since these plants don't look attractive once they've lost their conical shape.

If you want a 1.8 m high hedge, you're better off choosing slower-growing plants that can be kept to this height without too much difficulty. In fact, with many shrubs, pruning promotes rather than reduces growth; so while you may succeed in reducing the size of the shrub in the season you prune it, in the following year, you may be faced with an even more vigorous specimen that bears many more shoots.

THE PRINCIPLES OF PRUNING

Plants have a built-in reproductive system that works as follows: if you cut off the plant's leading shoot (from which it will eventually form flowers and seeds), you set in motion a secondary system, whereby the lower branches are galvanized into activity to do the work of the removed leading shoot. This then changes the shape of the plant from one with a strong, tall central stem to one with a more branching appearance.

If you follow this principle while pruning an apple tree, you'll find that if you remove the leading shoot, you get more secondary shoots. The fruit then begins to grow on these secondary shoots, and you increase the opportunity for more fruit to grow. The same applies to plants grown for their flowers: you increase the shooting ability of the plant and inevitably increase its flowering performance. In order to create a strong framework of branches, you need to prune every year.

WHEN TO PRUNE

Some shrubs produce their flowers on the current season's new wood, others on the wood made in previous seasons. To make matters more complicated, not every species in a particular genus performs in the same way. For example, in the *Buddleja* genus, *B. globosa* needs barely any pruning, *B. davidii* flowers on new season's wood and should be pruned in early spring, and *B. alternifolia* flowers on the previous year's wood and should be pruned after flowering in summer.

The best times to prune, therefore, are after flowering on any plant that will flower the following year on the growth made this year; for plants that flower on the current season's growth, no later than the end of winter or early spring. If you get this timing the wrong way round, and prune a plant that flowers on the previous season's growth in late winter or early spring, you'll remove the current season's crop of flowers.

PRUNING TREES AND SHRUBS

When growing trees and shrubs, your main aim is to create a really good shape that looks attractive and also encourages air circulation around the branches, because this helps to counteract disease. With fruit trees, you can use pruning to improve the quality and quantity of fruit.

Many trees and shrubs have a naturally balanced, attractive habit and require only a little pruning. Generally, evergreens belong in this category; this may be something to consider at the planning stage, especially if you don't have much time to maintain them.

TREE PRUNING

By and large, major tree pruning is best left to tree surgeons. The branches are large and heavy, and you can injure yourself if you make a mistake. Also, if you get it wrong, you'll be left with an eyesore. However, removing diseased or damaged branches from smaller trees is within the capabilities of most gardeners.

PRUNING CITRUS TREES

Pot-grown cirtus trees tend to grow slowly and require little pruning. However, sometimes they do need some attention.

- Remove all low-growing twigs and branches.
- Shorten back twigs that 'run away' outside the average periphery.
- Remove less vigorous shoots.
- As fruit are produced on last year's wood, any damage to this can cause the loss of a crop in the following year. Don't cut damaged wood until new growth is made, then cut it back to new sound shoot.

ABOVE Prune standard roses as you would bush roses.

Prune deciduous trees in late autumn or winter, when they're dormant. This applies especially to birch and maple: the sap will bleed if these trees are pruned during the growing season. When the trees are young, pruning will help to establish a balanced shape. For more mature trees, you should only prune to maintain the shape you have and to encourage growth. Removing any thin or crossing branches from the main structure of the tree will allow light and air into the centre of the framework.

Some evergreen trees, such as various kinds of magnolias, do not need pruning at all. If for some reason they do need pruning, do it during late spring. If the tree is immature, you can encourage a strong central stem by training a vertical shoot upwards and then removing any competing leaders. With well-established evergreens, you can simply remove any weak or unshapely branches by cutting back to a healthy shoot.

SHAPING SHRUBS

If left to their own devices, most deciduous shrubs will gradually become weaker and less attractive. The main goals are to maintain a good, open shape; to encourage flowering, if that's appropriate; and to remove any branches that cross over and rub each other, because these will almost certainly allow diseases to penetrate the plant. You should also encourage the branches to fan outwards in an open and attractive manner, rather than turn inwards.

PRUNING WISTERIA

Wisteria is a vigorous climber that needs annual pruning. In midwinter, cut back young lateral shoots not needed for the framework of the plant. These cam also be shortened in late summer if necessary.

1 Untwine tangled shoots. You may need to cut these out in sections to protect other shoots from damage. Space the remaining shoots over the support.

2 Next, carefully tie into position any shoots to be used as part of the plant's framework.

3 Cut back long lateral growths that are not to be used as part of the framework to just above a bud, 15–20 cm from where they emerge from the stem.

To achieve this effect, you need to make any pruning cuts just above outward-facing buds. If the buds grow in pairs, however, simply cut the stem straight across, just above the pair.

PRUNING AND TRAINING CLIMBERS

Climbing plants pose a few more challenges, because you need to make sure that the climbers grow in the direction you prefer rather than wander off.

Most climbing plants have a natural tendency to reach for the light, with the result that they flower at the top of increasingly long stems, which may not be the look you want. Therefore the chief aim when pruning and training climbers is to persuade the plant to produce flowering stems lower down where they can be more fully appreciated. Generally, this is achieved by creating a fan shape and encouraging the spread of horizontal branches.

Some climbers are notoriously vigorous and require a lot of pruning. For this reason, wisteria is not a plant for the faint-hearted gardener. In addition, the Russian vine (*Fallopia baldschuanica*) is frequently recommended for covering unsightly views quickly, but its common name is 'mile-a-minute', and this is really not much of an exaggeration. Avoid this plant unless you're prepared to do a lot of pruning.

HOW CLIMBERS GROW

The amount of pruning work you'll need to do on a climber depends on the natural habit of the plant. Some climbers attach themselves to any support with no help from the gardener. These are the plants that have aerial roots or small suckers that fix on to any surface. Others, such as many rambling roses, use the thorns on their stems to scramble over supports.

Most climbers belong to the twining group, and these do their work through twining tendrils, leaf petioles or stems. Stem twiners need suitable poles or wires around which to weave, with enough space in between the supports for them to bend their entire stems around them. In contrast, climbers that use twining tendrils or leaf petioles can support themselves happily on thin wires that are relatively closely spaced.

In their formative year or years, most twining climbers need the gardener's help in order to establish themselves on their support. Tie them in loosely to the support structure, using ties that are soft and loose enough not to damage any delicate stems.

PRUNING AND TRAINING ROSES

Some of the best-loved plants of all time, roses are often ill-treated by the gardener, due to a lack of understanding of their needs. There are many different types of rose, as breeders over the centuries have perfected hundreds of hybrids. These all perform in different ways. These groups include bush roses (hybrid tea and floribunda), shrub and species roses, climbers and ramblers. Climbers flower at least twice a year, ramblers only once. Most bush and shrub roses form a fairly wide-spreading plant that is about 1.5 m tall. Generally speaking, they require pruning in the same way

PRUNING BUSH AND SHRUB ROSES

1 Remove any old growth with a pruning saw.

2 Always prune to an outward-facing bud.

3 Leave a good air flow around the stems.

4 Remove growth that is less than pencil-thick.

ABOVE *Rosa* 'Aotearoa' is a pink, perfumed hybrid tea from New Zealand.

ABOVE RIGHT *Rosa filipes* 'Kiftsgate', one of the roses planted in Vita Sackville-West's White Garden at Sissinghurst (see page 281).

as other deciduous, summer-flowering shrubs. Prune bush and shrub roses in late autumn or very early spring.

CLIMBING ROSES

The different groups of climbing rose all demand different pruning techniques. The first group is the ramblers, which are vigorous, flower on old wood and produce new canes from the base. Generally, the best system is simply to cut out the old wood from the base (about one-third each year in winter), encouraging the new wood to grow and flower. A subsidiary group of ramblers produces few new stems, so prune these back in late summer to a framework where a new leader is developing. Repeat-flowering ramblers flower on new shoots. Prune these in early autumn by removing all but 15 cm of the laterals that have just finished flowering.

Prune pillar roses in a similar way in late autumn, but cut out some of the oldest stems and prune back some of the new lateral growth to improve the shape. Finally, the species roses, such as *Rosa filipes* 'Kiftsgate', are so vigorous that it's best to give them space to wander!

BUSH AND STANDARD ROSES

Prune hybrid teas and floribunda roses in spring, before new growth starts, cutting back new shoots to 15 cm and shortening laterals on remaining wood. On older plants, you may need to remove some old wood.

Roses grown as standards have been trained with a crown of spreading stems. These stems then form a flowering canopy above the long clear stem. Prune standard roses as you would bush roses. First, remove any dead, dying or damaged wood before cutting out competing shoots to leave a good flow of air around the stems.

TOOL MAINTENANCE

If you look after your garden tools properly, they'll repay you with a lifetime of service. The ideal time to sharpen your spade and secateurs as well as restore any cracked or splintery handles is probably winter, when there are fewer jobs to do in the garden.

Buy the best-quality tools you can afford, which doesn't necessarily mean the most expensive. Look for high-carbon steel with solid, well-balanced wooden handles. Stainless steel, which is alloyed with chromium and nickel, is an expensive but good rust-resistant option if you occasionally leave tools out in the garden!

Store each tool neatly by tying a string loop through a hole in the handle and hanging it on a tool rack. You can either buy one especially or make your own by mounting an old rake head on the shed wall. Alternatively, keep sharp hand tools clean and oiled in a bucket of sand mixed with oil.

SHARPENING SECATEURS

To sharpen a pair of secateurs, you'll need to disassemble them first. Using a spanner, loosen the bolt, then remove the spring and take the secateurs apart. Sharpen the cutting or bevelled side on an oilstone, making sure you hold the blade away from you. Finally, clean the cutting blade with an old rag, then put the secateurs together again.

STORING TOOLS

To prevent hand tools from becoming rusty, store them in a bucket filled with sand and some oil that have been thoroughly mixed together.

RESTORING HANDLES

To restore the dry and split wooden handles of old tools, you'll need: steel wool, a rag, a mixture of linseed oil and turpentine in an old jar, a sanding block and some fine and medium abrasive paper.

1 Sand back the spade handle with medium-grade abrasive paper. Then clean it with a soft rag.

2 Dip the rag into a mix of linseed oil and turpentine. Rub the handle with the soaked rag, then leave it to dry overnight.

3 Lightly sand with fine-grade abrasive paper. Repeat the process if necessary. Finish by rubbing the handle with some steel wool.

TOP TO BOTTOM An aphid; a caterpillar; and an earwig.

PESTS

There are many pests that can be a problem in your garden. Some are broad-spectrum, attacking a whole range of plants, while others are programmed to attack only certain species. The following list covers some of the most common ones. Suggestions for controlling pests are included wherever it's appropriate.

The critical thing in pest control is to check your plants frequently and to try to combat any infestation fast, before it has time to really catch hold. Some insects will simply cause a certain amount of damage to one plant; others will quickly destroy a whole crop. However, in general it's not in nature's interest to destroy the host plant, so most predator problems are annoyances rather than catastrophic. You'll need to decide whether to use chemical solutions or treat problems organically.

APHIDS

These common garden pests are usually green, brown or black winged insects that suck the sap from new shoots. Warning signs of an aphid infestation include distorted shoot tips and new leaves. Aphids leave a sticky coating, known as honeydew, that attracts ants; it's sometimes accompanied by black mould.

To treat an aphid infestation organically, spray the plant with an insecticidal soap or simply wipe off the aphids from the affected areas. If you wish to use a chemical solution, try using a readily available systemic insecticide, such as permethrin, at regular intervals.

CATERPILLARS

These are the larvae of butterflies and moths. They have tubular bodies in varying colours. Look out for telltale holes in foliage, flowers and seedpods as caterpillars can quickly strip a whole plant. Remove the pests by hand, or spray with permethrin if you prefer a chemical solution.

EARWIGS

Earwigs are small, shiny brown insects with pincer-like tails that leave circular holes or notches in leaves and flowers. To control them organically, balance upturned, straw-filled pots on canes. Leave them overnight and remove the pots (and trapped earwigs) in the morning. You can also treat earwigs with a permethrin spray.

LEAF MINERS

These tiny insect larvae tunnel through leaves and create distinctive wiggly lines. Leaf miners are more of an aesthetic problem than a damaging pest. Remove any affected leaves when you first sight the problem.

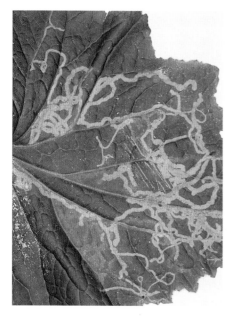
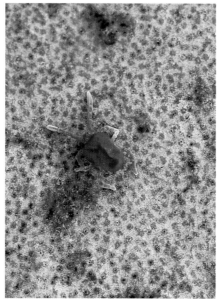

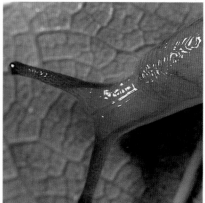

RED SPIDER MITE

Red spider mites are tiny sap-sucking insects that cause stunted, curled and finely mottled leaves. Keeping plants moist, particularly the undersides of the leaves, helps to prevent attacks. Spray with insecticide.

SCALE INSECTS

These are tiny insect pests resembling brown, blister-like bumps on leaves and stems. Look for stunted growth and yellowed leaves, as well as a sticky coating on the lower leaves, sometimes with sooty mould. Introduce a biological control, or spray with systemic insecticide at regular intervals in late spring and early summer.

SLUGS AND SNAILS

These slimy molluscs feed at night or after rain. You'll notice holes in leaves, and perhaps stripped stems. Look for a silvery trail on the ground around the plant. Collect slugs and snails at night, or use sunken traps of beer to drown them. Apply a copper band to containers. For a chemical option, sprinkle slug pellets around the bases of plants.

THRIPS

These tiny, brownish black insects gather on the upper surfaces of leaves and thrive in hot, dry conditions. They affect a wide range of ornamental and edible plants, in particular, peas and onions. You can identify them by means of a silvery discolouration with black dots on the upper surfaces of leaves. Regular misting with water helps prevent attacks, and you can also use several insecticidal chemicals.

CLOCKWISE FROM TOP LEFT Leaf miner; red spider mite; scale insects; a snail; and thrips.

TOP TO BOTTOM Botrytis, canker and downy mildew.

DISEASES

Just like human beings, plants are prone to diseases, particularly when they are not in good health. The key to dealing with diseases is to provide your plants with the optimum conditions in which to survive and thrive.

If you care for your plants, giving them the nutrients and conditions they need, they'll be more resistant to diseases. Irregular feeding and watering cause plants stress, making them more susceptible. Another common feature of disease-prone plants is poor pruning cuts, where the tissue has been torn rather than cut through cleanly. This makes the site more attractive to invading organisms.

While chemical controls are often effective, they may well be unnecessary, and nowadays few are available to private gardeners. Often a quick response using an organic treatment will serve the same purpose, so check your plants regularly and act swiftly if you find a problem.

BOTRYTIS (GREY MOULD)

Look for discoloured, yellowing leaves. Eventually the plant, or part of it, is covered with grey felt. Prune the affected parts and discard them. Try to improve the air circulation around the plant.

CANKER

This disease affects mainly fruit trees. Pitted areas of bark can lead to stem dieback. Prune the affected branches, and treat as much of the plant as possible with Bordeaux mixture or copper fungicide.

CORAL SPOT

This fungus is most commonly found on dead wood, but it also affects live tissue, covering bark with small pink blisters. Prune and discard the affected stems.

DOWNY MILDEW

This is a fungus affecting leaves and stems. The symptoms include discoloured yellowing leaves with grey–white patches on the undersides. Improve air circulation and use resistant varieties where possible. For chemical control, spray with a fungicide such as myclobutanil. Remove and discard badly affected plants.

FIREBLIGHT

This bacterial disease affects trees and shrubs in the rose family. It attacks soft tissue, causing blackened flowers, shrivelled young shoots and brown, wilted leaves. Discard any affected plants. There is no cure.

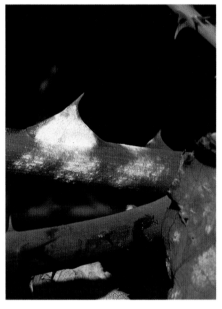

POWDERY MILDEW

Look for floury white patches on leaves, distorted shoots and premature leaf fall. Prune the affected stems, and if you wish to use chemicals, spray with fungicide at the first signs of infection.

RUST

This is a fungal disease that particularly affects roses. Symptoms include orange spots on the leaves. Improve air circulation around the plant by pruning. For chemical control, spray regularly with a fungicide such as mancozeb.

ROOT ROT

Root rot is often caused by poor growing conditions, such as wet or waterlogged soil or compost: the roots rot away and the top part of the plant wilts and dies. You can improve the situation with better drainage. Root rot can also be caused by the use of unsterilized compost in containers. The first indication of root rot is often wilting of the upper parts of the plant.

VIRUSES

Viruses are usually spread by sap-sucking insects. Look out particularly for distorted leaves and shoots, and for yellow mottling or streaking on the leaves. There is no cure for viral infection. Remove and discard any affected plants.

CLOCKWISE FROM TOP LEFT
Fireblight; powdery mildew; rust;
a tree with root rot; and leaves
affected by a virus.

ABOVE A mixed border of perennials based on a blue-and-white scheme.

ABOVE RIGHT A neutral colour scheme of pastel and white enlivened by splashes of red.

OPPOSITE The pillars of white climbing roses recede into the distance, throwing the spotlight onto the bold structural plants in acid yellow, purple, green and silver in the foreground.

DESIGNING WITH COLOUR

A well-designed garden requires both careful planning and the sort of skill that comes with practice and knowledge. Learning even a little about the theory of colour — harmonies, contrasts and single colour themes — will help you to use it effectively in your garden. You can either use the schemes and planting guides in this section as they are, or adapt them to suit your own taste.

CREATING GARDEN PICTURES

Most gardeners are guilty of impulse buying — perhaps falling in love with a new pink camellia — but however beautiful the new plant, it won't add to the beauty of your garden if it doesn't harmonize with the other plants.

The great gardener and gardening writer Gertrude Jekyll was an artist and embroiderer before she became famous as a gardener. She understood perfectly that gardening was about making pictures, not about strict rules or theories. Jekyll once said that the idea of gardening is 'the disposition of plants in ways that the whole effect is pictorial'. She wrote in *Colour Schemes for the Flower Garden*, first published in 1908:

A blue garden, for beauty's sake, may be hungering for lemon yellow, but it is not allowed to have it because it is called the blue garden... I can see no sense in this... any experienced colourist knows that blues will be more telling — more purely blue — by the juxtaposition of rightly placed complementary colour.

Once you've studied the colour wheel on page 262 and read about the relationships between colours, you'll understand what Jekyll meant.

ABOVE The colour wheel, showing the primary and secondary colours.

THE COLOUR WHEEL

The colour wheel is a summary of all colour relationships. The three major spokes are the primary colours of red, yellow and blue. Between them are the secondary colours — green, orange and violet — which are formed by mixing the primary colours. The linking colours, which include pink, lime green and violet-blue, are known as tertiary colours.

On the colour wheel, those colours on opposite sides contrast with each other, and this is why blue and yellow, and red and green work so well together. Those colours next to each other, such as blue and green, harmonize. This is why all blue and green gardens, while they can be restful, can slide into monotony. You can also see why a red, yellow and orange garden needs a green background to tone down any garish tendencies. White works brilliantly with all colours, making it a handy tool for the garden maker.

ASPECTS OF COLOUR

Just like an interior designer, you can use colours in the garden to influence the observer's perceptions of space and distance. For instance, warm colours such as red, orange and yellow seem to advance while the cool colours of blue and green retreat. In small gardens, for example, you can create an impression of a larger area by using soft, cool colours. Once you understand this principle, you can start experimenting with colour in your garden.

When thinking about colour, consider, too, the intensity of light. Light varies in different countries and at different times of the year. The stronger the light, the clearer the colours, because the amount of light affects your perception of colour. A pastel garden may look soft, pretty and muted in the early morning but totally washed out in the midday sun.

Bright scarlet, crimson and yellow look fine in the tropics — in fact, their intense colours seem to shimmer in the sun — but they may be overwhelming in a cooler, more northerly garden.

However, colour is only one aspect of good gardening practice: the design, shape and texture of plants are also important. See pages 320–7.

ABOVE LEFT Warm colours have a wide tonal range, from pale moonlight yellow to burning orange-red, yet they blend seamlessly together.

ABOVE White Monet tulips and bluebells densely planted beneath cherry trees in spring.

ABOVE A cool, harmonious theme of mauve and violet tones runs through this garden. Woven through this is a contrasting group, forming a subtle thread of yellow and white, lightening the plantings and making them less sombre.

HARMONIOUS COLOUR SCHEMES

In musical terms, harmony comes from the combination of simultaneous notes to form chords of sweet and melodious sounds. The same rules about composition apply to planning gardens. Your aim should be to create a sweet and pleasing harmony for the eye.

COLOUR COMPOSITIONS

Harmonious colours are those that are adjacent or close to each other on the colour wheel. For example, the primary colour red harmonizes with orange and yellow, while the primary colour blue harmonizes with all shades of green. Harmonies of shared colour follow natural laws and require no focal adjustment — unlike contrasts that, if used deliberately and with care, sharpen the eye.

For example, if you begin your composition with blue, the colour of many great flowers, then you can harmoniously extend your colour choice into the mauves and violets. Pink could be another easy starting point for an harmonious composition, as there are flowers in so many delightful shades of pink.

Consider too, the contribution that silver and grey can make to colour relationships in the garden. These inert colours tend to work well with all other colours, even white, making the overall effect of any planting lighter and brighter.

Combinations of silver and other light-coloured foliage (perhaps variegated) with pastel-coloured flowers work in a kind of two-way harmony — first, a pleasing harmony of tone with the grouping of different pale colours and, second, a harmony of saturation because all the colours are muted in hue. Silver and pink are natural partners; some pink flowers actually have a metallic sheen.

However, this kind of planting could easily fall into the feeble category, and it's important to make sure the beds have strong structural plants. This is where the cardoons, verbascums and perhaps some of the artemisias are needed to create vertical interest. If these silver-leafed plants don't suit your taste, you could install a more permanent structure — such as a trellis, wooden obelisk or frame — to hold the planting together.

Colour harmony also plays a part in establishing garden 'temperature'. If you plant lots of blue and blue-violet flowers and they dominate the colour scheme, the garden will have a 'cool' or 'cold' appearance; similarly, the harmony will be 'hot' if there are masses of red, orange and yellow flowers. It will be vibrant and busy, the very opposite of the restful and relaxing atmosphere that the cool colours engender.

LEFT Creating harmony doesn't necessarily mean a garden of pastels. This skilful planting uses well co-ordinated tones of green and yellow as well as foliage texture. Unusual plant choices, such as the fan aloe (*Aloe plicatilis*) in the centre and the grass of the *Carex* species in the foreground, add a unique touch.

HARMONY IN SUMMER BORDERS

Here are some simple guidelines for colour planting in summer beds and borders. In these gardens you can see that every colour scheme should include colour foils — for example, in a white and green garden you can use yellow or silver as a foil.

WHITE AND GREEN For a cool white or cream garden, use white and green and perhaps a touch of yellow. The background should be green — choose from box, spurge or cypress, for example. For annuals, choose from petunias, phlox, French marigolds, nicotiana, cosmos and Queen Anne's lace.

DARK PLUMS AND PINK For this look, exclude all white and yellow, although you could include some blue and red. Try setting petunias, phlox and salvia in shades of plum, burgundy and pink against a background of dark blue salvia, *Verbena bonariensis*, dark red zinnia, burgundy amaranthus and black hollyhocks.

HOT BORDER This is where the reds and yellows come into their own. The background should be green and could incorporate some dark burgundy or purple. Low-growing plants could include nasturtiums, verbena, calendula, petunia and zinnia. Choices for the mid-field include gaillardia and dahlias, while tall plants could include rudbeckia and sunflowers.

PASTEL COLOURS Use pink, blue and cream flowers. Grey- and silver-leafed plants, such as artemisia, are perfect for the background. Petunia, phlox and salvia are ideal for the front of the beds, with plants such as celosia, *Salvia farinacea* and gomphrena in the middle ground. For the tall plants, more than 1 m high, choose from hollyhocks, cleome and *Nicotiana sylvestris*.

LEFT Here's a scheme for lovers of pink. The vertical spikes of lupins are attractive on their own, but when placed in front of the bright pinky red rhododendron, they act as pointers to the drama in the garden behind them.

A PINK-BASED GARDEN

Pastel colours can provide some attractive combinations. Pink, for example, is comforting and easy to integrate into the garden. The pink colour tones are on the border between warm and cool colours. Pinks that contain blue blend and harmonize with cool schemes of blue and violet, while pinks that contain more yellow tend to harmonize better with the warm colours of yellow and red.

You can appreciate the enormous range of pink tones and tints by looking at massed azaleas: the flowers can be divided into those with blue tints and those with orange tints. The addition of blue makes a lavender pink, while a little orange results in varying shades of salmon pink. When grown together, the two groups (especially the more vibrant shades) usually need softening with white.

Depending on how much white it contains, pink covers many shades, from the exquisitely delicate shell pink to flamboyant magenta; however, some gardeners have called magenta 'the maligned colour', because it is difficult to use.

PINK AND WHITE

It's hard to think of a garden combination that is more pleasing than pink and white. You can use this classic duo all year round, starting from mid-spring, when you can partner flowering annuals such as primulas with bulbs like white tulips.

In summer, you can compose a romantic garden picture by combining stately white foxgloves with pink roses in many different shades. The reverse combination works well, too: deep pink foxgloves look marvellous with pale, pale roses, just off the edge of startling white. Perennials and annuals — from white penstemon to pink sweet Williams, from candytuft and alyssum to white stocks and love-in-a-mist — all work brilliantly together to make soft, gentle pictures.

White is very effective as a 'harmonizer': this might explain why the 'Iceberg' rose is still so popular. Alternatively, a pink rose such as the rose 'The Reeve' can be used as a centrepiece, perhaps surrounded by silvery *Helichrysum petiolatum* and *Verbena* 'Candy Stripe', with a *Leucanthemum* x *Superbum* cultivar as the white ingredient.

Another beautifully orchestrated scheme is the climbing rose 'Albertine' underplanted with white flowers, such as white foxgloves, love-in-a-mist and snapdragons.

RECORDING THE PICTURE

Keeping a garden diary is an invaluable help when you're planning colour schemes in your garden. It will also help you to remember just what you planted last year or exactly what flowered when. Use your camera as a tool, too, to record your successes. A photographic record of your garden over the years makes a great keepsake and archive.

LEFT The pink-and-white scheme along this driveway is provided by azaleas and cherry blossom.

OPPOSITE A cool-toned planting of muted pinks, violets and blues ends in a crescendo, with the cascading foliage of conifers forming a permanent backdrop to the shorter-lived foreground of colours.

ABOVE Clematis and roses are a classic and unbeatable example of harmony in colour and form; climbing clematis is supported by the branches of the rose. Here the fabulous flowers of *Clematis* 'lawsoniana' offset the rose's charming pink buds.

ABOVE RIGHT Chinese forget-me-not (*Cynoglossum amabile*), shown here in spring with peach blossom and white *Spiraea*.

OPPOSITE Tall flowers such as penstemon, salvia, lupins and lavatera create this cottage garden in violet, pink and white.

PINK, VIOLET AND BLUE

Other variations on the pink-based garden are combinations of shades of pink, violet and blue. For example, in spring, carpets of massed bluebells can underscore the rich pinks of rhododendrons. Deeper pink roses — for example, David Austin's 'Gertrude Jekyll' or 'Constance Spry' — look stunning when combined with tall delphiniums or planted among twining pale lilac clematis.

The fluffy mauve flowers of ageratum look very attractive when planted underneath rich pink Gallica roses, while on a smaller scale *Geranium sanguineum* makes a great background for cerinthe and tall, elegant lupins.

But simpler, less long-term double acts can work equally well. Pink cosmos or cleome will fill the bill, with campanula interwoven in the beds. Allium and borage also make effective foils for the roses.

Another pretty scheme to try is the rich blue of salvia (for example, *Salvia farinacea* 'Victoria') offset by the romantic, misty-looking *Gaura lindheimeri*. The little touches of pink in the gaura petals can be repeated in pink petunias at the front of the border, and at the back, choose bush roses with flowers in pink and white.

ABOVE One of the few coffee-coloured roses, 'Julia's Rose' is slightly fragrant and repeat-flowering. It will need careful attention and protection from diseases such as black spot to deliver blooms of the best quality.

ABOVE RIGHT A verbascum with copper pink blooms.

OPPOSITE Pink windflowers (*Anemone hupehensis*), also known as Japanese anemones, loll among the reddish brown leaves of berberis. This pretty and harmonious autumn duo isn't an obvious combination, but it works well in this country setting.

PINK AND BROWN

There are some other colour harmonies, based on pink, that are a bit off the beaten track. Some gardeners have used the glamorous modern hybrid tea rose 'Julia's Rose', with its distinctive coppery brown buds and its milk coffee-coloured flowers, as their starting point for a new wave of colour harmony based on pink and brown.

For example, you can team this rose with *Phormium* 'Maori Sunrise', which has sword-like leaves in bronze-pink and red. You could also include the verbascums, such as the coppery *Verbascum* 'Helen Johnson', which has large copper pink flowers, and the paler *V.* 'Cotswold Queen'. These tall and elegant plants could also introduce a change in plant texture and shape.

Digitalis ferruginea, a foxglove with flowers the colour of crushed raspberries, also finds a place in this grouping. Pansies in the 'Antique Shades' series can be used to fill any holes and extend the sense of unity, while those berberis plants with dull bronze leaves can be used as more permanent fillers.

Consider strengthening the colour register by including some of the darker, almost black flowers, such as the wonderfully rich sweet Williams, black violas and dark red scabious. These blooms are the colours of ruby and amethyst, and you could include the darkest possible roses from the colour chart, perhaps the deepest red of 'Mister Lincoln', the velvet purple 'Cardinal de Richelieu' or the near-black of David Austin's 'Fisherman's Friend'.

CONTRASTING SCHEMES

Contrasts in the garden are stimulating. There are several ways to achieve them, and much depends on the kind of dramatic effect you want to achieve. Bring excitement to the garden by juxtaposing strong colours, such as purple, with vermilion, magenta, orange, gold and crimson-red.

BASIC GUIDELINES

Some of the best colour contrasts can be achieved when complementary colours (those on the opposite sides of the colour wheel) are played out next to each other. It works like this: red is contrasted with green, blue with orange and yellow with violet. And while these are the basics of colour contrast, you don't have to stick rigidly to these rules. However, it does help to understand why some combinations work and some don't.

For example, consider the contrast of orange and lime green. Combine a fabulous marmalade-orange dahlia, such as 'David Howard', with a peachy orange canna, such as 'City of Portland', along with *Nicotiana* 'Lime Green' and a generous sprinkling of dill, for a brilliant result.

You can also use extremes of dark and light to create dazzling and vibrant colour contrasts. When done well, juxtaposing light and dark is eye-catching but not jarring. For example, try mixing pale lemon flowers with lots of dark purple or violet.

In a similar vein, consider a dark green hedge as a background for white flowers. It always looks fantastic — and it works on the same

BELOW The judicious sprinkling of what could be seen as the 'wrong' colours adds spice to this carefully planned garden picture — as well as a welcome element of surprise.

BELOW RIGHT Orange is one of the most vibrant colours on the gardener's palette. When you pair orange with its complementary colour blue, it's all the more intense, as seen in this pairing of Californian poppies and love-in-a-mist.

principle as that of a diamond brooch on a little black dress. The dark background shows off the contrasting lighter colour.

However, there is one rule you must always observe. Never plant mixed colours together as a way of achieving contrast. You cannot mix yellow, pink, orange and violet together in an annual planting. It's okay to mix violet and pink, or lemon and violet, but not the whole lot together. If you do, the garden ends up looking like a piece of hotel carpet designed to hide spots and stains.

LEFT Here contrast is provided by purple-flowered bearded iris, apricot-flowered *Geum chiloense*, white Queen Anne's lace (*Daucus carota*), red-hot poker (*Kniphofia* cultivar) and honey locust (*Gleditsia triacanthos*).

ABOVE Shocking garden colour in the bright blue of the Japanese iris and the vivid flowers of the Mollis azalea. Remember that the effect of such a combination depends on the kind of light in the area being planted: in a quiet leafy corner it could look terrific, but it may not be ideal next to a sunny, brick-paved terrace.

ABOVE RIGHT In this attractive planting of poppies and euphorbia, red and green work beautifully together as the two are complementary colours.

OPPOSITE A warm or hot scheme can be limited to just one season. Here brilliant autumn foliage lights up a woodland garden.

BREAKING THE RULES

Only an experienced and skilled garden designer like the late great gardener Christopher Lloyd can successfully break the rules of colour planting. In his garden at Great Dixter, in Kent, Lloyd decided that a great deal of colour planning seemed too unadventurous. Finding colour contrasts should be exciting: blockbuster bedding schemes featuring salvia and marigolds are 'numbingly uniform', he said. Among Lloyd's most famous schemes are lime green with yellow and red flowers — just think of the cheery picture created by red japonica, lime green euphorbia and daffodils in a spring garden.

Another of Lloyd's successes was a trio featuring the yellow *Achillea* 'Moonshine', purple *Salvia* x *superba* and a lively red penstemon with a touch of pink in its colouring. Lloyd admitted that even he felt a little ashamed of its garishness but that the flat plates of the *Achillea* flowers combined with spiky salvia made the picture work, even if the combination seemed a little too obvious.

The trick is not to have too many solid blocks of colour. Use airy flowers or lively green foliage to break up the spaces. Be careful, too, when using white as a contrast. It can be quite startling, and you don't want to create an effect that looks like a lacy white tablecloth thrown over the border. If you have a bank of orange daisies, you may need to break up the solid effect by adding in some green foliage or by incorporating different recurring shapes in green, such as box cones or spirals.

And don't overlook autumn foliage for its seasonal contribution to colour contrasts: the splendour of an ornamental grape vine down to its last ruby red leaf; the fiery brilliance of *Parrotia persica* as it sheds its leaves; or the fine butter yellow leaves of wisteria at autumn's end. Ash trees, too, are marvellous for their autumn colour: the golden ash (*Fraxinus excelsior* 'Aurea') and the claret ash (*Fraxinus angustifolia* 'Raywood') make wonderful spectacles of deep gold and ruby red light. And there are many, many others; all play their part in the colour parade.

ABOVE Think outside the box and introduce extra colour into the garden with paint. The brick-red gate contrasts beautifully with the green hedge.

ABOVE RIGHT Autumn colour in a tulip tree (*Liriodendron tulipifera*) complemented by a red garden seat.

USING STRUCTURES FOR CONTRAST

Plants are just one way of creating contrast in the garden. Another is to highlight the difference between the structural frameworks of the garden and the unrestrained exuberance of living plants. Try exploiting this contrast and see what dramatic effects you can achieve.

The best results come from taking a total approach — embracing the colour of your fence, the tiles on your roof, the colour of your brickwork and the colour of the window frames. If your house is rendered or painted, think carefully about whether the colour will act as an attractive background or clash horribly with your plantings.

A less permanent way of introducing colour contrast is with bold-coloured pots, obelisks, tripods and urns. At a 2000 garden festival at Les Jardins de Metis in Canada, the landscape architect Claude Cormier created a 'Blue Stick Garden', a contemporary take on the herbaceous border. He drew his inspiration from blue poppies (*Meconopsis betonicifolia*), and substituted a mass of blue-painted sticks. It sounds bizarre, but visitors were exhilarated by the humour and drama of the visual experience. You may not want to have blue sticks as a substitute for real plants, but it is a lesson in how colour contrasts can be introduced.

Try a bold blue pot next to a splash of vivid magenta petunias, or paint your trellis dark blue and train yellow roses such as 'Graham Thomas' over it. Take a fresh look at the front fence and see if it needs a touch of contrasting colour — perhaps the gentle, pale blue needs enlivening with the cheerful sprawl of a scarlet geranium? Or you could paint your front door a cheerful glossy red, then grow a rose in the same red on an arch over the front gate.

A pair of white Versailles tubs planted with handsome box and bay trees, or a dark green tub filled with white azaleas make a classic contrast. Ceramic containers, highly glazed in dramatic colours, often look brilliant in a contemporary garden; filled with flowers, they bring bright colour to even the dullest corner.

Another idea is to juxtapose brilliant colour on the entrance gates with soft planting, or to paint pots in bright hues to highlight the entrance.

Using painted screens or dividers is another way of introducing colour as a backdrop for unusual plants.

Buildings such as gazebos can work well in the garden, but they should be positioned with care to prevent them from clashing with the surrounding garden. They are usually at their most effective when coloured to match nearby landscaping features, such as brick or gravel paths. Perhaps a white gazebo could echo white gravel or the slate roof might pick up the dark bitumen on a path.

ABOVE The white colour scheme of this courtyard garden is reinforced by the airy, light-coloured table setting.

COLOUR-THEMED GARDEN FURNITURE

Before you choose garden furniture, consider the overall colour scheme of the garden. Bold reds and blues, dark green and dazzling white can all contribute to the garden picture, and enhance or detract from the effect you're trying to achieve.

Blue makes a great choice for garden furniture, partly because it enhances the many shades of green and yellow found in plants. For an effective yet restful duo, team blue paintwork on hard garden structures with lime yellow foliage.

However, exercise caution when considering whether to buy white furniture. Reproductions of cast-iron garden settings are better left on the verandahs of Victorian villas, not parked on green lawn. And while white seats have a classic look when combined with a background of geraniums scrambling over a garden shed, they can be dazzling in strong summer light.

Even so, white furniture can be successful, especially if a light, airy style of seat is blended with delicate plantings, such as white daisies and artemisias with silvery foliage, or *Gaura lindheimeri* teamed with clumps of pale-flowered lavender and perhaps an olive tree or two in a Mediterranean-style planting.

If you're following a Mediterranean theme, with appropriate silver-leafed plants, then seats in a silvery grey or a brilliant blue would look wonderful. If you live in rocky country, where lichen or moss thrive on rocks, take a little scraping of the plant material and match the colour of your furniture to it. You'll be surprised at how the colour of the painted surface, while blending with the natural elements, will still offer a contrast, although it will be a much more subtle one than the more obvious choice of dazzling white.

PASTELS AND NEUTRALS

Many gardeners find pale and delicate flowers especially appealing, perhaps because of their subtlety, or because they are a major element in the romantic garden. In nature, however, flowers must broadcast their appeal, and it's no coincidence that in many species the most insignificantly coloured flowers are the most fragrant. One of the happiest discoveries you'll make is that many of the white and pastel-coloured flowers you might choose for your garden are redolent with perfume.

Pastels are simply paler versions of colours, tempered by degrees of white, and, depending on their undertone, they too can be hot, cool or warm. Pastel-coloured flowers that are mixed together have a reputation for creating harmony and dreamy gardenscapes; however, these pale colours can also be used as contrasts or highlights.

Timeless and enduring, pastels are the soft hues of red, pink, blue and yellow. They're gentle rose pink, baby blue, cream and lime green. Pastels create a calm, gentle mood, quietening the senses. Use these delicate shades where bolder tones are too loud or where white is too stark.

For the best effects, use pale powder blues, soft pinks and creams in areas receiving first light or fading daylight. Pastels are romantic and soft as well as versatile companions. Plant them en masse with highlights of stronger colours for balance and effect. Create pockets of pastels to subdue bolder colours. Blend white with stronger colours, then add pastels to link them both.

Discreet and subtle in colour, pastels can suit any garden style, whether fused with more distinctive tones or planted alone. Use pastels to lift shady, dull areas, to bring out a soft glow or to add gentle colour against white walls.

BELOW The sweet flowers of *Ipheion uniflorum* are scattered over the foliage, creating a romantic picture. Decorative plants that are soft in outline but tough like this one are ideal both for easy maintenance and for softening garden plantings.

BELOW RIGHT Here the softness of pastel hues, with white highlights, complements the relaxed style of this rambling cottage garden.

WHITE GARDENS

One of the best examples of how to use pale colours can be seen in the renowned white garden created by Vita Sackville-West at Sissinghurst in Kent, a garden that became one of the icons of 20th-century gardening. Many gardeners have tried to emulate it, with varying degrees of success. Just before World War II, Vita first mooted the idea of a garden with an array of white flowers for a corner that was being drained and filled. She wrote:

I have got what I hope will be a really lovely scheme for it: all white flowers, with some clumps of very pale pink. White clematis, white lavender, white agapanthus, white double primroses, white anemones, white camellias, white lilies including giganteum in the corner...

But what is white? White picks up and reflects light — be it moonlight, sunlight or artificial light — from other sources. White light is created when all colours of the spectrum are combined and, therefore, all colours are incorporated in it. This is why white flowers mix happily with all other hues.

The key to a successful white garden, or to any garden filled with pale flowers, is to consider the light under which it will be viewed.

ABOVE Having made the decision to plant an all-white garden, don't be tempted to add other colours.

ABOVE LEFT With their stately vertical precision, foxgloves are an excellent way to introduce strong lines into a planting and thus provide some contrast with an all-white theme.

WHITE FLOWERS

- The sculptural beauty of white magnolias such as *Magnolia stellata* on bare boughs are a highlight of late winter and early spring.
- Viburnums comprise both deciduous and evergreen shrubs, with an amazing variety of flower forms. *Viburnum plicatum* has large, creamy white flowers in spring.
- Best in cool sites, lily-of-the-valley (*Convallaria majalis*) is renowned as a cut flower as well as for its glorious scent.
- Candytuft (*Iberis sempervirens*), among the purest of garden whites, blooms all summer with a pure mass of lace-like flowers covering wire-like stems.
- Hydrangeas love shade and thrive where the conditions are moist and the soil is rich in humus.
- Famous for their fragrant white flowers throughout late spring and summer, gardenias are wonderful cool conservatory plants. Position pots near a seating area for a waft of perfume.
- For a gorgeous white and silver pot, you could choose a combination of rock daisy, silver bush, variegated catmint and *Cineraria* 'Silver Dust'.

BELOW *Magnolia denudata.*

BELOW RIGHT *Viburnum plicatum.*

OPPOSITE, CLOCKWISE FROM TOP LEFT Lily-of-the-valley, candytuft, gardenias and a pot planted with rock daisy, silver bush, variegated catmint and *Cineraria* 'Silver Dust'.

RIGHT Snowball bush (*Viburnum macrocephalum*) flowers profusely in spring.

OPPOSITE This beautiful formal rose garden features pale pink standard roses underplanted with white dianthus and alyssum.

SPRING'S PASTEL PALETTE

Spring is the time when your dream of a white garden can become a reality — there is so much to choose from. It's a time when the freshness and frothiness of spring bulbs and blossoms look wonderful against a background of freshly unfurling leaves. The white show really begins a few weeks earlier, in late winter, when the first tiny snowdrops appear in borders, along banks and under trees. Later, paler flowered daffodils could add to the display, nodding under white camellia flowers, achieving perfection if protected from frost. Arum lilies spring from the ground amid dark, fleshy leaves, their tightly curled spathes a perfect complement to the white bark of silver birches.

As spring progresses, white and pastel flowers — cool, crisp and clean — appear on many plants, from the smallest bulbs to magnificent flowering shrubs. White, together with delicate pink, blue and cream, is the mainstay of this season. Everywhere you look pale flowers weave their magic. Tulips burst through a misty ground cover of forget-me-nots and pale primroses with rich green ruffs.

A succession of flowering shrubs can introduce further pale colours to the spring garden. Many shrubs and small trees have white or creamy flowers, often tinged with pink, and start to flower in late winter. The range of viburnums is extensive and includes old favourites such as *Viburnum* x *burkwoodii*, *V.* x *carlcephalum* and one of the most popular, *V. opulus* 'Roseum (syn. 'Sterile'), with its snowballs of white petals. The exquisite flowers held on the horizontal branches of *V. plicatum* 'Mariesii' are a magical sight.

The list of spring beauties is long — from the white, star-shaped petals of *Magnolia stellata* to the fleeting, confetti-like effects of Manchurian cherries as they burst into flower, from the stunning Japanese cherries such as 'Mt Fuji' to the enormous range of colour in rhododendrons and azaleas. Later in spring, rhododendrons in cream and white are yet another highlight. For many gardeners an all-time favourite in the smaller shrub category is *Rhododendron* 'Fragrantissimum', with its pretty, trumpet-like flowers and its wonderful spicy perfume.

PASTELS FOR SUMMER

As the days get longer, delicate spring flowers fade and the pale stars of summer emerge. Summer is the critical test for gardeners who want to create a white garden in the glare of strong sunshine. In the hot months the key is the light. As the sun climbs high in the sky, take the time to reflect on the dramatic difference between sunshine and shadow, and the interplay of light in your garden.

Strong shape in flowers is also important in bright, reflective light, and you can introduce dramatic impact to your garden with the huge tissue-paper petals of *Romneya coulteri* or the tall trumpets of *Nicotiana sylvestris*. Consider crisp white agapanthus, able to withstand high temperatures, or tall, stunning white poppies (*Papaver Orientale* cv.), whose great carnation-like heads make ideal vertical accents.

Knowing which shades of white and pale-coloured flowers work best together and then providing the right setting are critical aspects of planning a pastel garden. Clear, strong, summer light can handle the crispness of dazzling white flowers as well as parchment whites, pale yellows fading to white and whites tinged with pink. But do consider how they will look in the garden as they fade away — the petals of white flowers often turn brown and look unattractive clinging to the plant.

Beneath trees, especially where summer showers keep the ground cool and lush, the pale flowers of hydrangeas highlight a shady corner. *Hydrangea quercifolia*, with its luscious white heads amid exquisite cut-out green leaves, and *H. paniculata* 'Grandiflora', with its large, pyramidical flower heads, are both exceptional.

However, out in the bright sun, hydrangeas, hostas and impatiens will only look sad and sorry as they languish unhappily. Instead, you need plants that can thrive in the heat and dust of the Mediterranean summer — plants with leaves of silver and pewter-coloured hues, designed by nature to withstand the heat.

BELOW For a summer garden, tall pink cleomes and white cosmos are ideal for the back of the pastel border.

BELOW RIGHT A pastel garden with warm highlights of red and pale yellow.

AN ALTERNATIVE PASTEL GARDEN

White gardens don't have to consist of traditional shrubs and perennials. Consider creating a themed white garden based on plants from a particular part of the world. For a drought-resistant garden with an exotic ambience, try the Australian version. These plants are best in a sheltered site and require winter protection.

- Silver emu bush (*Eremophila nivea*) is a spectacular Australian native for both garden beds and containers. Growing to about 2 m tall and flowering from late winter to early summer, the tubular lilac flowers form an attractive contrast to the silvery grey foliage. It loves well drained soils in a sheltered spot.
- The masses of white flowers on coastal tea-tree (*Leptospermum laevigatum*) look marvellous in spring. This plant is wonderful against a sunny wall. *L. rupestre* is slightly more hardy.
- *Correa alba*, a delicate evergreen shrub, is another perfect choice for a sheltered site, growing to about 1.5 m high and wide. The oval green leaves are offset by the starry white flowers that appear over many months.

ABOVE LEFT Here drifts of pastel-coloured plants soften the edges of a gently curved pathway.

ABOVE, FROM TOP TO BOTTOM Silver emu bush (*Eremophila nivea*), coastal tea-tree (*Leptospermum laevigatum*) and *Correa alba*.

ABOVE This pretty combination
features cosmos, Canterbury bells
and ageratum. The trick when planting
out pastel shades is not to overdo the
pinks, as the effect of pink on pink
can sometimes be cloying.

RIGHT All the charm and romance of
pale-coloured flowers is encapsulated
in this lovely corner, where white
lunaria, violets, aquilegia and bluebells
mingle together.

FLOWERS FOR ACCENT

Beds of massed annuals can add a wonderfully frothy and airy appeal to the pastel garden. One private garden in northern France, Le Pontrancart near Dieppe, exemplifies this frothy style. It features one huge bed planted with white cosmos, its leggy bits at the base covered with grey-leafed dusty miller (*Senecio cineraria*), against a backdrop of a green hedge. In front of the bed a white seat rests on green lawn. The whole effect is one of simplicity and sparkling purity. This type of restrained planting can be hugely successful. You can mass plant annuals as seedlings and interweave them with silver- or green-leafed plants for relief.

If your house is painted white, you could build on this theme and plant your garden to enhance the house. Consider the simplicity of white wisteria trained over a pergola, massed plantings of cleomes with their spidery petals or banks of daisies.

If some annuals and perennials look dishevelled as they run to seed, cut them back well, add some extra fertilizer and some water, and they may reward you with a second flush of flowers.

Try to choose perennials that will carry on the pastel look between periods of annual flowering. These range from the silvery, heart-shaped leaves and white flowers of the ground-covering *Lamium maculatum* 'White Nancy' to perennial stocks, from fabulous shasta daisies to stately white foxgloves and aristocratic madonna lilies.

You might consider adding the casual yet soft pastel colours of the tough little seaside daisy, *Erigeron karvinskianus* (syn. *E. mucronatus*) is at its best on walls or beside paths. The Australian garden designer Edna Walling planted it in virtually every garden she designed, describing it as 'a little plant which never fails to thrive in every situation'.

BELOW This pastel garden is built on white, with snow-in-summer, white valerian, white lupins and *Centranthus alba* highlighted with blue-flowered campanula and red valerian.

SILVER PLANTS

Silver-foliaged plants such as artemisia, santolina and lavender — even verbascums with their felty leaves — are perfect for complementing a pale summer theme. They harmonize happily with cream and pink, and if you want to pursue an all-white theme, they will enhance the impression of lightness and add sparkle to what might otherwise be a monotonous garden bed.

The silvery sheen of these plants is created by masses of tiny white hairs on the leaf surface, their own protective screen against overheating in harsh sunlight.

Interestingly, many of these silver-leafed plants have fabulous shapes and textures, enlivening beds that could otherwise be rather insipid. The spear-like leaves of yuccas, the striking foliage of *Melianthus major* and the statuesque majesty of artichokes all help anchor a garden planted with pastel flowers. They lend extra strength or backbone to the garden. (See also 'Dramatic plants', page 324).

The low lance-like leaves of *Artemisia ludoviciana* 'Valerie Finnis' and the bushy *A.* 'Powis Castle', with its fine filigree of silvery leaves, are excellent for incorporating silvery highlights, as is lamb's ears (*Stachys byzantina*), which has downy, white-tinged leaves.

BELOW Alternate silver and green groundcovers spill over to cover the stonework of this raised garden bed.

SILVER PLANTS FOR PASTEL GARDENS

There is a wide variety of silver and grey perennials, herbs, ground covers, shrubs and trees available. Choose from *Convolvulus cneorum*, *Senecio cineraria* and its cultivars, catmints, snow-in-summer and lavenders.

- The grey-green tones of cotton lavender (*Santolina chamaecyparissus*) and lavender (*Lavandula* sp.) complemented by yellow-green euphorbia.
- *Melianthus major* is prized for its luxuriant foliage. The grey-green, deeply serrated leaflets offer a wonderful contrast in form and texture to other shrubs, and the flower spikes are also a striking feature.
- The silver-leaved pear *Pyrus salicifolia* is an ideal tree for the pastel garden. It has handsome, willow-like leaves, quite silvery while young, and small white flowers. Its semi-weeping habit is extremely graceful.

CLOCKWISE FROM TOP LEFT Some wonderful silver plants: artemisia and artichoke with echium; *Melianthus major*; and *Pyrus salicifolia*.

ABOVE Columbines (*Aquilegia* x *hybrida*) have dainty, grey-green foliage like maidenhair and charming spurred flowers.

TOP With its elegant, filigree foliage and spurred, many-petalled blue flowers, the aptly named love-in-a-mist (*Nigella* sp.) has a soft, hazy appearance.

TOP RIGHT The sky blue flowers of forget-me-nots (*Myosotis sylvatica*) create a soft, misty floor in spring.

ROMANTIC GARDENS

You can achieve a wonderfully romantic look with pastels. For a light, misty effect, concentrate on plants that have a certain softness about their appearance — plants such as cleome, cosmos, gypsophila, lavatera and old self-seeding favourites such as honesty, forget-me-nots, pyrethrum and centranthus. Quite often their fragile looks belie an inner toughness.

Perennials that further enhance a sense of lightness and airiness include *Gaura lindheimeri*, *Crambe cordifolia* and *Gypsophila paniculata*. Add Queen Anne's lace and *Thalictrum aquilegifolium* and you'll see that these plants make misty screens, softening the focus and almost dissolving any hard edges. They are essential for cultivating the romantic look.

If you're choosing a selection of roses, there are many variations in pale colours to help you achieve a romantic effect. For an immaculate white look, it's still hard to beat the ever popular 'Iceberg', closely followed by a selection of elegant David Austin roses. (See also the box opposite.)

Hunt through the gardening catalogues and nurseries for less common shrubs that will epitomize the sense of purity and elegance you're striving to achieve. Here are three suggestions that will give constant pleasure: pearl bush (*Exochorda racemosa*), a spreading deciduous shrub with pendulous branches and appealing chartreuse foliage; *Retama monosperma* (syn. *Genista monosperma*), which has pure white fragrant flowers and a weeping form of singular beauty; and snowy mespilus *(Amelanchier lamarckii)* with delicate white flowers in spring, bronze-green young leaves that are orange-red in autumn, and juicy fruits.

No matter which ones you choose, these plants with pale-coloured flowers will give pleasure on summer evenings. Much of the appeal of pastel gardens is their soft-edged look — dramatically different from a garden where the focus is on bold, strong colours in flowers and foliage.

ROSES IN PASTEL COLOURS

These pastel roses are ideal specimens for a romantic garden and they will all do well in dryish conditions. To grow healthy specimens, find a spot where the rose has plenty of room to spread, lots of air circulation to minimize fungal disease and preferably eight hours of sunshine a day. Start with robust varieties and keep the plants well watered and well fed. For the best results, pay careful attention to pest control, pruning and general care. Plant roses in well prepared soil, either as bare-rooted plants in autumn or any time of the year if they have been growing in pots.

The sweetly fragrant, soft pink double blooms of 'Fantin-Latour' appear in summer.

'Clair Matin' produces numerous clusters of decorative salmon pink flowers. This almost thornless, recurrent rose is a constant delight.

The flowers on 'Sharifa Asma', a David Austin rose, are a nearly translucent blush pink, with a touch of gold at the base. Austin describes this as a rose of rare delicacy.

'Glamis Castle' is one of David Austin's lovelier creations. Ruffled and cup-shaped, the white flowers have a strong, spicy fragrance.

Bred in 1940, 'Fritz Nobis' has all the charm of a heritage rose. During spring, masses of wonderful blooms — pink with a touch of salmon — cover the bush.

'Margaret Merrill' is noted for both the elegant form of its white flowers and its sweet fragrance.

COOL SCHEMES

All over the world, gardeners are drawn to cool-coloured blooms — from dark indigo to soft lilac to bright sky and azure. Cool colours are among the most popular of flowers, and they complement many garden styles.

In the garden, cool colours are based on blue, a natural complement to green. Cool-coloured flowers are eye-catching, but never clash. Even when they're used in uplifting contrasts, such as with white, yellow or red, they always seem serene. They can be gem-like in the shade, but also dazzling under the sun. Use blues and purples to harmonize with pastels and neutrals.

Cool colours appear to retreat, so when they're used in a small area, they give the illusion of more space and distance. Plant them in a warm spot to ease the temperature down. The green background is usually taken for granted as an integral part of the overall picture, and yet it makes an enormous contribution to a peaceful environment. Green shrubs and trees provide a perfect backdrop for a garden, and a green lawn acts as a calming device and counterpoint to the busyness of flowering plants.

BELOW This Australian garden demonstrates the effectiveness of a simple cool scheme. The main plantings are of white *Zantedeschia* towering over blue forget-me-nots and *Hyacinthoides*.

LEFT In a frost-free garden, potted kumquats underplanted with lobelia are softened by plantings of lavender and violas.

TOP Stars of the summer garden, agapanthus always lend a cool look to a scheme, even on the hottest days.

ABOVE *Echium candicans*, sometimes known as the tower of jewels, flowers from spring to early summer.

RIGHT In this green subtropical garden, Japanese box (*Buxus microphylla* var. *japonica*) defines the garden beds, complemented by the white flowers of arum lily (*Zantedeschia aethiopica*), *Gardenia augusta*, *Spiraea cantoniensis* and *Erigeron karvinskianus* as well as the purple blooms of bugle (*Ajuga reptans* 'Catlin's Giant').

GREEN GARDENS

Walk in any park or visit any city or country garden, and you will discover how many variations of green there are. The colour green offers almost endless change — consider the darkest of green needles on a pine tree, the brilliant lime green of *Gleditsia triacanthos* 'Sunburst', the soft green of an olive leaf, the dark green, glossy leaf of a camellia or holly, the grey-green of a eucalypt leaf and the acid green of euphorbia bracts. Yet we see all these leaves as green.

The rich tapestry of green ranges widely across the colour spectrum. There's the acidic yellow-green flower heads of euphorbia, which contrast superbly with soft grey-green leaves; the bright yellow-green leaves of golden privet; the dark, veined leaves of *Viburnum davidii*; the huge lime-coloured leaves of *Paulownia tomentosa*; the bright green, shiny leaves of citrus; the soft green leaves of *Hydrangea quercifolia*; the thick, dark green leaves of bergenias; and the purple-veined green leaves of the eupatoriums.

Foliage also comes in an extensive range of sizes, shapes and textures. For example, the strappy leaves of agapanthus contrast with the frilled, incised foliage of *Melianthus major*, and thick, sword-like grasses such as *Miscanthus sinensis* 'Gracillimus' are in complete contrast to the dark green glossy leaves of skimmias. The leathery leaves of bergenias are totally different to the soft green foliage of hostas, and the neat, small, green leaves of box are nothing at all like the drooping fronds of a palm.

A GREEN OASIS

In towns and cities, newer houses often have 'open-plan' front gardens while older ones have a tiny patch of green surrounded by a low wall or hedge, with very little scope for privacy. So the back garden should be organised to provide seclusion. This requires a particular style of garden — rather than busy borders with fussy beds of annuals in a parade of colour, you need a cycle of green throughout the year.

The basic elements required to produce this type of garden are simple — slender shrubs and trees, so long as they aren't rampant, plenty of climbers and possibly a lawn (depending on the size of the garden). Other necessities include a sheltered seating area and some form of lighting.

There may be a place for just one tree. For example, consider a weeping elm, *Ulmus glabra* 'Pendula' or a weeping birch, *Betula pendula* 'Youngii'. Hornbeam (*Carpinusbetulus*) and some pittosporums are also suitable. Choose such a specimen tree with care: you don't want any discordant colour, just a change of shape and texture. After all, you are selecting a graceful ornament for your green garden.

A number of plants are suitable for creating a green screen. Some, such as camellias and viburnums, are attractive flowering plants in their own right. Planted closely together, they can be allowed to grow into a loose, informal line that makes a wonderful boundary marker or fence screen. Or they can be pruned neatly into a hedge.

On the other hand, there are plants such as cypress, laurel, bay and holly that will give your garden a long-established air. A great idea for a green garden is to plant a tapestry hedge, although you will need to choose your plants with care and be prepared to keep them under control with selective pruning.

ABOVE Rhapis palms and dense foliage plants create a lush tropical garden in a small back garden.

ABOVE A walled and paved courtyard is softened with plantings of various palms with dashes of red impatiens.

ABOVE The greenish late summer flowers of the pineapple lily (*Eucomis comosa*) are scented and packed tightly onto a long spike.

ABOVE RIGHT Perfect for planting under deciduous trees, *Helleborus argutifolius* flowers in winter and early spring.

GREEN FLOWERS

The idea of green flowers might seem a little uninspired, but there are variations of green with white, yellow, lime and dark green that bring another dimension of light and sparkle to the green garden.

To begin with, there are green annuals to enhance the look — the light lime-coloured *Nicotiana* 'Lime Green' and *Zinnia elegans* 'Envy'; the stunning green arum lily (*Zantedeschia aethiopica* 'Green Goddess'), with its striking green flowers lightly patterned in cream; and the green 'bells' of *Moluccella laevis*.

You can begin the green-themed display with the viridiflora tulip 'Spring Green'. Its white petals are marked with green slashes. Then there are the lime green flowers on *Helleborus foetidus*. There's even a green rose, *Rosa* x *odorata* 'Viridiflora', although it is described by some garden writers as an 'ugly curiosity'. Euphorbia is popular because its acidic yellow bracts provide a contrast with many different plants.

You can also use variegated leaves to ring the changes on a green and white theme; this is sometimes a pretty way to bring sparkle to a shady corner. Variegated ivy, as long as you don't allow it to run riot and treat it with care, makes a great ground cover in a difficult corner; some of the smaller shrubs that have green and white foliage can also be used.

FOLIAGE FOR YEAR-ROUND INTEREST

Foliage has two great advantages over flowers: it is usually longer lived and it's much easier to maintain. Of course you need to trim and tidy it, but with many evergreens you can create foliage effects and patterns for different times of the year.

One of the most difficult times for gardeners is the end of summer. Green leaves look tired and badly in need of a wash, the summer cut-back has left mounds of perennials looking spent, and the dusty air saps the freshness from the garden.

This is a time when a dark green cone of box, a spiral of ivy or a twist of elegant topiary can hold the garden together. Green, clipped shapes act as visual resting points that bring a sense of order and structure to the green garden.

Ferns such as hart's tongue fern (*Asplenium Scolopendrium*), hostas and other choice shade-tolerant plants are perfect additions to a green theme. They are especially effective in creating an informal garden where the aim is to imitate nature by relying on combined shades of green, with different foliage shapes enhancing the total picture.

And don't forget that vegetables are a great way to add variety to a green planting scheme. For instance, a potager or even a garden bed planted with lettuce, cabbages, broccoli and peas will make an attractive and deliciously edible pattern of greens.

ABOVE An excellent example of a quiet courtyard garden. The green shade trees — maple and weeping elm — are underplanted with ivy, both softening and complementing the hard surface of the brick paving.

TOP With its distinctive bold and glossy foliage and stately flower spikes, acanthus is an excellent choice along this shady walk.

LEFT This harmonious green and gold scheme features carefully trimmed conifers.

PARTERRE GARDENS

For centuries, gardeners have been laying out parterre gardens, embroidering the ground with a distinct ornamental style. Many of these exquisite patterned gardens with their interwoven plants are still popular tourist attractions in Europe today.

One of the best known is Villandry in France. Its ornamental kitchen garden is divided into nine squares, separated by wide paths, and planted with vegetables and fruit trees in contrasting colours and flowers for ornament. The complex cultivation plans are prepared each year. No two squares are alike, and the result is a giant game-board effect.

The idea of formal pattern making in the garden is still very much in vogue, even if it's not on the grand scale of previous centuries. Small hedging plants, such as box, are set against a background of coloured earth, gravel or lawn, or filled with single coloured flowers such as bergonias or salvias. This style has never gone out of fashion — indeed, it has been a bit overdone in recent years — and once it's established, it's easy to maintain. Even the most scaled-down version, perhaps of zigzag dwarf box hedging infilled with annuals such as violas, is perfect for a small inner-city courtyard.

Box and bay are commonly selected for these designs, as they're tough plants that look smart all year round, requiring just a trim from time to time.

A simple cross featuring five clipped standard bay trees encircled by box is always a stylish solution for a townhouse garden.

BELOW In this garden 80 standard bay trees, each ringed by a hedge of box, have been laid out in a grid-like pattern. With well-established cypress and pines as a backdrop, the garden is a symphony in green, with sunshine and shadow making different patterns on leaves and grass.

OPPOSITE TOP A small topiary garden planted with box features a peacock design and geometric shapes.

OPPOSITE BOTTOM A parterre adds interest to the deep shade below a large evergreen tree.

BEAUTIFUL BOX

Growing box hedges requires vision and patience, but no other plant so perfectly defines boundaries and brings strong structure to the garden's design.

Box is tough and drought-tolerant and, once established, will withstand hot weather, frost, snow and anything in between. The formal gardens of Europe are testament to its adaptability: there box plants have survived for several centuries and still look immaculate.

Several types of box are available. The classic common box (*Buxus sempervirens*) has dark green, pointed leaves while *Buxus hartlandii* (syn. *B. microphylla* var. *japonica*) has lighter green, rounded leaves. *Buxus sempervirens* 'Suffruticosa' has a compact habit and very small leaves.

Box is one of the plants traditionally used for clipping into ornamental shapes. Spirals, cones and birds make a dramatic architectural statement in the green garden.

Well-placed topiary ensures the garden retains its structure all year round.

ABOVE In tropical climates jacaranda offers light shade and masses of beautiful lavender-blue flowers in early summer.

ABOVE RIGHT A peaceful, harmonious blue-and-yellow garden.

BLUE GARDENS

Blue is the ultimate cool colour. The magic sparkle of blue water is balm to our eyes on a hot summer's day; the blue water of any swimming pool is an enticing invitation. Blue is also the colour of space and distance: as we look to the hazy horizon, the blue hills and sky seem to stretch to infinity.

In the garden, blue has the same effect. And while blue flowers might be close physically, they are wonderful for conveying a sense of space and distance. Together with green, blue brings the twin qualities of coolness and calm to the garden.

It's not hard to see why blue flowers are favourites. The colour blue is peaceful, and blue flowers associate well with all other colours. They look particularly attractive in harmony with yellow, but are also very effective as a foil for green foliage. A bold bank of Californian lilac (*Ceanothus* sp. and cv.) adds a refreshing touch as it cascades over a fence, as does the more compact but also wonderful *Ceratostigma willmottianum*.

A wide range of foliage also contains blue tones. Pick a leaf of almost any eucalypt and you can see the blue in it quite clearly; that's why, in its native Australia, the hills and horizons in the distance take on a blue haze. There are species of eucalyptus that will flourish and grow into quite large trees in temperate climates. Some, such as cider gum (*Eucalyptus gunnii*) can be kept as small shrubs through frequent pruning, enabling their silvery blue leaves to be combined with the other blue plants in beds and borders. Sadly, though, the beautiful blue flowers of the jacaranda, from tropical America but common in all tropical countries, will only ever be a holiday memory.

The tree itself with its pretty filigreed foliage will grow slowly in a sheltered site, with plenty of winter protection, in warmer gardens.

There are blue floral delights in spring too, such as a carpet of woodland bluebells in full flower, or the sweet perfume of a stunning pot of blue hyacinths. Massed, self-sown forget-me-nots under newly sprouting trees in spring have an ethereal quality, while a stiff little ring of grape hyacinths has a wonderful richness, especially if they contrast with cheery yellow daffodils or the lime green heads of euphorbia.

ABOVE Himalayan blue poppies (*Meconopsis betonicifolia*) are a sight to savour when planted en masse.

ABOVE LEFT Grape hyacinths (*Muscari* sp.) and bluebells (*Hyacinthoides non-scripta*) are commonly planted in drifts under trees in woodland gardens.

BLUEBELLES

Head and shoulders above all other blue-flowered bulbs is the native bluebell (*Hyacinthoides non-scripta*) with its delicate stem of nodding scented bells which appear in mid-spring. It is at its best growing in swathes through deciduous woodland with a backdrop of bright green tree leaves. In some gardens it can spread quite rampantly, so if you like your garden neat and well organised, limit your apprecaition of it to country walks. Another rampant spreader is grape hyacinth, which has the added disadvantage in some species of the lax bootlace foliage appearing the previous autumn. However, *Muscari latifolium* has only a single strap-shaped leaf per bulb — a perfect foil for the neat bi-coloured flowerheads — and spreads only slowly.

BLUE FLOWERS FOR EVERY SITUATION

The range of blue flowers is immense, and they can claim a place in almost every garden. They are, in all their sizes and shapes, the stars of the garden. From deepest, darkest indigo to softest lilac to bright sky and azure, blue flowers complement many garden styles, from the mountains to the sea. Use them with pastels and neutrals to create harmonious pictures, or contrast them with white, yellow or red; blue flowers can be gem-like in the shade but also dazzling under the sun. They create the illusion of distance and evoke a sense of calm.

Japanese iris (*Iris ensata* syn. *I. kaempferi*) has stunning flowers in many shades of blue, violet and lavender that are displayed above sword-like foliage.

No other flower has the brilliance and stature of delphiniums, best planted in dense drifts of one colour or tone.

A highlight of the shady garden in spring, lungwort (*Pulmonaria* 'Lewis Palmer') has blue comfrey-like flowers contrasted with silver-spotted leaves.

The traditional colour of these Cornflowers (*Centaurea cyanus*), with thier thistle-like flowers, is so intense that 'cornflower blue' is a colour description in its own right.

Lobelia comes in many forms, including bushy and trailing types. The deep blue of the tiny flowers makes them a charming choice for edging a bed, or as a display in a pot or hanging basket.

A quick-growing annual with a spreading habit, baby blue eyes (*Nemophila menziesii* syn. *N. insignis*) has china blue, cup-shaped flowers with white centres, making them ideal for a two-toned border.

SOME BLUE-TO-PURPLE ANNUALS

- *Ageratum* sp.
- Alyssum
- Anemone
- Aster
- Forget-me-not
- Lupin
- *Nierembergia* sp.
- Nigella
- Pansies
- Petunia
- Statice
- Torenia
- Violets

ABOVE LEFT With its slender spikes of densely packed, lavender-like flowers in deep purple-blue, *Salvia farinacea* 'Blue Russian' adds a cool element to summer borders.

LEFT Larkspurs flower in spring in warm areas, but in cooler climates they bloom in summer.

RIGHT Zinnias look best in massed displays. Sow them in succession for a longer flowering display.

OPPOSITE The potency of red is well illustrated here — and made even more dramatic — by the brilliant placement of *Aeonium arboretum* 'Zwartkop' with its almost black foliage. This setting, with touches of yellow in the daylily flowers, has all the power and energy of a fireworks display.

WARM AND HOT SCHEMES

On the colour wheel, red, yellow and orange are the warm colours. When you combine the primary colours of red and yellow, shades of orange are created. Together, these complementary colours create an harmonious effect. Try experimenting. Mix rust, deep maroon or burnt orange to turn the temperature down. Add lemon, apricot or cream pastels to lighten. Warm colours are enveloping.

A dramatic, plum-coloured dahlia, a rich crimson rose, a neat bed of postbox-red bonfire salvia, a splash of yellow forsythia, a maple fired up in its autumn splendour — all these plants make 'hot' colour statements in the garden, and these bold, rich tones that were popular in the Victorian era are 'hot' again in contemporary gardens.

Hot colours are also evident in more subtle forms, in bud, fruit, bark, stem and leaf. Naturally, hot flowers always stand out because the opposite colour to red is green, but they can also be contrasted with lighter tones.

Warm colours can be happy, bold, beautiful and flamboyant. These refreshing colours stimulate and energize your mood. Warmth can imitate or reflect a climate, provide a tropical escape, or simply create a feeling of well-being. Warm colours appear nearer — perfect for making a large garden seem more intimate, and they also make an entrance welcoming.

VARIATIONS ON RED AND YELLOW

What are referred to as 'hot' colours are based on red, orange or yellow. They are all spin-offs from red and yellow, two of the three primary colours. If you look at the colour wheel on page 262, you can see that they are adjacent or near neighbours, with orange at the centre. They are all in harmony with one another.

When you think of the hot colours, they evoke a subconscious response: they make you think of fire and heat and, therefore, warmth. A dining room painted red has a warm, cosy feel, perfect for dining by candlelight. Similarly, yellow evokes the warmth of the sun: think of how, on a dull, rainy day, a patch of bright yellow brings a cheerful note to the garden. Whether it's a sweep of daffodils in a paddock, a stand of poplars in autumn or a bed of orange dahlias in a park, the warm effect is the same.

In the plant world, there are myriad variations on red, orange and yellow, ranging from the palest primrose through to the deepest plum. The colour red has seemingly endless mutations, from bright scarlet and vermilion, to crimson and deep red, and then into the smoky red and plum tones. The richness of a bed of yellow tulips featuring a blaze of red polyanthus, an edge of brilliant red bedding begonias with the faded dusky reds of heritage roses or even a bed of red-leafed lettuce can all play a part in your hot colour garden.

These warm and hot colours are not restricted to flowers. Coloured foliage is also an important component when you are designing beds with hot, dense colours. The rich decorative palette is worth exploring — for example, the virtues of cannas and dahlias, particularly the newer cultivars, have been rediscovered in recent years. The foliage of some trees, too, has a wonderful rich intensity. Think, say, of the purple-leafed cultivars of the magnificent maple family.

BLENDING HOT COLOURS

Colour themes based on bold, rich and hot tones can make powerful statements, as can be seen in two of England's finest gardens — Hidcote in Gloucestershire and Great Dixter in Kent. Both gardens have been enormously influential in their use of hot colours. At Hidcote, the Red Borders feature every shade of red, from vermilion to crimson, with orange daylilies and purple and maroon foliage. These borders were designed to be processional, exhilarating and uplifting, so that visitors can admire them as they walk through without stopping and resting.

At Great Dixter, the late Christopher Lloyd planted a dynamic hot garden where once roses stood in stiff formality. Lloyd's brilliant planting, with combinations of almost shocking colours, was deliberately designed to give an electric jolt to what he called 'the good taste brigade'.

Both these gardens and other successful hot borders rely on careful colour distribution. A flat block of solid colour, although perhaps initially arresting, soon loses its impact and becomes boring. The more subtlety you can incorporate, the more successful your garden design will be. As a general rule, the larger the garden is, the broader the effects: for example, in a long or deep garden bed you might start with scarlet at one

OPPOSITE TOP LEFT Californian poppies (*Eschscholzia californica*) come in many colourways, including all shades of yellow, orange, brick reds and even some pinks. Easy to grow, these self-seeders are a great way to add a splash of colour to a corner.

OPPOSITE TOP RIGHT Red canna flowers are a bold feature in a warm garden border.

OPPOSITE BOTTOM RIGHT Bright colour in the garden can come from different sources, and berries make cheery highlights. The fruits of *Arbutus unedo* look stunning against its dark green foliage.

OPPOSITE BOTTOM LEFT Cannas, especially the newer cultivars, often feature richly coloured foliage, perfect for hot gardens.

ABOVE Maples provide brilliant autumn colour in this established woodland garden.

ABOVE RIGHT Sometimes gardeners need to think laterally. Here's *Kalanchoe blossfeldiana* in a mass planting. Who would have thought that an uninspiring pot plant could look so good? These fleshy, succulent little plants have multiple heads of bright scarlet flowers that grow to 30 cm.

OPPOSITE The flower spikes of kangaroo paw (*Anigozanthos* sp.) come in shades of ochre, red, orange, pink and green. Here they are used to create broad sweeps of colour in a hot garden.

end, fade into orange and then deepen to dark red and purple, blended with magenta and yellow, at the other end.

Another possibility is to experiment with a combination of flowers and foliage in rich, deep shades of maroon, plum and red-violet, brightened with splashes of scarlet and crimson, and with a dash of orange here and there. In a small plot, which is seen from a close viewing point, the planting scheme can be quite intricate: in a sense, you are embroidering the ground with the colour of your choice.

An essential part of getting the hot colour marriage to work is to create variety in terms of shape and texture in the planting. Remember that trees and shrubs and their foliage colour — the permanent plantings — will be the backbone of your hot garden.

The flowers and leaves of trees and shrubs, perennials and even annuals create outlines against which plants in other colours react. Different shapes, from the delicately cut leaves of a maple to the rounded leaves of *Cotinus coggygria*, form distinct contrasts and create a more subtle level of interest in the garden.

Small leaf shapes can also be used to echo the shape of larger leaves. Similarly, texture can add contrast to your scheme: glossy-leafed plants such as dahlias can be massed against the purple-veined leaves of eupatorium, while black-leafed aconiums, drought resistant succulents, look stunning next to the strappy leaves of phormiums, such as 'Amazing Red' and 'Bronze Baby'.

FLOWERS FOR HOT BORDERS

- *Rosa moyesii* 'Geranium', a wonderful species rose with single crimson flowers, is followed in autumn by brilliant flagon-shaped, orange-red hips.
- Sunflowers (*Helianthus annuus*) are absolute show-stoppers and grow quickly from seed to 2 m or more high, making them ideal for the back of the border.
- Penstemons with red or purple flowers are useful in hot and warm schemes. The racemes of flowers appear from spring and throughout summer.
- The double blooms of *Rosa* 'L.D. Braithwaite', a David Austin rose, open vivid fire-engine red from dark crimson buds.
- There are hundreds of dahlia cultivars available, many in the warm and hot range. Grouped according to flower shape, there is one to suit every climate.

CLOCKWISE FROM ABOVE *Rosa* 'L.D. Braithwaite', a David Austin rose; sunflowers (*Helianthus annuus*); *Rosa moyesii* 'Geranium'; and a red penstemon.

WARM FOLIAGE COLOUR

When designing a garden featuring hot colours, you'll need to choose plants with complementary foliage, whether it's rich bronze, chocolate, crimson or purple-black. The magnificent Norway maple cultivar (*Acer platanoides* 'Crimson King') is an ideal plant to use here. It's a fabulous choice if you have rolling acres, but its size makes it unsuitable for a suburban garden.

Further down the scale in size, but not in beauty, are exquisite shrubs such as the delightful smokebush (*Cotinus coggygria* 'Royal Purple' or 'Grace') or the somewhat smaller *Berberis thunbergii*. The *Acer* family offers other possibilities, including the delicate blood-leaf maple (*Acer palmatum* 'Atropurpureum'), with its finely etched crimson-purple leaves. This is a slow-growing specimen that looks great in a large pot. Other wonderful purple foliage shrubs include *Sambucus nigra* 'Guincho Purple' with cut, elderflower foliage and flat heads of pink flowers in early summer, and its richer-coloured cousin 'Black Beauty'. Such dark colours need careful use if you are to avoid simply making black holes, so consider lightening the background with paler tones, underplanting with a complementary, but brighter flower, such as foxgloves, or even training clematis through them. All elders benefit from cutting back hard to produce a good crop of foliage for the following year. This does mean you have to forego the flowers though.

ABOVE Another dazzling sight in autumn is the smokebush (*Cotinus coggygria*). The fascinating summer flowers, which look like puffs of smoke above the leaves, are a bonus.

To give the garden a stronger look, providing a punctuation mark in a corner or a foil for soft leaves, it's hard to go past the strappy bronze leaves of *Cordyline australis*. Cannas, too, are making a comeback after a nose-dive in popularity. Their huge, translucent leaves and folded flowers are useful in the background. They like warmth and plenty of moisture. The boldly cut-out leaves of the castor-oil plant (*Ricinus communis* 'Carmencita') are also striking. These architectural plants hold the key to a successful permanent structure of shrubs and trees.

You can enhance these garden 'building blocks' by clipping and shaping them for further structural interest. For example, to help anchor the planting you can shape cotinus bushes into balls about 1.2 m in diameter and berberis into ones about 90 cm wide. These shapes may echo others used elsewhere in the garden, perhaps in box, bay or privet.

You can ensure year-round interest by including wonderful trees such as *Prunus serrulata*, with its dark, rich cherry-coloured bark. In winter the bare trunks glow as if polished.

Another way of looking at foliage colour is to organize the plantings in such a way that the seasonal crescendo of autumn creates a 'hot' time. The bright yellow of a silver birch as it turns from green to gold, the ruby richness of a claret ash, the setting sun through the brilliant leaves of an ornamental grape vine entwined on a rustic fence all make memorable garden pictures.

Plan so that summer is the 'cool' time and, as the garden goes to rest, it does so in a proverbial blaze of glory.

Bananas and coleus are among the more tender bright-leafed plants that will produce a tropical effect in sheltered gardens. During the height of summer, houseplants such as bromeliads might enjoy an outdoor holiday in a carefully chosen spot. Be very careful not to place them in the sun, no matter how tough they look, as it will scorch their leaves.

ABOVE Bromeliads weave brilliant colour through a shrubbery in a semitropical garden.

ABOVE LEFT A popular ornamental shrub, *Berberis thunbergii* is deciduous and grows to about 1 m high and wide.

OPPOSITE In this peaceful corner of the garden, the shapely leaves of the tulip tree (*Liriodendron tulipifera*) make pretty patterns as they fall onto the grass.

TOP Gaillardias are perennials, but often treated as annuals. They bloom for a long season and tolerate both heat and drought, as well as poor soils, if they must.

ABOVE In spring, use clumps of nemesia to create contrasts.

ABOVE RIGHT There are many cultivars of the red-toned *Salvia splendens*, and new forms are available most years.

ADDED DIMENSION WITH FLOWERS

Annuals and perennials are essential for adding to, and enhancing the effect of, a strong coloured planting. A summer-flowering collection of annuals could include zinnias, gaillardias, tagetes, particularly the French marigolds, and cockscomb (Celosia). Add some 'Giant Russian' sunflowers to the mix and you'll create a colourful piece of garden theatre.

Under softer skies, burgundy, cerise and magenta can look important and exciting, and add a jewel-like dimension to the garden. Wonderful plants in this colour range are the glossy black sweet William, *Dianthus barbatus* 'Dunnet's Dark Crimson'; almost-black delphiniums; self-seeding red valerian (*Centranthus ruber*), and some of the sedums and clematis.

YELLOW FLOWERS

Golden light in the garden is a visual treat at any time of the year. In late winter, a hedge of forsythia is a bright herald of spring. On a clear winter's day, when the sun is out, note the startling contrast between bright sun and blue sky; you can achieve this effect in your garden beds and borders by using yellow and blue plants, such as daffodils with blue grape hyacinths.

For real drama, try a yellow border. Daisies, coreopsis and daylilies — plants with a loose, relaxed growing habit — would look great framing a garden feature, such as a flight of steps.

ABOVE LEFT Coneflowers and yellow dahlias planted in a golden drift.

TOP Mass plant yellow iris as a solid block of colour for impact, or combine them with blue forms.

ABOVE Gaillardias have yellow, or yellow and red flowers.

LEFT A favourite with gardeners all over the world, daffodils provide a cheerful note wherever they're planted.

ABOVE The strappy green foliage of cliveas always looks smart; these plants are sensational when their orange flowers bloom in a shady Australian garden.

ABOVE RIGHT Plant pale-coloured hydrangeas to brighten a shady bed.

OPPOSITE The sunny yellow colour and strong vertical accent provided by the lupins set off the entire planting. The scheme has been strengthened by the use of yellow in the right aspect — the plants are perfectly positioned to catch the sunshine and light up an otherwise gloomy corner.

LIGHT AND SHADOW

Even if you have a wonderful collection of colourful plants, putting them all together requires skill and forethought. Designing and planning a garden with plants in hot colours means taking stock of your garden's aspect. Does it look predominantly to the east and, therefore, receive only bright morning sunshine, or does it face west, looking into the setting sun? Is the orientation to the north or south? It's worth asking yourself these questions so you can ensure that your plantings are enhanced by flattering natural light.

As the seasons change, the amount of sunshine your garden receives varies. In summer, long hours of sunshine cast a different light on the garden, especially in the middle of the day. And because the sun is high in the sky, it casts dense shadows. In winter that same midday sun is welcome, but rarely appears, shining on a garden so completely changed from its glorious summer self to be almost unrecognisable.

A bed of bright yellow coreopsis or *Achillea* 'Moonshine', where the plants are all of the same height, can look like a huge pond of melted butter in the garden when the sun is right overhead. A far more subtle display can be built by using plants of different heights and depths.

Along the western edge of his garden at Giverny, in France, the great French Impressionist painter Claude Monet planted a 'sunset' border that is still part of the garden today. Monet used a number of orange and yellow flowers, such as sunflowers and marigolds, to exploit the warm orange light of sunset so that this border glows like a fire's embers in the evening light.

You can easily see this effect on a late autumn afternoon when the sun's rays, low in the sky, light up an ornamental grape vine or a deciduous tree — birch, elm or claret ash — as the leaves turn from green to gold. The glorious effect resembles sunlight streaming through a stained glass window.

ABOVE This is a fabulous design to emulate. Pots of soft grey-green *Cupressus macrocarpa* 'Greenstead Magnificent' are set on each side of the gravel driveway. At the end of the vista is a sprawling ornamental grape vine.

FORM AND FOLIAGE

There's no denying that the flowers on a plant enhance its beauty. Pick up any book on plants and you'll find that much of the information centres on the flowering aspect of plants. There are detailed descriptions on the type of bloom, colour, perfume and flowering season. However, plants have a lot more to offer than just their flowers. And, when it comes to looking at plants as elements in garden design, flowers are transient details.

No matter how gorgeous the flowers in your garden are, their impact lasts for only a few weeks or perhaps months. Next time you choose a garden plant, don't be seduced by its bloom alone. Instead, ask yourself how this particular plant will look for the rest of the year, when it's not in flower but still taking up precious garden space.

Unless you're an ardent collector, there's probably no room, or time, in your garden for one-day wonders. Plants that give year-round interest are particularly important for small gardens and courtyards or in areas where plants are grown in containers. The structure of the plant becomes increasingly significant as more emphasis is given to enjoying gardens as living pictures viewed from indoors, framed through a door or window. And with the recent developments in garden lighting, plants can be on show at night as well as by day. Under lights, plant form and structure become all important while flowers and even foliage take a back seat.

Most plants offer much more than seasonal blooms. Indeed, there's an entire framework of vegetation and growth produced by the plant just to

support its flowers from bud to seed. Plants are made up of leaves, stems, branches and roots. These features are arranged so each plant has a distinctive and characteristic look. Some species are so captivating that they become living sculptures.

ABOVE Many beautiful foliage plants are shade lovers that add rich texture to the area under trees.

PLANT STRUCTURE

The key, then, to having a great-looking garden with year-round interest is to choose plants for both their form and foliage. This doesn't mean that you should completely ignore transient plants. Some short-lived plants have a fascinating shape and form that warrants their inclusion in the framework of the garden. Indeed, bulbs and herbaceous perennials, particularly the ornamental grasses, provide an eye-catching structure, even if the display lasts for only a couple of months.

So look for plants with good structure and long-lasting garden interest. Check the overall shape as well as leaf colour, texture and shape. These plants make a statement, either singly as a dramatic focal point, or massed together as solid shapes or blocks of texture. You'll find an enormous variety in plant forms, ranging from compact rosettes (including many of the succulents) to spreading carpet-like species, such as ajuga and dianthus. Some plants can offer lush and colourful foliage, just the thing for creating a jungle or tropical look. And there are others that make a dramatic impact. These bold and vibrant plants can give your garden an instant 'wow!' factor (see 'Dramatic plants' on page 324).

SPIKY PLANTS

Here are some suggestions for spiky plants. Some of these are not fully hardy so will need winter protection of some sort.

- *Agare* sp. and cv.
- *Anigozanthos* sp. and cv.
- *Cordyline australis*
- *Cynara cardunculus*
- *Cyperus* sp.
- *Dietes* sp.
- *Iris*, bearded hybrids
- *Kniphofia* sp. and cv.
- *Phormium* sp. and cv.

RIGHT In a succulent garden the emphasis is on leaf shape and form.

Some plants form clumps with both strappy and spiky leaves while others grow naturally into pleasing shapes such as buns, cones and balls. Plants with strappy leaves — such as agapanthus, irises and narcissus — take on a formal role when they are arranged in rows or blocks, giving uniformity and direction to a garden. But these plants can also acquire an informal air when they're planted in random groups.

By contrast, spiky plants make an exclamation point in a garden. They have a crisp, pointed outline that makes them an ideal choice as a living sculpture or when a certain sharpness is required. When mass planted, they contribute an exciting, active texture.

There's a host of ideas for creating rich variety and contrast in the garden. For example, select a bold, lush foliage plant, then accentuate its shape by partnering it with a sharp, spiky clump. Spiky plants also contrast well with strappy clumps or with plants that naturally form a ball shape. And don't overlook the power of carpet plants. Use these plants to soften hard edges in the landscape — such as steps, stairs and pathways — or as an underplanting beneath a single dramatic spire.

ABOVE You can provide interest in the garden with different leaf shapes.

ABOVE LEFT A warm foliage garden, planted with Japanese maples, conifers, hydrangea, viburnum and New Zealand flax.

PLANT SHAPES

Remember, too, that shrubs and trees are classified by their natural growing habits as evergreen, semi-evergreen or deciduous. They are also identified by their shapes. Trees, for example, may be broad-domed, columnar, conical or spreading, and shrubs may be prostrate, bun-shaped, vase-like or rounded.

ABOVE Fast growing and lush, the Abyssinian banana (*Ensete ventricosum*) instantly evokes a tropical ambience. Note the century plant (*Agave attenuata*), another dramatic plant, in the foreground.

ABOVE RIGHT The flower clusters of the tender spear lily (*Doryanthes excelsa*) sit atop long stems, 3 m tall or more.

DRAMATIC PLANTS

If you'd like your garden to have the 'wow!' factor, just plant a couple of strategically placed, drop-dead-gorgeous plants. Dramatic plants are nature's show ponies. They can be wildy flamboyant, colourful, unusually shaped, larger than life and strikingly beautiful. They can make an ordinary garden look spectacular.

It's best to use dramatic plants where they will have the biggest impact — as a single specimen, mass-planted, lining a fence or pathway, potted and placed on either side of a doorway or positioned where they're least expected to create an element of surprise.

You don't need a contemporary garden to enjoy these plants. For example, try planting the colourful spires of Russell lupins in a perennial border: these elegant flowers are bold and dramatic and have a wonderful peppery fragrance.

For warmer gardens, honey bush (*Melianthus major*) has huge leaves edged with a neat zigzag pattern, in shades of silvery blue and grey–green with purplish edges. Grow it in the background as it has a spreading habit that can become untidy.

VEGETABLE LEAVES

You can mix vegetables and herbs with flowers and foliage to create different colour and textural effects. For example, the bright flowers of red, yellow and orange nasturtiums look brilliant when mixed with red snapdragons, beetroot and beans, perhaps in a deep purple or red.

Look for other colourful vegetables such as dark-leafed lettuce, pink and mauve kale, beet, cabbage and Swiss chard.

Lettuce is an easy vegetable to grow. Choose varieties that have red-brown leaves, such as 'Rouge d'Hiver', a cos variety with brownish red, upright leaves, or 'Red Velvet', with deep red-bronze leaves that can be cut leaf by leaf. Similarly, 'Red Treviso', a radicchio chicory, produces variegated red and green heads.

Even if you don't like eating cabbage, consider planting 'Tuscan Black Kale'. With its slate-coloured savoy leaves, it makes a wonderfully dramatic addition to garden colour, while the 'Red Drum Head' cabbage creates equally arresting effects. And don't overlook the fabulous, very dark foliage of the annual red orach (*Atriplex hortensis* var. *rubra*) or the purple plantain (*Plantago major* 'Rubrifolia').

Burgundy-coloured lettuce provides contrast in a vegetable garden (left and above), while the red stems of ruby chard (top) add warmth.

BELOW In frost-free countries, versatile and undemanding, aechmea is mass-planted under trees, mounted on a log or used as a stunning feature in a pot.

BELOW RIGHT The spectacular foliage of cordyline.

OPPOSITE, CLOCKWISE FROM TOP LEFT A selection of rosette-forming plants for a frost-free garden. Neoreglia offers a range of bold designs — with stripes, spots, splashes and bands — in rich shades of green, red, burgundy, yellow and pink; like many succulents, *Aeonium* sp. provide foliage colour and interest all year round; agaves have some of the biggest and showiest rosettes of all — some resemble giant octopi, others are ball-like; and the exuberant Japanese sago palm (*Cycas revoluta*) are magnificent sculptural plants. They can live for 100 years or more.

SPIKY PLANTS

Spiky doesn't have to mean thorny or prickly. If you dismiss spiky plants you'll miss out on a wealth of marvellous texture, shape and form in the garden. The interesting shapes of some spiky plants come into their own when viewed against a background of small or regular foliage. They add the important punctuation points that break up what can be just a bland expanse of garden or wall. Of course, some plants have real spines or thorns, which are usually a defence against being eaten. However, these can work for you in the garden by forming a security barrier. Good candidates are berberis, hawthorn and pyracantha, but remember you will have to prune them, which can be an uncomfortable task.

ROSETTES

Named after the perfect form of a rose, the rosette shape appears in the flowers or leaves of a wide variety of plants. Whether it's their circular form, the rhythm of overlapping petals or leaves, or the spiralling effect of a whorl, rosettes are visually stimulating. They're very beautiful too, and because our eyes are drawn to the centre of rosettes, they make natural focal points in the garden, especially those plants that have large, bold leaves.

On a smaller scale, some foliage plants have flower-like radial symmetry; enjoy their beautiful forms by displaying them in pots. Rosette-shaped foliage plants generally require little maintenance as they seldom need pruning. Their neat and tidy appearance will also appeal to those who like order in the garden.

SUCCULENTS

Succulents, and some cacti, have a lot to offer the garden landscape. They come in a rich variety of sizes, shapes, colours and textures, some produce spectacular flowers and others look fantastic in a pot. Just make sure they have good drainage and be careful not to overwater them. Although most will not survive all year outdoors, they can be used in pots to make a desert garden in summer, and overwintered in a frost-free greenhouse.

FOLIAGE SHRUBS

Foliage shrubs are grown for their leaves, whether evergreen and brilliant throughout the seasons, brightly toned when fresh in spring, or deciduous and rich in autumn colour. Their beauty lies simply in their leaves and habits, even though many will also flower. Foliage shrubs provide structure and permanence as well as provide a green background to the garden all year round. Here are some shrubs with outstanding leaf colours or forms.

Brilliantly coloured Fijian fire plant (*Acalypha wilkesiana*) has large glossy leaves that are perfectly ovate. In warm gardens these shrubs are fast-growing and long-lived.

Dense evergreen shrubs, such as pittosporum and photinia make good hedging plants.

Fast-growing and low-maintenance, privets can be trimmed into bright green and gold hedges.

RIGHT A common but gracious sight in tropical climates, the poinciana (*Delonix regina*) has a dazzling flower display that covers most of its canopy for weeks in summer.

TREES

Trees are the most outstanding living features in any natural landscape, and also in our cities, parks and gardens. But when a tree flowers, it's a special occasion. All over the world, many of our cultural celebrations coincide with trees in bloom. In the garden, flowering trees are defining features. They highlight the seasons with their blooms, and can also inspire garden designs.

Some flowering trees have outrageously colourful blooms, or have spectacular tree-covering shows; others have flowers that are especially fragrant. There are also many other trees and shrubs that are prized for their foliage or fruit as well as their flowers. For gardeners, there are flowering trees to suit any style.

Deciduous trees influence our garden designs, but they also bring the seasons into our gardening lives. Their foliage colour, which occurs before the leaves are cast, is one of the delights of autumn, and they are the garden's architectural features of winter. In spring and summer, the trees' lush leaf canopies bring welcome shade, and sometimes they bear flower or fruit as well. By nature, deciduous trees are diverse and their seasonal characteristics vary depending on where they grow — an essential part of their charm.

And then there are fruit trees. The fruiting displays of fruit trees are seasonal highlights, as much as their flowers or leaves. Trees that bear fruits pods and berries bring an added decorative element to the garden.

ABOVE *Magnolia* x *soulangiana* is the most popular of the magnolia hybrids. It has goblet-shaped flowers in a range of colours, including ivory, white and pink through to purple and claret red.

ABOVE LEFT The oak tree (*Quercus* sp.) is not a tree for a small garden — it grows to about 20 m tall and wide and is capable of living for centuries.

TOOLS AND TECHNIQUES

Many of the landscaping and building tasks and projects described in this book require certain skills and tools. This section provides step-by-step instructions on some essential techniques — from setting out a project and checking for square to erecting posts and laying concrete slabs.

BASIC TOOLS

- Adjustable sliding level
- Bolster chisel
- Bricklaying trowel
- Broom
- Builder's square
- Claw hammer
- Hammer
- Edging tool
- Float
- Handsaw
- Hose
- Jointing tool
- Mattock
- Permanent black marking pen
- Plasterer's trowel
- Rake
- Rubber mallet
- Shovel
- Skutch hammer
- Spade
- Spirit level
- Steel float
- String line
- Tape measure
- Wheelbarrow
- Wooden float

BASIC TOOLS

There are a number of basic tools required for any construction project in the garden, whether it is a simple garden edge or a retaining wall. If you have the tools in the box at left, you can be sure you'll have all the tools you need for a satisfactory job.

CONCRETING

Knowing how to mix and lay concrete are handy skills that you'll be able to utilize in a variety of landscaping jobs, from laying paths to erecting post holes.

Different strengths of concrete are required for different applications, and you can adjust the strength by varying the proportions of the cement, sand and gravel components.

USING CONCRETE

Concrete is a mix of cement, sand and coarse aggregate. When water is added to the concrete mix, a chemical reaction occurs: the mix hardens or 'goes off' to form what is essentially a dense artificial rock. The advantages of concrete are that it's hardwearing and can be formed into almost any shape. Its usefulness is limited only by the concreter's ability to build a suitable mould or formwork, and the quality of the concrete mix (which must be designed not to crack when it's used in a large mass). Therefore it will pay off if you take the time to do concreting jobs properly.

DIFFERENT APPLICATIONS

Around the home, concrete is used for paths, driveways, retaining walls and terraces, as well as mowing strips, paving stones and even flowerpots and planters. A lot of the concrete, in the form of footings and floor slabs, is 'hidden'.

You can use concrete for many different applications, which often require the use of different kinds of concrete, as well as varying grades of sand, cement and gravel. For most of the projects around the house and garden, only standard mixes of concrete are required. In other situations you must use special mixes — for example, for concreting swimming pools and for core-filling concrete block retaining walls (for which you'll need gravel that is smaller than normal). In some large commercial and engineered structures, mixes are modified to speed up or slow down setting times and to limit the amount of heat generated by the chemical reaction.

The bulk of the coarse aggregate in the mix makes concrete an economical building material — the gravel that is generally used as the coarse aggregate in standard concrete is inexpensive when compared with the cement. Therefore, if you maximize the aggregate component of the mix, you'll reduce the cost of the concrete.

DEMOLISHING CONCRETE

One of the more difficult aspects of working with concrete is removing a slab or driveway in order to renew it. If you're lucky, the concrete to be removed may have already cracked and broken up, and you may only need to lift the pieces and put them in a waste-disposal bin.

Sound concrete needs to be broken up. If the concrete is not reinforced with steel, try using a heavy sledgehammer to break it into manageable pieces, starting at one corner and working across the slab. Lift broken pieces out of the way to keep the edge you are breaking up clear.

If the slab is reinforced, you will be facing a difficult job. The steel reinforcing holds the broken concrete together, and you will need access to the steel so you can cut it with bolt cutters. The concrete must be broken into smaller sections. This is a massive task.

You could hire a concrete saw, which allows you to make a series of regular cuts to create small manageable blocks that can be carried away — or a contractor could do the work for you. Jack hammers are sometimes effective for demolishing concrete, but well-cured, dense, reinforced concrete will take quite some time to break up.

Concrete that is not reinforced may be broken into manageable pieces with a sledgehammer.

BELOW Always take care to prepare and lay concrete properly. Poor curing, for example, can lead to cracking.

BELOW LEFT The early stages of spalling — the reinforcing steel is not yet exposed, but the signs of rusting are obvious.

CONCRETING TOOLS

- Measuring tape
- String line
- Plumb line
- Spirit level
- Builder's square
- Utility knife
- Handsaw or portable power saw
- Chalk or hydrated lime
- Tarpaulin
- Protective clothing (gloves, sturdy footwear)
- Mattock
- Shovel
- Club hammer
- Hose or bucket
- Wheelbarrow
- Bolt cutters or angle grinder
- Rake
- Screed board
- Wooden float
- Sponge float
- Steel trowel
- Edging tool
- Dummy jointing tool
- Stiff scrubbing brush

CONCRETING MATERIALS

The quality of concrete is directly related to the quality of the individual components — cement, aggregate and water.

CEMENT

For general use around the home, Portland cement is recommended. Light grey in colour, it's suitable for all home concreting projects and also for masonry mortar and sand-and-cement mixes. Where a lighter colour is required for the concrete or mortar, you could choose off-white Portland cement (although off-white cement is commonly used in preparing mortar to suit various brick colours and styles, it's rarely used in concreting because of the considerable extra expense).

Cement has a very limited storage life, so buy it fresh as you need it. Store it in an airy and dry place; in humid climates it can harden and start to set simply by drawing in moisture from the air. Never allow cement to get wet before it's used. This is also the case for premixed bags of mortar and concrete. Don't use the cement if it's too old, hard or lumpy. The bonding power of the cement is severely limited, and you will waste time making concrete that will be weak, hard to use and of limited durability.

Cement is sold mainly in bags of usually 25kg, and is readily available from DIY hardware and building supply outlets and landscaping suppliers. When mixing your own concrete, the most economical way to buy it is in 25 kg bags.

AGGREGATE

Two grades of aggregate are used — coarse and fine.

Coarse aggregate consists of crushed stone or 'metal', the most commonly used size being 20 mm. The gravel used in a concrete mix must be hard and durable, and it should not be made from soft or weathered rock (suitable rocks include basalt, dolerite and granite). Gravel should not contain any clay impurities or plant matter, or any other fines (the fine dust or powder produced by the crushing process) like those found in road base.

Smaller gravel sizes can be used for applications such as core-filling concrete block retaining walls. Normal concrete with 20 mm aggregate would choke up the small holes in the blocks, which also carry steel reinforcing bars.

Gravel is sold by the cubic metre, tonne or bag by large building suppliers. You can also buy it from soil, sand and cement suppliers and from landscaping suppliers.

Fine aggregate comes mainly in the form of sand, which is sold as a variety of types for different uses. Note that the sand used by bricklayers or plasterers is unsuitable for concrete because it contains a large amount of clay (this gives it the 'fattiness' required for bricklaying). River sand in general is quite coarse and rounded, and should not be used where 'sharp sand' has been specified for the concrete mix. The preferred sand for concrete is clean (washed) and sharp. DIY, building and landscaping suppliers sell it by the cubic metre, tonne or bag.

WATER

When mixing concrete, add only enough water to make the mix. You can use tap water — basically, if the water is drinkable, it's suitable for concrete. But don't use water from the sea or from bores, because this has a high salt or mineral content.

MIXING ON-SITE

You can mix concrete on-site or order it premixed. The choice will depend on the size of the project, the location of the project relative to concrete plants, and the speed at which you can work. For example, filling cores in concrete block retaining walls is slow, painstaking work and is often best done by hand.

Nevertheless, many local concrete suppliers will deliver very small quantities of concrete — it's certainly easier on your back to obtain the concrete premixed, ready to pour into the formwork.

CHOOSING A MIX

You can adjust the strength of concrete by varying the proportions of cement, sand and coarse aggregate. Use a mix of 1 part cement, 2 parts sand and 3 parts coarse aggregate or gravel (1:2:3) for water-retaining structures, heavy-duty floors and precast items. Use a mix of 1 part cement, 2 parts sand and 4 parts coarse aggregate/gravel (1:2:4) for paths, driveways and patios, and garage and shed floors. A 1:3:6 mix of concrete components is suitable for fence post installation and for filling large holes.

For everyday tasks you only really need to remember the 1:2:4 mix, which can be substituted for the 1:3:6 mix. It's slightly stronger but not quite as economical. All mixes are measured by volume.

Add only just enough water to give the mix adequate workability, as adding excessive amounts of water reduces the strength. As a rough guide, each 25 kg bag of cement you use will require 12.5 litres of added water, which translates into half a litre of water per kilogram of cement. The amount of water required will vary to an extent, depending on the moisture content of the sand. Sand that has recently been in the rain holds a large amount of water, so you may need to reduce the total amount of added water.

HAND-MIXING

When mixing concrete on site, you can either mix by hand or use a concrete mixer, depending on how much concrete you need to make, the size of the job, the access available for the mixing machine and the hire costs for a mixer.

When mixing by hand, use a container such as a bucket to measure the components by volume. Don't use a shovel for measuring ingredients: a heaped shovel of damp sand has a greater volume than the average shovel-load of cement or gravel.

The quality of the concrete will depend on how well you mix the concrete. To make small quantities, mix the dry cement, sand and gravel on a hard flat surface until they become an even grey colour. Mix slightly

ABOVE For safety as well as aesthetic reasons, keep concrete steps clean of dirt and moss.

CLEANING CONCRETE

Concrete is porous, so it's subject to staining; however, removing these stains is often difficult. You should always try scrubbing with water first, perhaps adding a little detergent. Acids and cleaning solutions can react with the concrete, often altering its colour.

Different types of stains usually require different treatments.

DIRT, GRIME, MOULD AND MOSS REMOVAL

To remove years of grime and dirt, first try cleaning with a high-pressure water washer. These machines are available from most equipment-hire outlets.

High-pressure water is also the first step in trying to remove mould and moss growth. An alternative is a chlorine bleach solution. Apply the solution to wet concrete and scrub vigorously. This will usually kill the moss or mould. Scrub off the residue after a few days. Keep further growth at bay by using the solution occasionally.

Stubborn stains from timber can often be removed by applying chlorine bleach. Hold the solution in place on the concrete for a few days with a cloth and plastic cover until the stain has bleached to an acceptable level.

RUST REMOVAL

Rust stains can be difficult to remove. If using proprietary cleaners, make sure you follow the manufacturer's instructions.

Another method is to make a moist mass (a 'poultice') of cat litter with a solution of 1 part sodium citrate combined with 6 parts water. Apply to the stain, then scrape off after it has dried. A single application should remove light staining. Rinse off the concrete well with clean water. Oxalic acid (poisonous) may also be effective.

OIL REMOVAL

Oil tends to soak into concrete and is almost impossible to remove entirely. If your car drips oil, park it over a drip tray.

Soak up as much of a new oil stain as possible with absorbent paper towels or newspaper, changing the paper often. Then apply a poultice made of 2 parts mineral turpentine and 1 part lime. If the stain is older, scrape off as much as you can without spreading it, then apply an engine degreaser. This emulsifies the oil, allowing you to hose the residue into the garden. Several applications may be needed.

If mixing sand and cement or mortar, try doing so over the oil stain. The powder components and mixing action may help to clean up or at least disguise the stain.

LEFT When mixing concrete by hand, add only enough water to make the mix workable.

larger amounts in a wheelbarrow, as this will contain the fluid concrete efficiently and make it immediately transportable.

1 Form a hollow in the middle of the mix and then add some water to the hollow.
2 Fold dry material from the sides of the mix into the water and begin mixing with a shovel or mattock.
3 Keep adding water as needed and mix until the concrete is of uniform colour and consistency.
4 To test if the concrete is ready, use the back of your shovel or a trowel to work the surface of the mix in a circular motion. This should produce a shiny smooth surface that has no irregularities and is free from excessive amounts of water. You should then lay the concrete without delay.

For smaller jobs, use premixed bags of concrete mix. These contain a standardized mix of cement, sand and fine gravel, and they're ideal for small jobs, such as bedding-in fence and pergola poles, pouring small blob footings for decks and pergolas, and making bases for birdbaths. Premixed concrete is also useful for projects where work could be interrupted, in which case you should mix only small batches.

Premixed bags of concrete are also available in a quick-setting formula. This concrete sets in about 30 minutes, yet retains the characteristics of normal concrete — you just need to work quickly before it sets. Quick-setting concrete can be useful for small jobs such as pergola poles, where waiting for the concrete to set overnight would hold up the progress of your project.

Premixed bags of concrete contain enough concrete to fill a volume of 0.011 m^3, so you need 91–92 bags for a cubic metre. For small quantities, pour the contents of one or two bags into a wheelbarrow and add water.

MACHINE-MIXING

For larger jobs, it might be more economical to hire an electric or petrol-driven mixer.

1 Accurately measure the concrete components by volume.
2 When adding materials to the mixer, start with 40–50 per cent of the water and the coarse aggregate. Follow this with the sand and cement, adding them alternately in small batches, then mix in more water as required.
3 Continue mixing for 2–3 minutes until the mix is an even grey colour. If you start with dry components and add water, the mix will stick to the sides of the mixer and have an uneven consistency.

PREMIXED CONCRETE

Using premixed concrete on a job will save you a lot of time as well as a good deal of hard and messy work. Also, you won't need to store and handle the individual components. Good-quality concrete is virtually guaranteed, and if you live in a major population area, you can order concrete in quantities as small as 0.2 m³. This is the amount of concrete needed for a 100 mm thick slab measuring 1 x 1 m — a useful guide if you're doing DIY jobs around the home.

When ordering premixed concrete, tell the concrete supplier how many cubic metres you require, the slump (see 'Slump' below), and the purpose for which the concrete is to be used. The supplier will then suggest the appropriate strength grade or concrete mix to use.

SLUMP

The slump is a measure of the 'workability' of the mix (see 'Pouring and screeding', page 349). Concrete suppliers know the mix to use for a given slump, which is largely dependent on the amount of water in the mix. An 80 mm slump is standard for most household work; a 100 mm slump is more fluid and harder to control.

STRENGTH

Premixed concrete is sold on the basis of strength, usually given as megapascals (mPa). The strength is also often written as an 'N', followed by a number. The N refers to 'normal' and the number is the concrete strength in megapascals.

N32 is suitable for water-retaining structures, heavy-duty floors and precast items. N20 is used for paths, driveways and patios, and for garage and shed floors. A strength of 10 mPa is appropriate for fence-post installation and for filling large holes.

ACCESS

When using premixed concrete, remember that the truck requires reasonable access to the concreting area. Time penalties may apply if the truck has to spend too long on site while you pour the concrete. If access is remote, you will need to make long trips with a barrow. If the wheelbarrow route does not travel over a flat or gently sloping site, consider having a concrete pumping truck on site. This costs extra, but is worthwhile if you have to move several cubic metres of concrete.

Another consideration is that concrete does not travel well when wheeled over long distances in a wheelbarrow, as the heavy coarse aggregate tends to separate out and settle to the bottom. If long distances are involved and the premix truck or concrete pump can't get close to the concreting area, it may be better to use a portable cement mixer.

ESTIMATING QUANTITIES

Quantities of concrete are calculated by volume — that is, by the cubic metre. To calculate the quantity you need, simply multiply the area by the depth required. First calculate the area of the work being concreted:

area (square metres) = length (metres) x width (metres)

Then multiply the area by the depth of concrete required, also in metres. If the thickness or depth of concrete is to be 100 mm, it needs to be converted to 0.1 m to give the correct volume.

volume (cubic metres) = length x width x depth

If the plan is more complicated or has curves, make a scale drawing on a sheet of graph paper. Use this to divide the plan into a number of parts (say, 1 x 1 m). Add these individual areas together to arrive at the total area. In the diagram at right, counting the whole squares and adding the partial squares gives an area of about 4.5 m². To cross-check, measure the length of the path down the centre line and then multiply by its width — that is, 4.5 x 1 m = 4.5 m².

The second step is to calculate the volume. The thickness of concrete in a path will typically be 75–100 mm. Convert this to metres (0.075–0.1 m). In the example given, the area is about 4.5 m². If the thickness of the path is 100 mm (0.1 m), the volume of concrete required will then be 4.5 m² x 0.1 m = 0.45 m³. If the path is 75 mm thick, the volume is 4.5 m² x 0.075 m = 0.34 m³.

Volume is the only measurement you need for ordering premixed concrete. If mixing on site, you must calculate the individual quantities of sand, gravel and cement to give the volume of concrete required. This will depend on the specific mix you use (see the table below).

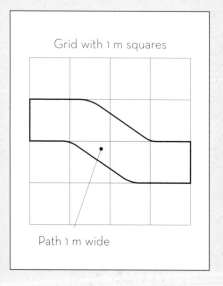

Grid with 1 m squares

Path 1 m wide

ABOVE Calculation of area for a curved path.

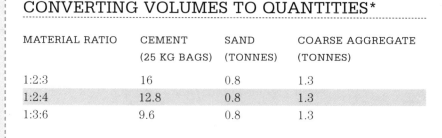

CONVERTING VOLUMES TO QUANTITIES*

MATERIAL RATIO	CEMENT (25 KG BAGS)	SAND (TONNES)	COARSE AGGREGATE (TONNES)
1:2:3	16	0.8	1.3
1:2:4	12.8	0.8	1.3
1:3:6	9.6	0.8	1.3

* Per cubic metre.

WASTE ALLOWANCE

Discovering at the last minute that you don't have enough concrete or materials can ruin an otherwise successful day of concreting. It's not a good idea to halt a pour halfway through, as the join between the original and later concrete will always be a plane of weakness. It's essential that you make some allowance for error or waste.

The amount of waste allowance depends on the application. If you are uncertain about any of your calculations, allow for greater waste.

No matter how accurate your calculations, you're likely to have some concrete left over. Plan some standby projects to use up any leftover concrete — for example, a base for a birdbath, pavers (make sure you have the formwork ready), garden edges or mowing strips, re-securing clothesline posts, resetting fence posts or patching damaged paths.

LAYING THE CONCRETE

The sophistication of your concrete set-out and pour depends on the complexity of the job. A slab for a garden shed, for example, is one of the simplest concreting projects. Whatever the job, the basic steps stay the same: decide where to pour the concrete, prepare the site, measure exactly, build and level formwork, and pour and cure the concrete.

PROPERTY BOUNDARIES

If you're building near a boundary, you may be affected by building or party wall requirements. Your local Building Control office can advise you of these, and can offer guidelines about any new buildings and work. In order to locate the appropriate position precisely, you must locate your boundary.

If your fence is accurately located on the boundary, work from the fence line (if not, get a surveyor to mark the corners of your property). Run a taut string line between corner pegs, ensuring it isn't caught on plants. To find the position of the boundary on the ground, drop a plumb line from the string. If your slab is not parallel with the boundary, you only need to check the point nearest the boundary. A surveyor may put intermediate boundary pegs close to where you want to build.

PREPARING THE GROUND

1 Measure the rough position of the slab on the ground, trying to make all measurements in the horizontal plane. If you're measuring down a steep slope, correct the distance to allow for the slope. You're only marking out the area to be cleared or excavated.
2 Mark out the length by the width of the job, and allow for the thickness of the formwork, if any.
3 Push small pegs into the ground to mark the position of the corners.
4 Use a tape measure to check that the diagonals are roughly equal, which in turn means the angles for the slab are at right angles.
5 Dig out all vegetation and rocks within the marked area.

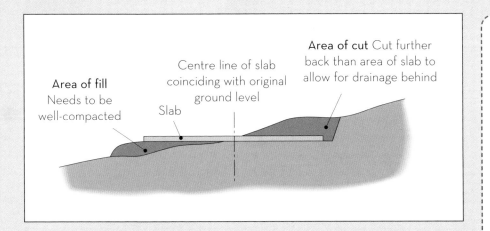

Area of fill Needs to be well-compacted

Slab

Centre line of slab coinciding with original ground level

Area of cut Cut further back than area of slab to allow for drainage behind

A SLAB ON A SLOPE

Bear in mind that if you're cutting a slab into a slope, you will need to provide drainage in the cut section of the slope in order to control water runoff. Ideally, you should limit the depth of fill and position the slab thus: the short dimension of the slab should run into the hill and the long dimension should run across the hill.

6 If you have to dig out large plants, or even trees (check with your Building Control office whether this can be done), you will be left with soft ground requiring re-compacting. Dig out all soft material, backfill with road base, adding 150 mm of fill at a time, and compact it using a tamp (see the diagram below). Keep filling the hole in 150 mm layers until it's at the same level as the rest of the site.

7 Most slabs should be level. Using a long, straight length of 100 x 50 mm timber, together with a spirit level, measure the existing slope. Chock up the low end so the level gives a horizontal reading, then measure the height from the ground to find the depth of the excavation required at the high side.

Alternatively, you can halve the difference to be cut from the high side and fill the low side, as long as the fill is well-compacted (see the diagram above). Check levels in both directions until the site is quite level. You can then set out the slab exactly.

FINDING THE SLAB HEIGHT

The height of the slab may not be critical for a shed, but you may want to match an existing level. There are several ways to do this.

METHOD 1

If the level to be matched is immediately adjacent, use a long straight edge with a level to establish the heights.

METHOD 2

If the new slab is more than a few metres from an existing structure and the ground falls away, mark the required slab height at a convenient point on the existing structure. Drive in a stake at a corner of the new slab position. Take a 5–10 mm clear plastic tube (long enough to reach easily from the existing slab to the far corner of your new slab), fill it almost completely with water and eliminate all bubbles. With a helper, bring the bottom of the meniscus (the water surface) to the level marked on the existing slab. When the water steadies, mark the level at the corner stake to give exactly the same height.

ABOVE LEFT Typical cut-and-fill preparation for a small slab.

BELOW A tamp is used for compacting road base. *Note:* The hardwood block is fastened to the handle with a single 10 mm coach bolt that is 125 mm long and counterbored.

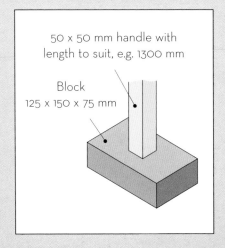

50 x 50 mm handle with length to suit, e.g. 1300 mm

Block 125 x 150 x 75 mm

CHECKING FOR SQUARE

When you're setting out a project, there's a simple way to ensure you've made a right-angled corner before you start digging trenches or post holes.

1 Set out a base line (string line or profile board, or the house wall if you are working from it). From the corner point, measure along the base line 3000 mm (or any multiple of this, such as 6000 mm) and mark.

2 Attach string lines to the corner point and the 3000 mm mark. On one string line measure and mark 4000 mm (or the appropriate multiple such as 8000 mm). On the other line measure and mark 5000 mm (or the appropriate multiple).

3 Bring the 4000 mm and 5000 mm marks together. The 4000 mm string line forms a right angle with the 3000 mm line.

METHOD 3

After you've excavated the area, if the new slab is to be laid in higher ground than the existing level, start with a datum, a measured height of H above the desired level. Set the water level to this mark and transfer it to a stake adjacent to the proposed slab. To find the correct height of the distant slab, subtract the height H from the level given by the water level.

EXCAVATION

Work out the fill depth from the required finished height. Subtract the slab thickness from the finished surface (say, 100 mm) and add to this the thickness of any sand bed below (say, 25 mm) — a total depth of 125 mm.

REFERENCE POINTS

Establish a point (usually a corner) of the project to which you can refer in all aspects of setting out. Errors can be compounded if you progressively measure each new point from the previously established point, and the final layout won't be quite right.

PROFILES OR SADDLES

Once you've established the slab's position, the best method of setting out is to erect a series of 'profiles' or 'saddles'. A profile consists of two pegs, each 600 mm long, driven into the ground about 450 mm apart. A rail is nailed across the top of the pegs.

Place the profile beyond the end of the slab and perpendicular to the line to which you are working, and tie a string line to the rail. The width of the profile allows you to adjust the position of a string line until it's exactly right.

RIGHT Using a water level to position a new slab at the same height as an existing one. *Note: H* = the height to the meniscus.

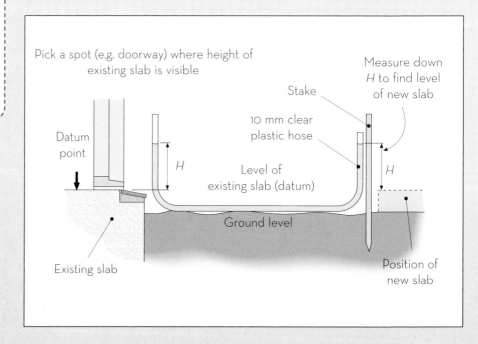

Pick a spot (e.g. doorway) where height of existing slab is visible

Datum point

Existing slab

H

Level of existing slab (datum)

10 mm clear plastic hose

Ground level

Stake

Measure down H to find level of new slab

H

Position of new slab

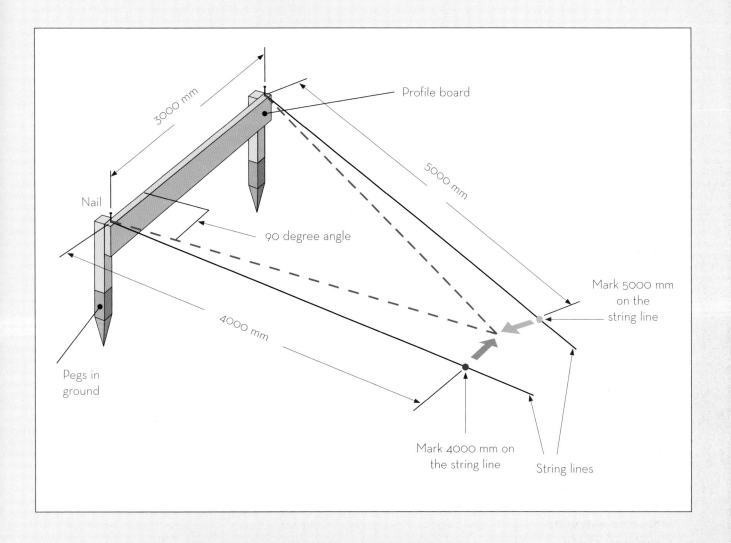

Profile board

3000 mm

5000 mm

Nail

90 degree angle

Mark 5000 mm
on the
string line

4000 mm

Pegs in
ground

Mark 4000 mm on
the string line

String lines

Then drive a clout nail part way into the timber to mark the position. When repeated all around the slab edges, this process makes setting out highly accurate. To find the excavation and formwork positions on the ground, even if it's uneven, simply drop a plumb line where the strings cross to give the exact position of a corner (see the diagram on page 345).

You can remove string lines while you excavate and then reinstate them without measuring their position again. When excavating for the slab, mark the ground with chalk and remove the string lines. Leave the profiles in place.

ABOVE Checking for square using the 3-4-5 method.

BUILDING FORMWORK

The formwork is the timber mould that holds the concrete while it's wet and fluid. Formwork must be strong enough to withstand not only the pressure of the fluid concrete but also the vibration of the concrete as it's being worked. For a simple small slab, formwork should be at least 25 mm thick, although 50 mm thick timber would be better. Nail the timber pieces together at the required angles and hold them in place with pegs driven into the ground on both sides of the timber.

RIGHT Making horizontal measurements on sloping land, from *X* to *Y*.

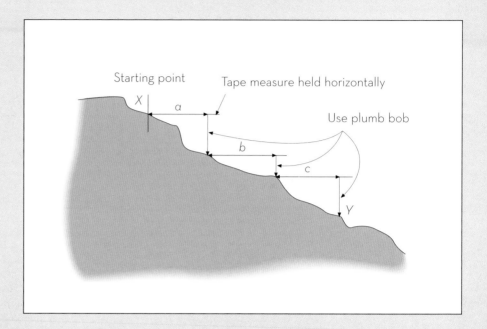

Starting point

Tape measure held horizontally

X

a

Use plumb bob

b

c

Y

MEASURING ON SLOPES

All distances given on a plan are horizontal. When building on a steep slope you must compensate for the slope, either by using trigonometry or by measuring a series of horizontal distances down the slope.

1 Ask a helper to hold a measuring tape at the base of the highest point and measure the space between it and a plumb line or vertical stake further down the slope. The tape measure is horizontal when you have the smallest measurement to the plumb line. Note the measurement.

2 Mark where the plumb bob hits the ground, drive in a stake, then start the procedure again.

3 Repeat until the whole distance down the slope is covered, then add up all the horizontal measurements to give the total horizontal distance.

When constructing formwork, remember that it has to come apart (or 'be stripped') once the concrete has set. Don't use any fixings or brackets that will be embedded in the concrete, as this will make the formwork impossible to dismantle.

Spend time accurately setting out the formwork to the correct dimensions and levels. If the formwork is levelled to the final required height of the concrete, it will give the correct levels of the concrete — and you won't need to refer to a spirit level in the middle of a pour. When building formwork, use a spirit level and a long, straight piece of timber to check that it is level in all directions. Measure the diagonal distance

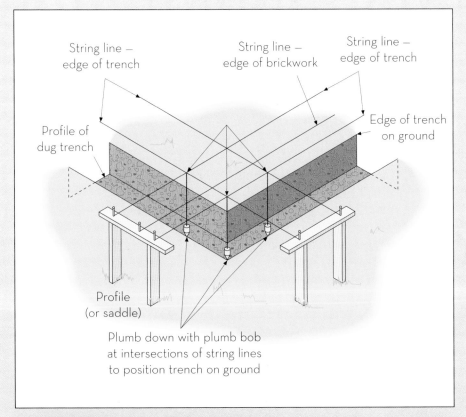

String line — edge of trench

String line — edge of brickwork

String line — edge of trench

Edge of trench on ground

Profile of dug trench

Profile (or saddle)

Plumb down with plumb bob at intersections of string lines to position trench on ground

LEFT Set-out of footings.

BELOW LEFT Reinforced concrete is ideal for footings. One of the profiles used in marking out is shown here.

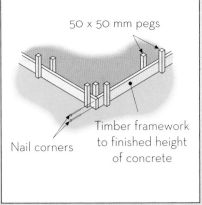

50 x 50 mm pegs

Nail corners

Timber framework to finished height of concrete

ABOVE Simple slab formwork set-out.

MOULDS FOR SMALL ITEMS

If you're making small concrete items such as pavers or stepping stones, use moulds such as buckets, trays, polystyrene boxes or plastic bowls, depending on the required shape. In order to give a concrete surface a rough appearance, drop some sand or gravel in the form first. Line the mould with rope to create grooves, or make plywood cut-outs to produce various shapes. Use containers with a slight taper to the base. Paint the mould formwork with a release agent before pouring the concrete. This will make it easier to remove the concrete item. Painting diesel oil on the surface is just as effective.

between opposite corners of the formwork set-out: if the two distances are the same, the formwork is square. If the distances aren't equal, you should reposition the formwork.

WATERPROOF MEMBRANES

For most landscaping and garden concreting jobs you'll need to install a waterproof membrane. And if you're building a slab for a shed or garage, it's vital that the building has a dry floor. This can only be guaranteed if you lay a waterproof membrane under the concrete.

The membrane is normally made of polyethylene (or 'polythene') and is laid over a bed of sand, lapping up over the edge of the formwork. The sand provides drainage under the slab and membrane and also acts as a soft bed to protect the membrane from being punctured by sharp stones and debris. When pouring the concrete, press and fold the membrane carefully into the corners to avoid creating air pockets and thin edges of slabs.

You can buy waterproof membranes that are up to 3 m wide. If you need a wider membrane, overlap the sheets by 200 mm and tape the joint with waterproof tape. When positioning steel reinforcing (see below), don't spear sharp steel rods through the plastic.

REINFORCEMENT

Concrete is very strong in compression — that is, it can bear a great deal of weight placed on it. However, concrete on its own doesn't have great tensile strength, or ability to resist bending. Over time, thin slabs of concrete will bend or crack if they are unsupported. Concrete also shrinks as it cures and dries; this leads to minor cracking, which can develop into structural cracking if the two sides of the crack are not held together. For these reasons you must add steel reinforcing to the concrete.

In the case of floors and structures supported by the ground, a structural engineer would specify the steel required for the concrete so that it maintains its structural integrity. The reinforcing becomes an integral part of the slab or beam and must be placed exactly as specified.

Steel reinforcement may come in the form of bars or prefabricated meshes. For most domestic projects you will need either a sheet of welded mesh or trench mesh (used for narrow footings).

Welded mesh is sold in 4.8 x 2.4 m sheets (or occasionally in 3.6 x 2 m sheets) and has different strengths and thicknesses. There are a number of different thicknesses and aperture sizes, all covered by British Standards. Because soil conditions vary widely between areas, consult a structural engineer for which type you need.

The reinforcing steel may also be welded into strips comprising 3–5 thick bars with thin spacer rods joining them. This is trench mesh. For domestic work you need to choose between three, four or five bars, depending on the width of the footing (3-bar trench mesh is 200 mm wide, 4-bar 300 mm wide and 5-bar 400 mm wide). Again, get advice from a structural engineer regarding which type of trench mesh is best for a particular job.

Steel bars are used for larger footings and stressed corners and are usually specified by a structural engineer. The most common bar is T12, a 12 mm thick steel bar with a rough surface.

The steel reinforcement must be protected from long-term corrosion by a good surrounding cover of concrete, at least 50 mm all around.

By holding the concrete together when a crack starts to develop, steel reinforcement also helps to control the development of small shrinkage cracks in slabs supported by the ground. Although it won't stop the crack, it does hold the concrete in alignment and prevents more serious cracking. Slabs on the ground typically only have the top layer of reinforcing steel. Once edge beams (perimeter and intermediate ribs of thicker concrete below the slab) become part of the slab, steel bars are included for structural reasons.

SUPPORTING REINFORCEMENT

There are several ways to hold steel in place while the concrete is being poured.

- **Reinforcing set on chairs** The steel fabric may be supported on bar chairs. These come in a range of heights and allow the steel to be held at the desired height off the ground or off the side of an excavation. Plastic chairs usually sit directly on the ground, whereas steel chairs are placed on 'plates' or 'saucers' to stop the prongs sinking into the soil. The plates also stop steel chairs from putting holes in a waterproof membrane, laid under slabs for homes or garages.
- **Suspended reinforcing** When installing reinforcing steel in footings or trenches, it's common to make it up into cages (by wiring the top and bottom reinforcing together to form a 'cage') and hang it with wire from timber battens laid across the excavation. The bottom of the suspension wire is bent into an open hook, shaped to support the steel. Once the concrete is poured, the wires holding the trench mesh in place are unhooked so no steel is exposed at the top of the concrete.
- **Reinforcing placed after a half-pour** This is an easy method of building a small slab (as well as pathways). Begin by pouring half the concrete and raking it level, then lay the reinforcing mesh on top and bed it down carefully. Pour the rest of the concrete on top immediately.
- **Reinforcing pulled through the concrete** A variation of the previous method is to lay the reinforcing on the ground and pull it up through the concrete to the level required. However, this can mean the steel will rest in the concrete at levels of varying heights, and in places the steel may be too close to the surface.

EXPANSION OR CONTROL JOINTS

As concrete loses water, it shrinks slightly, and this can go on for some time after the concrete has set. Carefully curing the concrete (see page 351) helps to reduce the amount of shrinkage by ensuring complete hydration of the cement, but in large areas or masses you must take shrinkage into account. As a rule of thumb, control joints are included every 6 m unless otherwise specified.

LEFT TO RIGHT Welded mesh, steel bar, plastic bar chairs, trench mesh.

The control joints are a complete break in the concrete from the top to the bottom of the slab. They can be formed by breaking a pour with formwork, allowing the concrete to set, then replacing the formwork with expansion joint material. Alternatively, you can include the expansion joint material at the time of the pour.

The control joints are made from either bitumenized fibreboard or foam material. To allow for expansion and contraction of the concrete, joint material must be compressible. At the time of the pour the material is likely to be compressed slightly, due to the pressure of the fluid concrete.

JOINTING STRIPS

When laying larger areas of concrete, break the work into manageable sections over several days. Set out the formwork for the first day in the normal way, and include formwork at the joint where the next section is to be laid. After the concrete has set, strip the formwork and replace the section where the next area of concrete will join with a length of expansion joint material. Build the formwork for the new section. Ideally, space pouring breaks in multiples of 6 m (the required spacing for control joints).

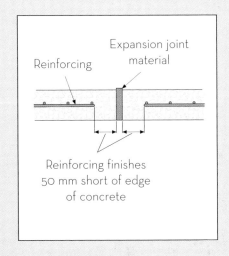

ABOVE Control joint.

PREPARING FOR A POUR

On the day of the pour everything — the site, materials, suppliers, helpers, access — should be organized, so you can concentrate on the pour and finish laying the concrete in the shortest possible time. If you're mixing your own concrete, the time or pressure won't be the same, but you must make an early start so you don't run out of daylight. At this stage you should have:

- prepared and levelled the site;
- built, levelled and squared the formwork;
- laid any membrane required on a bed of sand;
- fixed and secured in place the steel reinforcing;
- ensured there is access for a concrete truck, or ordered and set up a concrete pump if you're using premixed concrete;
- rallied extra helpers and barrows if you have to move the concrete by wheelbarrow; and
- already decided where any excess concrete is to be used.

CONCRETE TRUCK ACCESS

The closer a concrete truck can get to your site, the less work and expense there is for you. Most concrete companies limit the amount of time a truck can be on site, and after that you may be charged extra. You must balance the extra charge against organising concrete pumping or paying for extra labour.

The roadway into the site must be sound enough for a heavy truck — you don't want a truck filled with concrete bogged halfway down the driveway you haven't yet concreted.

PUMPING

Pumping is often used on difficult sites or where access is restricted, but remember that it will cost at least a few hundred pounds to hire the machine and operator. It's best to book early and confirm the booking the day before the pour.

POURING AND SCREEDING

Concrete is poured into formwork, built to withstand the pressure of the fluid mix. For a standard slab, pour concrete into the formwork to a level that is 5–10 mm above the top edge of the forms and rake it level. On a large slab, do this standing in the concrete (wear Wellington boots to protect your feet and legs). If any pegs are left inside the formwork, remove them as the concrete is poured.

The corners are important. If they are hollow or full of air bubbles, they will be weak and will crumble away. Hold a short length of 50 x 50 mm

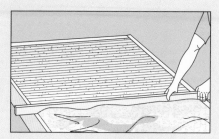

Use a screed board to work the concrete into the formwork with a sawing and chopping motion.

timber on end to 'rod down' the concrete until it's dense and well compacted into the corners. If the edges are low, add more concrete and rake until the surface is even.

Once the concrete is evenly distributed, begin screeding — that is, compressing the concrete with a screed board, which is a stiff piece of timber usually 50 x 125 mm in size. The board should be 450 mm wider than the area to be concreted. On a narrow slab one person can do the screeding, but on a slab over 1 m wide it's much easier if two people work together.

Hold the screed board on edge, and use it to work the concrete into the formwork with a backward and forward sawing and chopping action, ensuring no air bubbles are left. Screed until the concrete is level with the top of the formwork, which is the exact height and level required. Avoid standing on the freshly finished concrete by working from one end back towards the other end. The result is a fairly level area ready for trowelling.

Use a hammer to tap along the side edge of the formwork. This helps to settle the edge concrete and prevent 'honeycombing'.

The surface may have a few holes where the screeding action has pulled out loose gravel. It will also be very wet, as screeding brings water and many of the fine particles in the concrete slurry to the surface. If there are any hollow areas, take some concrete from behind you and rescreed it into place.

FLOATING/TROWELLING

When the concrete is very wet on top, it's difficult to float or trowel — the surface will show major swirl marks, and hollows will tend to fill with water. Allow some initial evaporation to take place so that the concrete is still wet and workable but has only a little free water at the surface. Check the condition of the surface every half hour or so.

You can leave the concrete with a rough-screeded finish if you require a grip on steep driveways and pathways. For a smoother surface, use a float or trowel.

WOODEN AND SPONGE FLOATS

A wooden float is normally about 300–400 mm long. It's worked in broad sweeps across the concrete, leaving the surface with a slightly sandy texture, ideal for most purposes. Use the float at a slight angle, as it tends to stick to the surface by suction if you use it completely flat — this makes it hard to 'sweep' the float over the concrete and will leave suction marks on the surface.

Using a wooden float also brings more cement and water to the surface, helping to achieve a smooth, fairly dense finish. Non-slip and durable, it's suitable for driveways, paths and surfaces that are to be tiled. The finish can be further smoothed with a sponge float.

STEEL TROWEL

For mirror-smooth concrete, use a steel float after you've finished the surface with a wooden float. Sweep it across in broad arcs to achieve a much smoother and denser surface, which can even have a sheen. This finish is mainly used indoors as a base for thin, resilient tiles or for finishes such as paving paint.

Work a wooden float in broad sweeps across the concrete, leaving the surface with a sandy texture.

EDGING

You'll need to round over the edges of concrete paths, as the edge resulting from trowelling up against the formwork is sharp and brittle when the formwork is removed. Run an edging tool backwards and forwards along the formwork. Don't go too deep. If the tool digs out small pieces of aggregate, discard the gravel, fill the hole with some fine material from the concrete and trowel over.

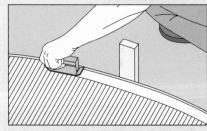

Run an edging tool backwards and forwards along the formwork to round over the edge of the concrete.

DUMMY JOINTS

When building concrete paths you'll also have to provide dummy joints, shallow grooves running across a path at intervals of about 2 m. If the concrete is prone to cracking, the dummy joint will serve as a plane of weakness — the crack will occur along the joint. Run the dummy jointing tool (or groover) along a straight edge laid gently on the concrete.

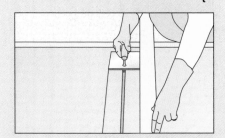

Run a dummy jointing tool along a straight edge to make shallow grooves in the concrete.

CURING CONCRETE

If concrete is to be strong, it's essential that the cement hydrates (combines with water) completely. You'll need to continually apply additional water to the surface of the concrete for quite some time after it sets. If the cement is not fully hydrated, the concrete formed will not be as strong as it should be, the surface may become powdery, and the steel embedded in the concrete will not be protected against corrosion as effectively as in fully cured concrete. The chance of shrinkage will also be increased.

Concrete reaches about 60 per cent of its strength after about one week, but only if it has been cured properly. Curing should be carried out for at least a week. Normal concrete reaches about 98 per cent of its strength after a month of curing. The simplest method is to water the concrete with a gentle spray from the hose morning and night, so that it does not dry out. In hot, windy weather you may need to do it more frequently. You could also cover the concrete in plastic: moisture evaporating from the concrete is trapped, condenses and then returns to the concrete surface. Alternatively, cover the concrete with hessian bags or sand and keep them wet: these materials hold water much longer than the concrete surface. Curing agents are not necessary for home projects.

BUILDING FEATURES

Whether you're building a screen to block out your services area, or a pergola to shade your outdoor dining area, you'll need to know how to erect posts and cut housings.

ERECTING POSTS

First, set out the area — see 'Preparing the ground' and 'Checking for square' on pages 340 and 343, respectively.

1 For 90 x 90 mm posts, dig holes 200 x 200 mm and 600 mm deep. In damp areas, dig 150 mm deeper and place 150 mm of coarse gravel in the bottom.

2 Stand the first post in the hole, lining up the face with a string line. Use a spirit level to check it's vertical both ways. Prop it upright with two timbers nailed to adjoining faces 900 mm from ground level. Stand the other posts in their holes in the same way.

3 Mix concrete and pour it around the posts, packing it down with a piece of scrap timber. As soon as you finish packing the concrete, check that the post hasn't moved. Let the concrete set for 24 hours and then remove the props.

4 Find the lowest post and measure up the required height. Mark this point and then transfer this level to the other posts.

CUTTING A HOUSING

A housing is a groove cut in timber to form part of a joint. To mark out a housing, measure to the required point and square a line across the face. Then measure up the width of the housing and square a second line across. Continue these lines down each edge, set a marking gauge to the required depth and mark both edges between the lines. Or, if you are using a power saw, set it to cut the required depth.

Cut down the shoulders on the waste side of the marked lines to the required depth. Then make a number of relief cuts between the shoulders to the same depth. Space them about 6 mm apart. Use a 25 mm chisel and hammer to remove the waste and clean out the housing, levelling and smoothing the bottom.

To cut a housing at the end of a timber, cut down the shoulder to the required depth, then cut along the timber from the end. When you use a power saw, the cut does not finish square to the surface it's running along, so finish the cut with a handsaw, keeping the saw square to the end of the cut. Clean and smooth the housing with a chisel if required.

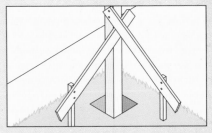

2 Stand the post in its hole, then check that it's vertical and nail props to adjoining faces.

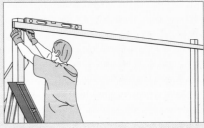

4 Rest the timber on top of the nail in the lowest post and raise the other end until it's level.

To make a housing, cut down the shoulders at either end and then make relief cuts between them.

Use a chisel and hammer to remove the waste, levelling the bottom of the housing.

OPPOSITE This garden screen requires various carpentry and building skills, including accurate setting out.

INDEX

PHOTO CREDITS

Joe Filshie
3, 33, 86 right, 104, 117 left, 133 bottom, 148, 149 left, 153, 166 right, 169, 189 right, 192, 195, 196, 201, 203, 213 top, 219 left, 221 bottom, 252 top, 261, 262 (purple, green), 280, 285, 291 left, 295 left and bottom right, 301 bottom, 305 bottom, 325 left, 329 right, 336, 354–5.

Denise Grieg
257 top left and bottom right, 258 centre and bottom, 259 (top centre; right top and bottom).

Marcus Harpur
191 left, 214 left, 215, 224, 325 bottom right.

Ian Hofstetter
29, 49, 330–1, 333, 336–7, 347–8.

Tony Lyon
14, 17–19, 21, 24, 27, 31–2, 38–9, 44 bottom, 45, 46, 52–3, 54 bottom, 55–7, 61, 65, 66–8, 70–1, 74 top, 78, 80–1, 82 right, 83 left, 84–5, 86 left top and bottom, 87, 89, 92, 96–9, 101, 103, 111, 114, 118, 124–5, 127 right, 128 top left, 131, 133 top, 137–41, 143, 146, 150–1, 156, 159, 161, 164, 165, 167, 168, 174, 176–7, 179–80, 182, 187–8, 190, 191 right, 194, 199, 332.

André Martin
44 top, 145, 171, 175.

Murdoch Books Photo Library
73, 189 left, 220 top, 233, 250, 256, 257 right top and centre, 280 right, 287 bottom right, 304 bottom left, 315 left, 327 right top and bottom.

Robin Powell
325 top right.

Howard Rice
95, 102, 105, 116, 117 right, 120–1, 123, 211 left, 278 left.

Lorna Rose
12, 16, 59, 64, 69, 91, 94, 186, 197 (right top to bottom), 198, 208–9, 210, 211 right top and bottom, 212 bottom, 214 right, 217, 223 top, 226, 227 top, 237 left, 241 bottom, 244 top, 254, 257 top centre, 259 top left and right centre, 260, 262 (red, blue, yellow, orange), 263, 264–77, 278 right, 279, 281–2, 283 (all but bottom left), 284, 286, 287 (all but bottom right), 288–9, 291 top right, 292–4, 295 top right, 296–300, 301 top, 302, 303 left, 304 (all but bottom left), 305 top, 306–8, 310–14, 315 right, 316–21, 323–4, 326, 327 top and bottom left, 328, 329 left.

Sue Stubbs
15 bottom, 83 right, 218, 220 bottom, 230 top, 234 bottom, 255 top, 283 bottom left, 290, 291 bottom right, 322.

Juliette Wade
10–11, 34, 36, 41–3, 90, 93, 126, 127 left, 128 right and bottom left, 132, 134–6, 149 right, 166 left, 185, 212 top.

Mark Winwood
15 top, 54 top (pix 1–3), 58, 62, 74 bottom (pix 1–3), 76, 82 left, 109, 115, 183, 197 left, 213 bottom (pix 1–3), 216, 219 right (top to bottom), 221 top (pix 1–3), 222, 223 bottom (pix 1–3), 225, 227 bottom (pix 1–3), 228–9, 230 bottom (pix 1–3), 231–2, 234 top, 235–6, 237 right, 239–40, 241 top, 242–3, 244 bottom (pix 1–3), 245–9, 252 bottom (pix 1–3), 253, 255 bottom (pix 1–3).

James Young
303 right.

The publisher would like to thank the following garden owners for allowing photography in their gardens:

Olwen Abbott, Huonville TAS; Dell Adam; Anthea and David Adams, Ngosevwa, Waiuku, New Zealand; Sally Allison, Lyddington Garden, North Canterbury, New Zealand; 'Al-ru Farm, One Tree Hill, SA; J and P Andrew, Molong NSW; Sarah Baker and John Spence, Leichhardt NSW; Bankstown Municipal Park, Bankstown NSW; Bay Cottage, TAS; 'Bebea', NSW; 'Billinudgel', NSW; 'Bringalbit', Sidonia VIC; Bronte House, Bronte NSW; Burnbank', Ladysmith NSW; 'Buskers End', Bowral NSW; G Campbell, Church Point NSW; Heather Cant, Burradoo NSW; 'Cherry Cottage', Mount Wilson NSW; Christchurch Botanic Gardens, Christchurch, New Zealand; T and M Collins, Kenthurst NSW; Convent Gallery, Daylesford VIC; Mrs P A Cooper, Exeter NSW; E Cossil and T Carlstrom, Frenchs Forest NSW; R and W Davidson, 'Windyridge Garden', Mount Wilson NSW; Zeny Edwards, Turramurra NSW; Ellerslie Flower Show, Auckland, New Zealand; K Ferguson, Cremorne NSW; Johnny Fields, Marulan NSW; Finches of Beechworth, VIC; 'Foxglove Spires', Tilba Tilba NSW; 'Gemas', Leura NSW; Gethsemane Gardens, Christchurch, New Zealand; Betty Harowickle, Pymble NSW; 'Heronswood', Dromana VIC; Heysen Family, The Cedars, Hahndorf SA; S Hill, Thornleigh NSW; 'Hillview', Exeter NSW; Kevin Hobbs, Sydney NSW; E Hogbin, Mount Kuring-gai NSW; T and J Howie, Orange NSW; 'Kennerton Green', Mittagong NSW; Kevin Kilsby Ceramics, Mount Albert, Auckland, New Zealand; 'Kiah Park', Jaspers Brush NSW; Graham and Doris King, 'Westbrook', Mount Hunter NSW; Kings Park Botanic Garden, Perth WA; Meredith Kirton, Putney NSW; 'Kooringal', Wagga Wagga NSW; K and M Law, Roseville NSW; 'Lindfield Park', Mount Irvine NSW; Ree and Wilton Love, Tanah Merah QLD; Sarah Magoffin, Marrickville NSW; Beverley McConnell, Ayrlies, Howick, New Zealand; K and A Mills, Orange NSW; 'Moidart', Bowral NSW; 'Morella', Bruny Island, TAS; Mount Tomah Botanic Garden, Mount Tomah NSW; 'Noroo', Mount Wilson NSW; Ruth Osborne, Beecroft NSW; Out of Town Nursery, Beechworth VIC; Parkers Nursery; Tony Petracca, Cronulla NSW; 'Pockets', Billinudgel NSW; Rainbox Ridge Nursery, Dural NSW; Sue and Robert Read, Pennant Hills NSW; Red Cow Farm, Sutton Forest NSW; R and D Reid, Turramurra NSW; Renaissance Herbs, Warnervale NSW; Michael Rennison; J Robb, Pennant Hills NSW; Katy Rogers, Marrickville NSW; Linda Ross, Kurrajong NSW; Ross Roses Nursery and Garden, Willunga SA; Janet and Lee Rowan, Newcastle NSW; Royal Botanic Gardens, Sydney NSW; Saumarez Homestead, Armidale NSW; Dora Scott, Wahroonga NSW; M Shepherd, Canberra ACT; Silky Oak Lodge, Mossman QLD; Diana Smith, Ranelagh TAS; Derek and Karyn Sprod, Netherby SA; J Staley, Willoughby NSW; Swanes Nursery, Dural NSW; Sydney Wildflower Nursery, Marsden Park NSW; Lance Symington, Castle Hill NSW; Tasman Bay Roses, Motueka, New Zealand; The Folly, Chewton VIC; The Garden in the Forest, Stanley VIC; The Hedgerow Roses, Tumbarumba NSW; The Olive Branch, Ferny Grove QLD; The Orangerie, Stirling SA; The Rose Garden, Watervale WA; The Wildflower Farm, Somersby NSW; D & B Thomson, Barkers Creek VIC; 'Titoki Point', Taihape, New Zealand; University of British Columbia; Urrbrae House, Urrbrae SA; 'Waterfall Cottage', Bayview NSW; 'Yengo', Mount Wilson NSW.

The publisher would also like to acknowledge these garden designers:

Jonathan Baillie, 191 left; Robyn Cunningham Garden Design, 61, 194; Robyn Cunningham Garden Design and Manna Landscapes, 55, 71 top right, 143 bottom right; Marsupial Landscapes, ph 02 9486 3944, 67, 127, 140 left, 199 right; Mother Nature's Landscapes, ph 02 9997 8929, 39, 56 right, 86 bottom left, 103 top, 151 right, 187 right, 199 left; Andrew O'Sullivan, design and construction, 297; Piet Oudolf, Pensthorpe Waterfowl Park, Norfolk, England, 215; Profile Landscapes, NSW, ph 02 9568 5868, 12, 14 right, 31, 38, 71 top left, 80, 87 right, 102 left, 103 bottom, 143 left, 150, 176 right, 180, 190; Anne Thomson Garden Design, ph 02 9983 0111, 8, 45, 53, 124, 125 top, 131, 141 bottom, 151 left, 177 right, 188 bottom left; Annie Wilkes, The Parterre Garden, Woollahra NSW, 12; Michael Rennison and Darryl Zahra, front cover, title page, 169; Geoff Whiten, RHS Chelsea 2001, 325 bottom right.